40
24
144
52
25/9
48
-25/9
22/9
19

NINTH EDITION

# Acting Is Believing

**Charles McGaw**
Late of the Goodman School of Drama
A School of the Art Institute of Chicago

**Kenneth L. Stilson**
Chair, Department of Theatre & Dance
Southeast Missouri State University

**Larry D. Clark**
Dean Emeritus, College of Arts & Sciences
University of Missouri, Columbia

**THOMSON**
™
**WADSWORTH**

Australia • Brazil • Canada • Mexico • Singapore
Spain • United Kingdom • United States

## *Acting Is Believing,* Ninth Edition
### Charles McGaw, Kenneth L. Stilson, Larry D. Clark

Publisher: Holly J. Allen
Assistant Editor: Lucinda Bingham
Editorial Assistant: Meghan Bass
Senior Technology Project Manager: Jeanette Wiseman
Senior Marketing Manager: Mark Orr
Marketing Assistant: Alexandra Tran
Senior Marketing Communications Manager: Shemika Britt
Project Manager, Editorial Production: Catherine Morris
Creative Director: Rob Hugel

Executive Art Director: Maria Epes
Print Buyer: Karen Hunt
Permissions Editor: Bob Kauser
Production Service: Interactive Composition Corporation
Compositor: Interactive Composition Corporation
Text Designer: John Edeen
Copy Editor: Beth Chapple
Cover Designer: Marsha Cohen
Cover Image: Richard Finkelstein
Text and Cover Printer: R.R. Donnelley/ Crawfordsville

Library of Congress Control Number: 2005938201

ISBN 0-495-05033-4

**Thomson Higher Education**
**10 Davis Drive**
**Belmont, CA 94002-3098**
**USA**

For more information about our products, contact us at:
**Thomson Learning Academic Resource Center**
**1-800-423-0563**

For permission to use material from this text or product, submit a request online at
**http://www.thomsonrights.com.**
Any additional questions about permissions can be submitted by e-mail to
**thomsonrights@thomson.com.**

With love to Emma

# Contents

CHAPTER **3**

## Discovering Physical Actions   35

CHAPTER **4**

## Defining Simple Objectives   60

CHAPTER **7**

## Investigating the Subconscious  133

PART **II**

## The Actor and the Play

CHAPTER **8**

## Creating a Character  150

P A R T **III**

# The Actor and the Production

C H A P T E R **12**

## Getting the Job    236

C H A P T E R **13**

## Transforming into Character    258

A P P E N D I X **A**

## Suggested Plays for Scene Study    277

A P P E N D I X **B**

## Acting Power Verbs    285

A P P E N D I X **C**

## Theatre Resources    289

# Foreword

by Chris Cooper

The scenario has become familiar to me: I'm in an airport, mall, cinema, or supermarket. A young man or woman approaches and asks: "Aren't you that actor? I want to be an actor, too. How did you get started?" These questions could make for a pretty long conversation with a stranger I've just met. At this point, I try to gauge the passion this unnamed person has for acting. I offer: "I'm guessing you recognize me from work in film. What you may not know is that before my first film, I worked for fifteen years in theatre; I had years of study and training before that." I see the light drain from their eyes, their feet shift, shoulders droop. I have my answer: "all that *work?*"

For years now, I've heard the stories of actors, some personal, most through articles, interviews, and documentaries. They speak of their respect for the craft, the actor's problems, its demands, disciplines, the competitiveness, the rejection, successes, failures, and how they got started. What ignited their imagination, inspired them, or what life experiences started the wheels turning?

I have my mother to thank for getting mine to move. She was not a follower and some would call her eccentric. She had a gift for enthusiastic storytelling. When I was five years old, my mother and I would often escape the blast furnace heat of a Missouri summer day in the cool of her bedroom, listening to symphonies, musicals, jazz, or popular singers of the day. One particular day she introduced me to the music of the *Grand Canyon Suite*. As we followed the movements, she would say, "Use your imagination. Here's the part where the sun is rising. Imagine the early morning light working its way down the canyon walls. Imagine the constant change of color: the purples, yellows, and reds." I began to see everything. "Here the donkeys make their way up the canyon trail. They trot at first and now the trail gets steeper. They're tired and struggle to reach the top." I could picture every scene, in detail.

My mother was a great film buff. Luckily for me, she hated kiddie movies. Instead of cartoons, I went with her to an amazing variety of films. Little did she know what an impression certain films and actors made on me. As a young boy, these actors didn't so much entertain me as transport me to another world. They

Used by permission of Wolf Kasteler Van Iden & Associates.

took me on a journey. This was a period well before videos, yet these single viewings stay with me to this day.

Years later, in my teens, these films were aired on television, usually late at night. With a touch of maturity, I could now follow the story lines more completely and once again found myself thoroughly engrossed in the performances. Over time, I understood that these actors brought a more believable kind of acting to the screen; they rendered an emotional truth that set them apart from other actors. All had trained first on the stage and studied with renowned teachers.

The big three teachers I was aware of were Lee Strasberg, who founded the Actor's Studio, Stella Adler, with whom I would later study, and Sanford Meisner, who ran the Neighborhood Playhouse. All were veterans of the Group Theatre. They were teaching and making adjustments to Constantin Stanislavski's observations and precepts that address the problems of presenting a character with absolute truth.

I began to collect the books of Stanislavski. With wonderful understanding and advice in each chapter, he gives examples of the things that have always troubled actors and fascinated students. Reading and re-reading the chapters, I picked up terms common to actors and privately practiced the exercises suggested. At the same time, I offered my services at a community theatre: hanging lights, building and painting sets. In the evenings, I stood in the wings as a scene shifter, observing the performances. These actions gave me a respect for all involved in every aspect of mounting a theatrical production.

My first real application of Stanislavski's practices began at the University of Missouri in acting class and later in mainstage productions directed by this text's second author, Dr. Larry Clark. Stanislavski's books, the tutelage of Dr. Clark and practical experience in productions gave me a foundation of craft that I regard as an ever-evolving process. That's the great thing about this work: you will always have more to learn. And now, with this book, *Acting Is Believing,* you have a distillation of a century's worth of observation, advice, and exercises that will help you find your way. You also have the advantage of learning, in later chapters, how to approach the business end of an actor's profession, something I had to learn belatedly, pounding the pavements of New York City.

Read, travel, listen to the great music, observe, ask questions. Fill yourself with all that living a life has to offer. For if you choose acting as your profession and career, the craft and demand of executing a fully formed character in performance will require your all. *All that work?* Yes. Yes, and gladly.

# Preface

"I don't believe you." This simple statement was the primary force behind Charles McGaw's groundbreaking text, *Acting Is Believing*. "An actor must believe to make his audience believe." Based upon the teachings of Constantin Stanislavski, McGaw's method of acting was centered on the concepts of action and belief. Fifty years and eight editions later, the formula of discovering true emotions onstage through belief in physical actions remains as relevant as ever. Like Stanislavski, McGaw also understood that having talent wasn't enough to forge a successful and enduring career in acting. He recognized that natural ability had to be cultivated. Just as a rigorous music teacher drills his most gifted and advanced students in preparation for careers as concert pianists, acting talent must be nurtured and sustained through serious training, McGaw believed.

Today, with hundreds of acting programs across the country graduating a multitude of talented young professionals each year, technique training is more important than ever. In the twenty-first century, acting continues to be one of the world's most glamorous and yet elusive professions. Thousands of actors vie for a limited number of jobs in theatre, film, television, and other forms of multimedia. Competition is fierce. Without training, connections, and a relentless will to succeed, actors cannot hope to survive in this profession—no matter how great their talent.

Between 1955 and 1986, Charles McGaw's brilliant interpretation of Stanislavski's System inspired generations of young actors. It endured through four editions, until the authorship was passed to Larry D. Clark, who expertly co-authored the next three editions to meet the demands of actors in the late twentieth century. From 1985 to 1991, I had the honor of studying with Dr. Clark at the University of Missouri–Columbia, and in 2002, through his recommendation, Wadsworth/Thomson Learning asked me to co-author the eighth edition to continue the core foundation of my illustrious predecessors. As a Stanislavski-based, twenty-first-century artist who grew and Clark, I vehemently believe that this system of acting today than ever. With the eighth edition, I tried to bring the generation of actors, students who thrive in a world even more aggressive than previous decades.

Over the past three years, I have continued to refine the text, expanding and yet streamlining the chapters and the arrangement of material. I have also persisted with my own experimentation with Stanislavski-based exercises, revising long-standing ones and developing new ones that better speak to today's students. I have continued to seek fresh outside sources, infusing them into the practice material and examples. Additionally, I have tried to illustrate points using more contemporary actors to whom this generation can relate.

Throughout the book, I hope you will find a fresh and creative exploration of acting theories and exercises that remain as grounded as the original text. Much of the material, particularly in Part I, has been revised or rewritten with undergraduate students in mind. In every chapter, exercises have been added, deleted, or modified to help keep the book current and relevant. In all the chapters and appendices, many of the references have been modernized, and most of the script examples have been updated.

To help clarify important and intricate concepts, I have merged the two chapters called "Relating to Things—External Stimuli" and "Directing Your Attention" into one new chapter, "Exploring Circles of Attention." To better reflect revisions made to this edition, I have changed numerous chapter titles: "Finding a Purpose" is now "Defining Simple Objectives," "Seeing Things" becomes "Developing Your Powers of Observation," "Relating to Things—Internal Stimuli" changes to "Investigating the Subconscious," and "Communicating the Lines" is now "Communicating the Subtext." I have also changed many of the subheadings within the chapters to better reflect modifications.

The order of chapters has also changed slightly to help the instructor with a more logical way of presenting the material to students. To help simplify assignments and navigation, I have numbered and titled all exercises, and I have greatly expanded the "Table of Contents." Additionally, to keep the book fresh and to help illustrate ideas, I have again updated most of the photographs and captions found in this edition. In my own teaching, I have found that students frequently have trouble articulating their objectives with simple statements that motivate action. Therefore, I have added a new, self-explanatory appendix entitled "Acting Power Verbs," which has been an enormous help to my own students.

In the eighth edition, some reviewers expressed mild dissatisfaction with the decision to replace the "Learning the Lingo" chapter—found in editions one through seven—with a "Glossary" at the end of the book. I understand their concerns and have tried to incorporate their suggestions into this edition. After much research, discussion, and pedagogical consideration, I have deleted the "Glossary" at the end of the book. In its place, I have added a new "mini-glossary" at the end of each chapter, entitled "Terms and People to Know." All the terminology from the seventh edition is included and even expanded in this text. I have also added simple entries identifying key acting theorists, and the terms and people are included with the most relevant chapter. I believe this will satisfy the aforementioned concern and, in fact, enhance discussions and help with examinations. I hope you agree.

Many people have graciously donated their time, energy, and resources to the completion of this edition. I again want to thank Dr. Larry D. Clark for his guidance and tutelage. He is an inspirational teacher. He also influenced Chris Cooper's early career, and it was that association that allowed me to contact him regarding the Foreword to this edition. I deeply appreciate Mr. Cooper's words of advice and the time he took out of his busy career to endorse and enhance this book. I also want to thank his wife, Marianne Leone Cooper, a writer who encouraged him and served as the liaison for most of the communication between us.

I greatly appreciate the help of my publisher, Holly Allen, as well as Darlene Amidon-Brent and Sarah Allen at Wadsworth/Thomson Learning. I again want to thank Dr. Robert W. Dillon, Jr. for our ongoing discussions about how to improve the quality of our teaching and this text. Philip Nacy also provided sound advice, and Beth Scherer helped me in more ways than she will ever know. I also want to thank Dr. Martin M. Jones, Dr. Carol Scates, my style specialist, and my other colleagues at Southeast Missouri State University. I appreciate the work of my student assistants, Meagan Edmonds and Christine Maire, as well as the constant feedback from my students in acting classes and productions. I also want to thank my professional colleagues for their ongoing reactions and criticisms.

I appreciate the comments of reviewers from the University of Missouri–Columbia, West Chester University, Red Rocks Community College, Saginaw Valley State University, and Virginia Union University.

For his willingness to share his extraordinary photographs and his help with obtaining permissions, I want to thank Richard Finkelstein and his colleagues at James Madison University, the University of Colorado at Denver, and the New York Theatre Institute. For their considerate help with their companies' beautiful photos, I also want to thank: Cara Tripicchio, Wolf Kasteler Van Iden & Associates; Bruce Lee, Publications Director, Utah Shakespearean Festival; Robin Barnes, Senior Marketing Manager, Philadelphia Theatre Company; Judith Midyett Pender, Director of Acting, University of Oklahoma; Suzi McLaughlin Russell, Allied Theatre Group/Stage West; Glynn Brannon, Director of Public Relations & Graphic Design, and David Leong, Chair of Theatre, Virginia Commonwealth University; Pat Atkinson, Chair of Theatre, University of Missouri–Columbia; Alice Rainey-Berry, Director of Publicity & Promotion, University of Memphis; Peter Smith, University of the South; Ken McCoy, Stetson University; Linda Sabo and Lauren Zapko, Elon University; Kevin Marshall, University of Florida; Bill Buck, James Madison University; David Roweli, Florida State University; Bill Black, University of Tennessee; Joe Kreizinger, Northwest Missouri State University;

Jay E. Raphael, Chair of Theatre & Dance, and Mark Templeton, Marketing Director, Missouri State University; and Dr. Felicia Londré, Tom Mardikes, and Kristi L. McKee, University of Missouri–Kansas City.

Finally, I want to again thank my wife, best friend, and colleague, Rhonda Weller-Stilson. She is always there.

*Kenneth L. Stilson*
*Cape Girardeau, Missouri*
*September 2005*

## CHAPTER 1

# Training Your Talent

*"Acting is the life of the human soul receiving
its birth through art."*

–Richard Boleslavsky

$A$cting is believing: what a simple definition for arguably the most complex of all the arts—giving birth to an imaginary character. As an actor, you must hone your ability to believe in everything that takes place onstage. You must believe in your every action within the existence of your invented circumstances. You can only fully believe in the truth; therefore, you must know how to find it at all times in your character, this fictitious person that has sprung to life through you. But if everything onstage is nothing more than invention—a lie—how can you find truth there? The stage is filled with mere imitations of life—painted scenery, artificial furs, faux jewelry, makeup, costumes, stage lighting, blunted swords, and plastic crowns. All lies. How can you *believe* where no truth exists?

According to **Constantin Stanislavski,** whose theories have influenced every generation of actors since the early twentieth century, "There are two kinds of truth and sense of belief in what you are doing. First, there is the one that is created automatically and on the plane of actual fact, and second, there is the scenic type, which is equally truthful but which originates on the plane of imaginative and artistic fiction." You are not searching for factual truth; rather, you must seek "scenic" truth, an emotional or inner truth. It is the kind of truth that comes from deep within your being and surges through your body to find outward expression. With every character you create, you must find truth in your memories, images, and emotions, as it defines your relationship with every person, thing, and event onstage.

"Truth cannot be separated from belief, or belief from truth," wrote Stanislavski. Truth and belief cannot exist without each other, and you must have both to create and truly live your part. You must fully commit to everything that happens onstage, just as you must fully connect with your acting partners and the audience. Your behavior must inspire the audience to momentarily accept that the people and events onstage are real. They must recognize the possibility that these events could actually happen, allowing them to experience emotions analogous to those being experienced onstage by you, the actor. Each and every moment must be saturated with a belief in the truthfulness of your actions and emotions.[1]

Of course, you must realize that everything around you onstage is false. You are not really the crown prince of Denmark living in the tenth century seeking revenge for the murder of your father. You are not really living in the 1930s and standing on a balcony of the French Riviera with your new husband in a condominium adjacent to his ex-wife's. You know you are really wearing costumes and makeup. You never completely lose yourself in your part. You know you are engaged in scripted dialogue, performing a sequence of rehearsed actions working opposite fellow actors. You feel thousands of watts of light flooding down on you. You are aware of the stage manager and backstage crew, the actors waiting in the wings. You know you are standing before an audience. You are even aware of noises and events occurring outside the theatre—planes going overhead, cars honking, rain hitting the roof, etc. You would have to be mentally imbalanced to lose your awareness of your real self and the factual things around you. However, as an actor breathing life into a character in a completely fabricated "secondary" reality, you must enter into the magical world of "if." You must say to yourself, "*If* these clothes upon my back were real, *if* this space actually existed at this particular time, *if* I were this person with this distinct personal history who had these perceptions, biases, desires, fears, and relationships, this is what 'I' would say. This is what 'I' would do."

Only reality exists. You cannot help but believe in the truth of reality. With the help of this "**magic if,**" however, you can **suspend your disbelief** and enter into this new world with greater enthusiasm than you believe in your own reality. *If* allows you to part from your own plane of truth and allows you to enter into your secondary reality as a new person. You cannot create another existence without *if*.

As an actor, you are searching for truthful behavior within the **given circumstances** or unchangeable facts of the play. Each script, however, redefines reality. Different levels of truth exist in every production. Some worlds closely

**Figure 1.1**   Kaliea Devi Schutz, Jenifer Alonzo, & Jennifer Velarde in a scene from the University of Colorado at Denver's production of *On the Verge*. Directed by Laura Cuetara, scenic and lighting design by Richard Finkelstein, costume design by Jane Nelson Rudd. With help from the "magic if," actors suspend their disbelief and enter into the world of the play with greater enthusiasm than they believe in their own reality.

resemble our own; they "hold a mirror up to nature." In other worlds, however, people may break into song and dance, speak in verse, or live an existential life following a nuclear holocaust. It is your responsibility to understand the reality of your character's circumstances and then behave with absolute truth.

Of significance to an actor is what Stanislavski called the "reality of the inner life of a human spirit." You will be seeking the inner spiritual world of an imaginary person with your own resources. As an actor you will face the daunting task of building a three-dimensional being who may be your polar opposite with regard to every conceivable issue. How do you portray a young female runaway, hooked on crack, and who has turned to prostitution? How do you justify the actions of a violent alcoholic who beats his wife? How do you play a young nun who has fallen in love with a priest? Where do you find the reality of a young Jewish girl trapped in an upstairs apartment surrounded by the atrocities spawned by the rise of Adolph Hitler? For that matter, how do you enter the mind of a notorious dictator? Regardless of how deranged, loving, eccentric, drugged, spiritual, hateful, or naive your character, you must never judge them. You must never approach your characters from the third person, passing a verdict on their moral, social, religious, and political beliefs and behaviors. If you do this, you will never sustain conviction in your actions onstage. Not everyone holds your personal viewpoints—the same holds true for your characters. All people justify their thoughts and actions. An abortion clinic bomber doesn't see himself as immoral; rather, he justifies his actions as doing the work of God. Part of the craft of creating a character means looking at the world of the play through his eyes, wearing his clothing, walking in his shoes.

Although this imagined character will have a completely different inner and outer existence from your own, you must find your work of art by stirring your own inner life, for each character you create must spring from your own being. Each portrayal is a unique creation derived from three sources: the given circumstances, your imagination, and your personal history, including everything you have experienced, felt, read, or observed in life or fiction. For each character, you must touch a different wellspring from within your lifetime of emotions and experiences. You are your own instrument. Pianists have their pianos. Painters have their canvases. But actors have only their own bodies and spirits. Unlike artists in other fields, you are the creator, the material, and the instrument all in one.

Throughout Stanislavski's life and career, he watched in awe as many great actors of his time brought to life night after night the most complex characters ever conceived. And perhaps more astonishing to him, it was as if these stage events were happening for the first time. Were these actors merely inspired to greatness? From where did their creations come? How did these actors know what would happen next when their characters did not know? Stanislavski became obsessed with discovering this **mystery of inspiration.** Is great acting limited only to those who are gifted enough to summon inspiration upon demand? What of those would-be actors who are occasionally inspired but haven't the ability to beckon it with each subsequent performance? Are there no technical means for the creation of art, the "craft of creation," so that this inspiration may appear more often than not?

You cannot create inspiration merely by artificial means. That is impossible. Rather, Stanislavski created a favorable condition for the appearance of inspiration by means of the will. He produced a positive environment for the inception of artistic stimulation during the creation and performance of a role. For stage characterization and behavior that appeared as spontaneously and naturally as in real life, he designed a "system" of actor training that is as relevant to today's actors trying to establish a career onstage or in film or television as it was to actors one hundred years ago.

Some people may ask if a training system for the creation of characters can actually exist. Can so-called laws be founded for all time? The answer is yes. For example, there exists a proven link between the relationship of your

**Figure 1.2**   Seth Gilliam in a scene from the Philadelphia Theatre Company's production of *Topdog/Underdog,* by Suzan-Lori Parks. Directed by Leah C. Gardiner, scenic design by Louisa Thompson, costume design by Andre Harrington, lighting design by Traci Klainer. Inspiration that can be repeated at every performance comes through technique training, a system of acting that provides a conscious means through which to enter the super-conscious region of creativeness.

psychological inner self and your physiological body. This law exists for all eternity and can be used in the actor's artistic process. Such laws are completely conscious, tried by science, and binding on everyone. In his book, *My Life in Art,* Stanislavski stated that each actor must know them and "dare not excuse himself because of his ignorance of these laws, 'which are created by nature herself.'" For you, the actor, these laws exist for the purpose of stimulating your inner emotions and a "super-conscious region of creativeness." This is an area outside our comprehension. Yet, once we reach this creative state, it affects all our conscious decision making. It is a place where inspiration rules, a miraculous mental and physical state without which no true art can exist. Therefore, the purpose of your acting training serves one objective. It is a *conscious means through which to enter the super-conscious region of creativeness.* It is the key to unlocking the elusive mystery of inspiration that can be repeated at each and every performance.

If your goal is to perform consistently at a level of professional competence, you need thorough and demanding training in a reliable technique—whether you are performing the works of Anton Chekhov, August Wilson, Stephen Sondheim, or **William Shakespeare.** Like musicians and dancers, actors must master their art in small steps. Stanislavski said that the most dangerous dilettante is the one who denies the need for technique and insists that it interferes with inspiration. Performing a significant role requires both talent and technical skills fully as great as those necessary for a professional pianist to perform a major concerto, and this talent can be developed and these skills acquired only through proper training. In today's highly competitive world, such training will play a vital role in your success in this business. Years ago, actors had no formal training; however, what was the rule has become the exception. You must train to prepare yourself for a successful career in this field. Unless you are related to powerful individuals in show biz or people who have connections with or influence over those groups, the odds of launching a career without training are remote. And even then, without extraordinary talent, your career will be limited.

Prior to the flood of training programs across the country, fledgling actors received their training by working as walk-ons and bit players in stock companies or by touring with road shows, learning their skills in the "school of hard knocks." Stories abound of actors discovered in drugstores and young aspirants who descended on Broadway or Hollywood and found fame and fortune merely on the basis of their charm, physical attractiveness, or unique personality. Those days are over. Stock companies have practically disappeared. The number of touring shows has been reduced greatly, and employment with those that remain is certainly not available to untrained actors.

Today, stage, film, television, and even CDs afford you an extremely competitive market in which thorough training is necessary for even moderate success. For the first time in history, most of our professional actors at least began their training in a college, university, or conservatory. Furthermore, your best opportunities today are often in small professional or regional theatres, which usually offer a mixed repertory of classics, modern plays, and musicals that require range and versatility. In the past several decades, the growth of these theatres, along with the rise of alternative theatres, children's theatres, theatres associated with colleges and universities, conservatories, and community theatres has given both actors and playwrights many opportunities to practice their profession away from the boom-or-bust syndrome of Broadway and from the major production centers for TV and film.

Even so, it is still commonplace for acting teachers to announce to their students that "there are no jobs" in acting. True, professional union actors earn, on average, less than $13,000 a year (and included in that average are a significant number of actors who make several million dollars annually!). Out of more than 100,000 professional actors in the United States, less than 50 percent earn an income higher than the national poverty level in any given year, and less than 10 percent of those actors consistently earn a middle-class income.[2] Acting is one of the most deceivingly difficult art forms and one of the most difficult careers with which to make a living. Nevertheless, the best acting students are those who are so irrepressibly committed to this ephemeral and often heartbreaking profession that they persist in trying it against all odds.

## Acting with Professional Competence

The successful stage performance is a carefully planned feat of artistry. It effectively communicates a viable interpretation of a play's meaning to an audience. Rather than a casual world in which actors behave impulsively in chance events, the stage is a world of controlled design in which all parts of the pattern serve to illuminate a vision, usually that of a playwright as interpreted by a director. Of course, improvisation and discoveries are an exciting and extremely important part of the process, and we will talk about them later. But, from the beginning, you must realize that acting is not doing simply what "feels natural." Spontaneous responses are most valid (and most likely to appear) only after careful groundwork, and remember, preparation spawns inspiration.

Like Stanislavski, legendary acting theorists have for decades attempted to harness these sparks or flashes of genius. There are endless examples of actors who are brilliant on opening night and then fail to achieve any semblance of this initial insight in subsequent performances. True inspiration must not be an opening night discovery. "Drama is absolutely and elaborately 'scored,' and the greatest acting contains a minimum of spontaneous invention and a maximum of carefully calculated effects repeated with only minute variations at every performance of the same part," wrote Tyrone Guthrie, one of the most eminent twentieth-century directors in a 1966 *New York Times* article. "Dramatic performance, therefore, is concerned with repeating a series of intelligibly prescribed actions in order to form an intelligibly prescribed design."

All we have said thus far makes acting seem to be incredibly complex and demanding, and indeed it is. Nevertheless, in addition to the proper motivation to succeed, we can state the essential qualities of a successful actor quite simply. Remember them as the *two t's:* talent and training.

**Talent** lies deep within your core, and sometimes it is extremely difficult to capture from its hiding place. Talking about talent is easy, but defining it precisely is extremely difficult. Talent is relevant to the observer. Certainly, a "stage mother" and a casting director have two different opinions with regard to talent. But even to a trained professional, it frequently seems to be unrecognizable in its undeveloped state, because biographies of many actors of great prominence tell how they were advised early in their careers to consider another profession. In other words, "Don't quit your day job." Certainly, talent must not be confused with being stagestruck or "screenstruck." Many such people lack the requisite talent and are attracted to the profession only by the most superficial elements of show business.

Perhaps the best way to define talent is to delineate the personal traits of successful actors. They have an aura—also referred to as personal magnetism, stage presence, star quality, and the unspoken television rating system known as TVQ—that makes people want to watch and listen to their every action and thought. Working actors exude confidence and control over their own personality. They have an awareness and readiness to accept their own inner and outer selves. They have expressive bodies and voices and a desire and need to share experiences with others. Professional actors have a sensitivity to the world at large and a curiosity and understanding about diverse people's modes of behavior and the human condition. They radiate courage and self-confidence and are unafraid to reveal their inmost feelings on a public stage.

If you possess these attributes, you will probably be considered talented. You will probably be cast in major roles that test your abilities on a regular basis at your university or community theatre. Although you may lack technique and experience at this point, your talent will probably be recognized at an early age. Without it, however, you will face an uphill and perhaps insurmountable battle.

Some people claim that talented actors do not need **training,** the second "t." "Great actors are born!" However, painters, musicians, and dancers must also be born with talent, and yet do any of these other visual or performing artists achieve greatness through talent alone? Laws certainly do not govern extraordinary talent, but it is unlikely that you will ever hear a working actor say that technique is unnecessary. In fact, it is quite the opposite; the greater your talent, the more development and technique you will need. Technique must be applied to talent. Not everyone who studies the piano will learn to play music. By the same token, not everyone who studies dance will become a prima ballerina, and not everyone who explores acting will become an actor. You may study technique for many years, but it in no way guarantees that your work will be considered outstanding. On the other hand, talent that goes untrained will never reach its full potential. Concert pianists rehearse scales every day of their lives. Prima ballerinas spend hours at the barre each day working all the muscles of their bodies. Painters, creative writers, and sculptors practice their art seven days a week. It is your responsibility as an actor to train and develop your talent on a daily basis—especially when you are not in rehearsal. Too many so-called actors sit idly between "gigs" doing nothing but speaking of their art. Once cast, they expect inspiration to magically appear. All art demands virtuosity, and virtuosity demands regular training. In book after book, biography after biography, this simple fact becomes abundantly clear: Good actors work hard, train hard, and take their work seriously. They know that artistic achievement can come only after practicing their technique so frequently and so thoroughly that it becomes a natural part of everything they do.

Training requires time, patience, hard work, and self-discipline. Enthusiasm, a striving for perfection (although it can never be achieved), and a willingness to work cooperatively with others; all are important. In fact, as necessary as abundant talent is to your chance for success, it can be a trap in the early stages of development if it tempts you to get along with a minimum of effort. Before you know it, persons of lesser talent but with uncompromising discipline and a better attitude will be accomplishing more. You must take complete control of your art, your discipline. Otherwise, you will become no more than a talented proletarian actor, what the legendary actress and teacher, **Uta Hagen,** referred to as a "hack." You will soon be disappointed and discouraged. Talent by itself is a waste, but a talented actor with a strong work ethic has the potential to become an extraordinary artist.

We can divide actor training into seven parts, the development of *mind, body,* and *voice,* plus training in *auditioning, rehearsal technique* and *performance skills,* and cultivating the ability to *self-assess* or objectively critique and learn from your own work.

1. **Mind.** Internal training begins with cultural development, an important and inadequately emphasized aspect of the training process. As an artist, you must be a student of life. A broad education in the liberal arts is essential— no matter where you study. The material from which you draw is the entire realm of human knowledge and experience. You cannot afford to be ignorant of historical or contemporary events, linguistics, literature, music, visual arts, design, psychology, sociology, religion, politics, sports, economics, travel, business, circus arts, eroticism, etc. The list is endless. "An artist who has not mastered his profession is a dilettante," wrote Goethe, "and an artist who has limited himself to his profession is a corpse." Another part of your mental training involves a keen understanding of human psychology, **historical imagination,** and learning how to control and to make effective use of sensory and emotional responses. Your internal acting training also includes learning to read a script, examine the plot, explore your character and his relationships, break the dialogue into small structural units, determine the simple objectives (by way of action verbs) and obstacles (both physical and psychological), unearth the subtext of the verbal and physical actions, and determine the "through-line of action," the chain of consecutive simple objectives, all of which lead to the discovery of the character's superobjective within the play as a whole.

2. **Body.** External training includes the development of your entire physical apparatus. Not only must you train in dance, combat, fencing, athletics, etc., but also you must learn that your body—through alignment, gestures, and movement—is one of your principal tools through which to create a character. You must train your body to be a responsive and expressive instrument

with the ability embody your character's inner thoughts, desires, and fears. Your body is your only real means by which to create a physical form that gives comprehensible meaning to others and has intrinsic artistic value. Body training also includes learning to endow your characters with an appropriate dimension, energy, and clarity that can communicate the meaning to an audience of a certain size occupying a certain space.

3. **Voice.** Vocal training, which may or may not include singing and musical training, develops your oral dexterity as a speaker and involves detailed work in diction, rhythm, tempo, resonance, projection, pitch, inflection, and dialects. Like your physical body, your voice is another primary means to externalize your character's inner life. As an actor, you must have the ability to speak your lines with clarity of thought and purpose through the eyes of your character. To fully explore the subtext of each thought, you must acquire the skill and habit of putting the greatest possible meaning into every word you utter.

4. **Auditioning.** Whatever else acting might be, it is a business, and a very cold and heartless business at that. Although you may—and perhaps should—be getting cast on a regular basis as a student, the world of professional acting is extraordinarily competitive. Whereas you may be one of two or three leading ladies at your university, in the so-called "real world" there always seems to be someone else who is taller, shorter, blonder, more ethnic, or less ethnic. The person in line next to you will be able to sing a higher note, handle more complex dance choreography, or manage Shakespearean verse better than you. Beautiful and distinctive people, who are equally talented and equally well trained, will surround you. You may feel overwhelmed, insignificant, even depressed by your lack of connections. You may find it extremely difficult to juggle your "regular" job, to keep your head above water financially, while simultaneously staying active in the audition circuit. Professional acting is a business of rejection. The odds are always against you. For every fifty auditions you attend, you may receive one offer. Even established professionals—unless you are Brad Pitt or Julia Roberts—must frequently face rejection by producers and casting directors. And once you have secured a job, you must start the process all over again—even before your current job has ended.

A hunger to succeed isn't enough. Ambition alone will not land you a callback. Being discovered is a myth. You must have the tenacity and confidence to handle rejection on a daily basis. You must have the ability to present yourself in a professional manner and sell your talent in an extremely tight job market. Thus, audition training includes the capacity to prepare marketable headshots, résumés, business cards, postcards, thank-you notes, and various audition materials and the communication skills to handle yourself in callback or interview situations.

5. **Rehearsal Technique.** Most actors do not know how to rehearse. Or they know how to rehearse but are too lazy to put in the requisite work needed to fully develop a three-dimensional character. First, you must know how to prepare for rehearsals at home. Research and script analysis skills, which infuse your observations and past experiences with your imagination, are prerequisites when preparing to enter the rehearsal process. Once they have begun, you must become skilled at experimentation, making discoveries, and learning from failure. You must know how to explore various rhythms and how to commune with yourself, the environment, your images, the text, and with other actors. You must also possess the learned skills of working with the director, the stage manager, and the production staff, and you must understand and observe the principles of rehearsal ethics and discipline.

6. **Performance Skills.** Truthful performance skills (without pandering or **indicating**) come through in-class exercises and scene study and through actual experiences. Once you have developed the capacity to create a character and rehearse, you must learn how to mentally and physically prepare yourself before a performance. Once onstage, establishing a communion with your audience is paramount. You must have the skills to maintain and control impulses, energy, and various tempo-rhythms. Finally, you must know how to focus your stage energy and how to capture and repeat an inspired portrayal as if your character were living the events of the play for the first time each time you put on your character's clothing.

7. **Self-Assessment.** Stanislavski warned, "Young actor, fear your admirers!" Once you enter the magic circle of self-deception, it is difficult to escape the mendacity. Indeed, it is pleasant to hear the flattery and praise of your adoring admirers because you desperately want to believe them. However, you should not enter into this profession simply to amuse your followers, and do not discuss your artistic process with anyone other than trusted mentors and colleagues. The naive compliments of friends and family—who are not themselves actors—will not help you grow as an artist. Talk to your admirers, but listen, understand, and even love the observations of a true professional. There is nothing more beneficial to your growth than the brutally honest words of someone who knows. Unfortunately, however, you will not always be lucky enough to have an acting coach who knows or cares standing over your shoulder giving you expert advice. Therefore, you must know how to objectively observe your own work.

Self-assessment is a learned skill. Beginning with your first acting class, you must make honest appraisals of your own work. You cannot be totally reliant upon any one person, always seeking their approval for your choices and discoveries. One of your teacher's primary responsibilities is to train you to become self-reliant—to serve as your own critic. In the commercial world of theatre, film, and television, directors expect you to deliver a product. They are not your teachers. They will not hire your potential; rather, they contract your skills. Therefore, you must be experienced and honest enough to continue your own growth and development as an artist once you leave the security of the classroom. And although the general public may be satisfied with your work, you must objectively look at your own creation, assessing your choices and continually working on weaknesses. You must believe that inner reward is better than applause.

With the exception of cultural development, which must come as a lifelong commitment to expanding your knowledge of and sensitivity to the world around you, these processes roughly constitute the information presented in this book. You must be cautious, though, about thinking of acting as a step-by-step, logical process. Professional actors never stop honing their abilities in all these areas. You should always bring the skills and understandings of previous lessons to bear on your current exercise. With each assignment, you should explore and practice in a way that continually expands your skills. The ability to perform at a professional level is accumulated over time. You must never cease to study and practice your basic training, just as accomplished musicians devote a tremendous portion of every day to practicing scales.

However talented or tenacious your desire to succeed, you must realize that technique training cannot be accomplished simply from studying this or any other book. It requires the guidance of able teachers, coaches, and directors. Because theatre is a highly cooperative endeavor, working with others in exercises and in scene study is essential. After acquiring the basic skills, you should be given an opportunity to work before an audience, preferably first in a laboratory situation and later under conditions that approximate those in professional theatre.

Much of this book is based on a twenty-first century interpretation of Stanislavski's System. "As a seeker for gold, I can transmit to future generations not my searching and my privations, my joys and disappointments, but the precious 'mine' that I found," proclaimed Stanislavski. "This 'mine' in my artistic field is the result of my whole life's work. It is my so-called 'System,' the technique that permits the actor to create a character, to reveal the life of a human spirit and to incarnate it naturally onstage in an artistic form."[3] Stanislavski's method is based on laws of the organic nature of an actor. Most everything in his "System" was developed naturally throughout his long career, and it has survived the test of time over the past one hundred years. Once mastered, technique training provides you with a means for keeping your performance fresh. With proper technique your work will not grow stale, no matter how long the run. When these actions are harmoniously and artfully integrated, they help reveal the purpose of the play as interpreted for a particular production. Only then can acting be said to be "good,"

Kenn Stilson

**Figure 1.3**   Mike Culbertson as Reverend Eddie in Southeast Missouri State University's production of *Some Things You Need to Know Before the World Ends: A Final Evening with the Illuminati*. Directed by Kenn Stilson, scenic design by James VonDielingen, costume design by Jennifer Sturm, sound design by Adam Leong. Actors must continue to hone their internal and external acting skills throughout their lives.

no matter how "beautiful" it may have looked or sounded or how "exciting" the event itself may have been to an audience. Only then will "acting" and "believing" become synonymous.

What part should a textbook play in the complex task of training an actor? It should organize your study in a logical progression; it should create an awareness of recurring problems and suggest solutions, thus guiding you toward technical proficiency; and it should provide you with useful practice exercises. No text can be comprehensive; this one, without ignoring any aspect of your overall training, focuses on the psychophysical process through the development of your body, mind, and voice.

## Exploring Your Resources

This book proceeds from the fundamental belief that student actors begin their training with self-exploration. The tools you will use as an actor, although they may be sharpened by practice and stretched by learning and exercise, are present within you even as you read these words.

The need for you to develop a well-trained body and voice—which we will refer to as your **external resources**—should be obvious. A musician forced to perform on an inferior instrument is at a disadvantage. And you will have a similar disadvantage if you lack muscular and vocal control. In fact, the training of the actor's voice and body as an instrument occupied the almost exclusive attention of acting teachers well into the twentieth century.

Today's theatre practice demands that this external training—as essential as it is—be accomplished in conjunction with other studies and exercises fundamental to your development. A fine speaking voice and a well-coordinated body in themselves do not make an actor, any more than possessing a Stradivarius makes a violinist. Your primary task is to create a character who "behaves logically in imaginary circumstances," and truthful behavior begins deep inside your being and is externalized through your body and voice. Thus, your body, mind, and voice will join through this psychophysical process as the fundamental basis for the study of acting.

The need for internal truth surfaces the moment you start to think seriously about performing a role in a play. Suppose you have been cast in a part that requires you to create a character who lives in a different time and within a culture that is completely foreign to your experiences. For example, you are playing a young Russian princess in fear for your life just prior to the Bolshevik Revolution. If you are like most untrained actors, you will go to your first rehearsal without any ideas about what to do when you get there. Who are the Bolsheviks? And why do they hate "me"? Before rehearsals have begun, you should have asked a thousand questions about your character. Who am "I"? What are "my" relationships? What are "my" desires, "my" fears, "my" points of view about the world? Without in-depth answers to all your questions, how could you possibly perform, or indeed even imagine truthful actions for your portrayal of this young royal? The process begins the moment you are cast, and the comprehensive answers will come only after an arduous journey—a voyage filled with exploration, discoveries, and failures—in which you systematically discover what you have in your historical imagination that might help bring your portrayal of this princess to life on the stage.

You have now encountered the world of the actor at rehearsal. All actors face the same dilemma when they prepare to perform a role in any play, no matter how common or how foreign the situation and setting. Your goal as a student of acting is to bring to rehearsal a method of studying a role that will enable you to access the necessary raw materials for creating and performing it. These raw materials, simply put, constitute the accumulation of your own knowledge and are composed of everything you have experienced or imagined in your lifetime. Your actions onstage are limited to your personal history and imagination. For the role in question, you will need to find elements within yourself that will allow you to create and believe in the circumstances of the unfamiliar character. Just as you are dependent on your voice and body to carry out your actions, you are also dependent on your mind to provide the proper impulses for those actions.

Fortunately, your history is not confined to what you have experienced in person; it comes from reading, listening, and observing countless sources. Research and the expansion of your historical imagination are important parts of your quest to unearth the truth in the world of the play. And part of talent is the ability to deepen and extend experiences in the imagination.

Let us suppose you have been cast as Shakespeare's Romeo or Juliet, and that the scene for rehearsal is Act III, Scene 5, sometimes called the second balcony scene. To illustrate the current point, we need only recall the chief facts of the situation. Romeo and Juliet are the son and daughter of two powerful and wealthy families who have long been bitter enemies. Having met by chance, they have fallen deeply in love and have married secretly. Within an hour after their marriage, Romeo, involved in an outbreak of the ancient hostility, has killed Juliet's cousin and has been banished from his native city of Verona. There seems to be no hope of happiness together as the young couple say farewell in the dawning light.

What an exciting prospect to play one of these famous lovers. You have now learned that you must be prepared to explore and expand (through research) your own personal history before you can possibly create a character in whose behavior you, the other actors, and the audience can believe. But how do you know where to find these inner sources that may be deeply rooted in the subconscious regions of your mind? How can you begin to match your own experience with that of the character? You begin with the script, first discovering the physical actions the character must perform. Before that, however, we shall begin by giving rise to an environment that encourages maximum inspiration for the discovery of these actions, a truly creative state where you will be able to achieve full artistic expression.

# Terms and People to Know

**Boleslavsky, Richard (1889–1937)**   An original member of the Moscow Art Theatre's first Studio, he left Russia in 1920, settled in the U.S. in 1922, and founded the American Laboratory Theatre in 1923. His book, *Acting: The First Six Lessons* (1933) introduced Americans to Stanislavski's theories.

**external technique**   The development of the body and voice as responsive and expressive instruments; vocal dexterity, speech, movement, and gestures are the actor's principal means of external expression.

**Group Theatre**   Founded in 1931 by Harold Clurman, Lee Strasberg, and Cheryl Crawford, the Group was a pioneering attempt to create a theatre collective influenced by the teachings of Stanislavski and modeled on the *Moscow Art Theatre*. In their ten years of existence, they produced the most important group of theatre practitioners and teachers in U.S. history.

**Hagen, Uta (1919–2004)**   Preeminent German-born actress known for her portrayals of Blanche DuBois in *A Streetcar Named Desire*, Martha in *Who's Afraid of Virginia Woolf?*, and Mrs. Klein in *Mrs. Klein*, Hagen was perhaps known best as a great teacher of acting at her second husband's HB Studio and through her two books, *A Challenge for the Actor* and *Respect for Acting*.

**historical imagination**   A subjective approach to convince yourself that "you" exist in the world of the play. Historical facts are not the issue, but rather the external behavior of a unique individual in a particular social order with its own culture, values, fashion, and mores.

**indicating**   A derogatory term in psychologically motivated acting in which actions are presented without objectives.

**inspiration, mystery of**   The goal of Stanislavski's System. When actors find a consistent and repeatable conscious means to subconscious creativity, they are said to be inspired.

**internal technique**   An actor's keen understanding of human psychology, *historical imagination,* and learning how to control and to make effective use of Stanislavski's theories onstage.

**magic "if"**   Key to unlocking the imagination, it describes the process by which actors place themselves in the given circumstances of the scene. The actor asks, "What would I do *if* I were this character in this circumstance?"

**Moscow Art Theatre**   Founded by Constantin Stanislavski and Vladimir Nemirovich-Danchenko in 1898, the MAT is the best known Russian theatre and arguably the most influential company in the history of theatre.

**Shakespeare, William (1564–1616)**   Author of such plays as *Romeo and Juliet* (1595) and *Hamlet* (1600), Shakespeare is the greatest playwright in the history of Western civilization. Because his plays transcend time and place and because of their continued twenty-first century popularity, the authors of this text continue to use many common Shakespearean references.

**Stanislavski, Constantin (1863–1938)**   Russian co-founder and director of the Moscow Art Theatre from 1898 until his death in 1938. The creator of the world's first and best known systematized study of the acting art. Most of today's acting technique training is a derivative of Stanislavski's System.

**suspension of disbelief**   The audience's willingness to temporarily accept the actions on stage as truth, although they never completely forget they are watching fiction.

**talent**   A natural ability to create art of a superior quality. Although talent is innate, it must be enhanced with technique training.

**training**   Using any number of teaching methodologies, actor training is divided into seven parts, the development of *mind, body,* and *voice,* plus training in *auditioning, rehearsal technique* and *performance skills,* and cultivating the ability to *self-assess.*

## CHAPTER 2

# Approaching the Creative State

*"Tension is the artist's greatest enemy."*

–Lee Strasberg

Stanislavski referred to muscular rigidity as the actor's occupational disease. In *My Life in Art,* he wrote, "In searching for a way out of the unbearable state of a person who is being forcibly exhibited and who is compelled against his human will and need to create . . . we resort to false, artificial techniques of theatrical acting."[1] Once the actor discovers these false or indicated means to cope with this unnatural setting, she begins to rely upon them. They become habitual. Having become sharply aware of the damage and the artificiality of an actor's physical and emotional being while onstage, Stanislavski began to search for an alternative frame of mind, a mental environment in which imagination and inspiration could thrive. He referred to this as the **creative state.** Characterized as the state of "I am," it means "I am not simply on a stage. Rather, I think, feel, and conduct myself in the same way as the character I am portraying."

As long as physical anxiety exists onstage, you cannot focus on the delicate shadings of feeling or the spiritual life of your part. Consequently, before you attempt to create anything you must get your muscles in proper condition so they do not impede your actions. You will never be entirely liberated from these enemies because they cannot simply be outgrown as you gain experience.

Therefore, you must develop more or less conscious techniques of relaxing. While onstage, you must strive to eliminate all tension not absolutely needed to execute a movement, say a line, or maintain a position. Economy of effort characterizes both good movement and good speech.

The ability to relax is necessary to the internal as well as the external aspects of acting, for the tense actor finds it impossible to focus on the subtle process of creation. Excessive tension inhibits freedom of action and clarity of objective, a point Stanislavski made clear by demonstrating that it is impossible to multiply thirty-seven times nine while holding up the corner of a piano. The actor's unwanted tension is often just as great as that required to lift a heavy weight, and playing a clear objective certainly demands as much mental acuity as solving a multiplication problem.

The inability to relax shatters your ability to perform a believable character. If you are overly tense onstage, the audience inevitably focuses on the resulting nervous mannerisms rather than on the actions of your character. These mannerisms belong to you, not your character, so they destroy the believability of the scene.

In addition to learning proper relaxation technique, theatre artists around the world recognize that physical exercise to develop coordination and muscular control is an essential part of acting training. Indeed, most theatre programs require fencing and dancing to help the student develop poise and alertness. Most actors also value the regimen of some sort of athletic training such as gymnastics, yoga, t'ai chi ch'uan, or martial arts. Many actors also undergo training in stage combat, mime, and circus techniques. Anyone seriously interested in acting understands the need to develop a coordinated and responsive body.

## Training Your Body

Creativity comes from within. Your body and voice are simply instruments, subordinate to the beckoning of your internal virtuosity. An out-of-tuned musical instrument, no matter the emotional and physical health of the musician, will never produce beautiful music. If an actor possesses a faulty instrument (his body), it will cripple creativity and alter interpretation.

"All artistic people, from geniuses to the simply talented, are capable to a greater or lesser degree of arriving at this creative state in mysterious intuitive ways; however, they are not empowered to regulate and to control it arbitrarily," wrote Irina and Igor Levin in their recently published book, *The Stanislavsky Secret*.[2] You cannot rely on intuition any more than you can rely on inspiration. How do you create an environment that is conducive to inspiration? Are there any technical means by which to accomplish this? Be forewarned that technical does not translate as artificial; more accurately, it means scientific and procedural.

The Levins go on to quote Stanislavski as having asked, "How to go about making this state not appear unexpectedly, but be created by the actor's own will, on his 'order'? And if it should be impossible to acquire this state immediately, could it be done piecemeal—put together, so to speak, from separate elements?"

Intensive efforts have been made to discover a genuinely effective program in body training for the actor. These efforts have produced significant changes both in concept and practice, together with an emphasis on carefully directed work in stage movement. Several influential approaches to actor training were developed by such modern "pioneers" as Jerzy Grotowski, Peter Brook, Joseph Chaikin, and Arthur Lessac, great innovators who were oriented to physical training as a means of developing the actor's total instrument. Literally hundreds of teachers and "systems" have sprung from the work of one or another of these individuals, some of brief duration and others that have made genuine contributions to actor training throughout the world. All these people would agree with Grotowski in his groundbreaking book, *Towards a Poor Theatre,* that "the most elementary fault [of the actor], and that in most urgent need of correction, is the over-straining of the voice because one forgets to speak with the body."[3]

Practically, body training is designed to accomplish two basic, closely related objectives: *proper body alignment* and *freedom from excess muscle tension.* Accomplishment of these objectives enables the actor to move in any direction from a standing, sitting, or lying position with a minimum of effort and without a preparatory shifting of weight. Together they produce strong, efficient, unforced movement.

Proper alignment, occasionally called **centering,** is sometimes misunderstood to imply something that is static or artificially frozen. Many people believe that "correct" posture is synonymous with a stiff and artificial carriage. Correct alignment is our body's natural position. Look at babies who have just learned to sit up by themselves. Notice their relaxed and yet perfect posture. Poor alignment usually happens as a result of a lifetime of bad habits. As we age, we habitually distort and misshape our bodies. We slouch in our chairs; we slump our shoulders; we drag our feet; we hang our heads. As an actor, you must understand that each character is entirely different from you—both internally and externally. The manner in which they walk, sit, stand, and gesture is unique. Until you fully realize your own body alignment, your own habitual carriage, you will never go beyond yourself as you adopt the physical body of your character. Until you make a conscious effort to return your body to the alignment intended by nature, you remain blissfully ignorant, limiting your range as an actor. Natural alignment is best achieved under the guidance of a skilled instructor; however, a description of the ideal will help you understand the work required to attain it.

You unconsciously achieve proper body alignment as you recline on a reasonably hard surface. From this prone position, you can eliminate excess tension, bringing your body weight naturally into correct relationship. As an actor, you must transfer this relationship and this feeling of relaxation from a prone to an upright position.

When you do so, you will be *standing tall,* and the "tip at the back of the top of your head" will be the tallest point. The bottom line of your chin is parallel with the floor, as you relax your front neck muscles—a condition essential to eliminating vocal tension. Your shoulders will be rounded forward to obtain the widest possible space between the shoulder blades. You should think of the shoulder blades as a double gate that is always kept open. Square-shouldered, closed-gate, military posture produces tensions and inhibits the body's natural expressiveness. Your abdominal muscles will be held firmly in place and the buttocks tucked under, properly aligning the spine from top to bottom. When you stand in this position against a wall, little or no space will remain between the wall and the small of your back. Your arms swing freely from the shoulders, and your knees will be relaxed.

The second objective of body training—muscular relaxation—is a quality that characterizes all fine acting. The goal of relaxation is not dormancy. Instead, it should provide a state of alertness in which you can attain your utmost capacity for accomplishing any activity. Relaxation bolsters your courage and increases your self-confidence. Stanislavski's creative state has also been called "blissful relaxation" (Morris Carnovsky) and the "potent state" (Moshe Feldenkrais). Robert Benedetti, in *The Actor at Work,* summed up the creative state as a "kind of relaxation . . . in which you are most ready to react, like a cat in front of a mouse hole. Tensions that would inhibit movement are gone, and you are in a state of balance that leaves you free to react in any way required."[4]

Actors who have not attained a state of muscular freedom will often be told, "Just relax; take it easy." These words can easily produce the opposite of the desired effect by causing actors to become more aware of their tension and, consequently, to become more uptight. Unfortunately, no exercise program will eliminate excess tension in a few easy lessons. You achieve the creative state through a lifelong regimen of training, relentless in its demand on your time and energy.

## Conquering Inhibitions

From an actor's perspective, live theatre can be extraordinarily dangerous, while film and television, on the other hand, are relatively safe. Aside from the director, producers, writers, technicians, and crew, no audience watches the filming of a movie. Television programs sometimes accommodate studio audiences; however, if an actor forgets a line or misses an entrance, the director can simply shout "Cut!" In both film and television, the director can re-shoot a scene as many times as he wishes. He can cut away, splice, and edit until most mistakes are virtually erased. For the actor, the camera is a safety net. The medium protects them from errors, and the finished product is frozen in time. Even such shows as *Saturday Night Live* are simply taped live before a studio audience, but the broadcast occurs later that evening. No film and virtually no character-driven television program today is shot live. Many early TV shows were presented in front of both the studio and televised audiences simultaneously. Today, however, outside of newscasts and some sporting events, almost everything is frozen in celluloid or by digital means. Following Janet Jackson's infamous wardrobe malfunction at the halftime presentation of Super Bowl XXXVIII, even football has a fifteen-second delay.

Because danger lurks around every corner onstage, the idea of performing in live theatre terrifies many film and television actors. Mistakes happen. Lines are forgotten; entrances are missed. Telephones and doorbells fail to ring. Only your improvisational skills can sometimes save you from utter embarrassment and shame. Once the curtain rises, no director can rescue you. No one can shout "cut." There is only you and your partners standing emotionally naked before an expectant audience.

On the other hand, the communal experience that occurs between theatre performers and spectators is indescribable. To hold an audience spellbound by your actions, to speak powerful words to a group of people who are mesmerized by your interpretation, to deliver a punch line which in turn causes a thousand viewers to spontaneously laugh is invigorating beyond words. As a stage actor, you will never be more alive than at that moment. But the stakes are high, and inhibitions may be present. Stage fright can overtake even the most seasoned professional. At the height of his career, Laurence Olivier, arguably the greatest twentieth-century actor, was so terrified of standing before an audience that he refused to perform for over two years. The phenomenal Barbra Streisand is reclusive to the point where she hardly performs live any longer. If Olivier and Streisand suffer from this greatest of inhibitions, what chance do we mere mortals have in overcoming stage fright?

Phrases frequently heard in describing an actor's state of being are "He forgets himself onstage" or "He forgets the audience and loses himself in the part." Actors who *lose* themselves in their characters also lose control of their actions. They are extremely dangerous people to play opposite. Instead, you must "find yourself" in your role, and you must share a spiritual connection with your partners onstage and with the audience. *To enter into the creative state and to overcome stage fright, you must forget your limitations and inhibitions by concentrating on your character's justifiable actions.* "Forgetting yourself onstage" implies that you must enter into a trancelike state in which you are unaware of your surroundings and thus lose control of the situation. Actors can forget neither themselves nor the audience, and those who insist they do are either lying

Reprinted by permission of Robin Barnes, Philadelphia Theatre Company. Photo by Mark Garvin.

**Figure 2.1**   Nicole Van Giesen in a scene from the Philadelphia Theatre Company's production of *The Last Five Years,* written and composed by Jason Robert Brown. Directed by Joe Calarco, scenic design by Michael Fagin, costume design by Anne Kennedy, lighting design by Chris Lee. Removing excessive tension frees this actor to relax and make more creative physical choices.

or insane. Instead, through a sixth sense, you must remain conscious of the "publicness" of your performance, but you must focus on the actions of your character.

While onstage, you must maintain an awareness of the audience, but you must not agonize about them. It is not your responsibility to keep them entertained. Instead, you must incorporate the magic if. What would I do *if* I were this character in these circumstances? Worrying about the audience produces instant tension. Like actors, athletes also cherish the approval of the spectators, but during the game they must concentrate solely on their actions. As LeBron James soars to the goal, he is certainly aware of the audience, yet he has one thing on his mind—the basket. While Serena Williams rallies against Lindsay Davenport up match point, she knows she is being watched by millions of tennis fans around the world; nevertheless, she stays focused on one thing—her next stroke. The moment the audience becomes their center of attention, anxiety will overtake them. James will overshoot the basket; Williams will pull her shot wide. During competition, great athletes have exceedingly short memories, quickly forgetting minor errors or shortcomings of form. The small mishaps are irrelevant; their job is to win the game or match. Afterward, as a way of making mental and technical adjustments and improving their next performance, they reflect upon their errors—usually at the behest of an announcer who grabs them before they retreat to the locker room. As an actor, you too must have a short memory while onstage. Miscues will occur, but you will "win" by creating a believable character who behaves truthfully. To accomplish this, you must free yourself from worry over nonessentials. You must justify your actions and then focus your energies to pursue your character's objective freely and fully. If you are absorbed in your activity, your personal tension will disappear. Once the performance has ended, however, you must immediately and objectively evaluate your own work. Otherwise, you will never grow as an artist. Like the athlete, self-assessment is one of your primary means to improve your next performance.

Other emotional inhibitions can also be a tremendous obstacle for an actor. An honest portrayal of King Lear's descent into madness or Blanche DuBois' painful deterioration requires great depth of feeling. For the actor playing the role of Alan Strang in *Equus,* being physically naked in front of an audience may not compare to the difficulty of revealing this young man's internal anguish. Great pieces of dramatic literature sometimes demand extraordinary things from you, actions that will force you to confront your personal "hang-ups." Some roles compel you to stand emotionally exposed before an audience as you reveal your character's inner self. Phèdra's uncontrollable passion for her stepson and Ophelia's emotional decline and subsequent suicide force the actor to face a number of inhibitions. An onstage kiss is so incredibly simple, and yet kissing is one of mankind's most intimate acts of affection. Therefore, it is one of the most difficult things for some actors to do "fully." Romantically touching "your" lover, hugging, holding hands, touching someone's face, even the act of really looking into someone else's eyes can all be very intimidating to the young actor. Intimate speech involving painful and emotional memories can be extraordinarily difficult. For that matter, foul language and violence may be just as awkward as affection. All human beings have a unique sense of moral rightness, and each person carries a lifetime of emotional baggage. You may consider yourself to be an extremely affectionate and passionate person who has no problems with touch and intimacy. You may think of yourself as socially liberal, free from "hang-ups." On the other hand, you may be rather shy and reserved. You may have difficulty demonstrating love—particularly with someone whom you have just met or whom you consider a friend. No matter how extroverted or introverted, how liberal or conservative you consider yourself, chances are you harbor some inhibitions—whether they are personal or spring from the mores of society.

Social inhibitions take many forms. They vary substantially from society to society, from era to era, and from individual to individual. In our society, for instance, men rarely touch one another except to shake hands or to engage in playful banter. But in other societies, such as Mexico or Italy, it is perfectly acceptable for men to kiss, embrace, and walk arm in arm in public. Even succeeding generations within the same culture have different sets of social inhibitions. Social embarrassments may have prevented our great-grandparents from wearing bikinis to the beach or shorts on a hot day. An important key to freeing inhibitions, then, is to understand them by assessing your character's society, customs, and traditions.

Still, the relationship between social inhibitions and the individual person remains complex. Why is it that some actors are less hindered by social inhibitions onstage than others are? Can an actor from a conservative background learn not to wince (either internally or externally) at using suggestive behavior or foul language onstage? What are the actor's rights and responsibilities in these delicate areas?

These questions have no easy answers. You must develop your own moral compass, turning down roles in which you feel yourself exploited. On the other hand, once you have accepted a role, you have a responsibility to behave truthfully from your character's point of view, even when his or her actions differ from your own personal choices. The question is not "What would *I* (the actor) do?" but rather "What would 'I' (the character) do?" Also remember the comment from Chapter 1, "You must never judge your character; otherwise, you will never be able to sustain belief in your actions." If you believe in a play and in your role and concentrate on the reasons that characters behave the way they do, you soon will lose your inhibitions. They will slip away as you involve yourself in your character's simple objectives. Internal logic will prevail as you increase your empathy with the character.

Finally, it is realistic to expect that today's actor may have to decide whether playing a character in the nude is artistically justified. For example, the nudity found in Arthur Miller's *Playing for Time,* set within the confines of a Nazi concentration camp, is completely substantiated. Mrs. Kendall's intimate removal of her top for the benefit of John Merrick (the Elephant Man) is artistically justifiable. David Storey's *The Changing Room* takes place in the locker room of an English rugby team. At one time, all the players appear nude while changing from street clothing into their uniforms. The nudity is not central to the meaning of the play, but it is a necessary and rational part of the play's locale. Obviously, too much self-consciousness would work against an actor's ability to create the easygoing, uninhibited locker room banter. If you consider the nudity to be gratuitous, you may wish to refrain from auditioning. If you are not comfortable enough with your body to rehearse and perform the play in the nude, regardless of its necessity to character, forward movement of the plot, and artistic justification, you obviously should not consider the role.

## Entering the Creative State

Let us now turn to a sequence of exercises designed to help you remove tensions and promote the creative state. Please realize that these exercises are a mere taste of the organized, rigorous physical-training regimen that serious acting students should undertake. We have also included a small number of vocal exercises, for voice training parallels body training. Again, however, we assume you are taking voice classes simultaneously with your courses in acting. We cannot emphasize too strongly that we agree completely with Kristin Linklater, Arthur Lessac, and others who believe that the creative impulse emanates from a synthesis of a sound, tension-free voice and a healthy, relaxed body. Excellent exercises may be found in their writings, which are detailed in the Bibliography at the end of this book.

Incidentally, various combinations of the following exercises can serve as an excellent warm-up routine before classes, rehearsals, or performances. Just as athletes warm up before practicing or playing the game and pianists do finger stretching and relaxation exercises before rehearsing or performing, you must always prepare your body, mind, and voice for the work at hand. You should *never* commence a sustained period of rehearsal or performance without warming up.

The following exercises are sequential and move logically through eight basic phases: *focusing, meditating, tensing and releasing, centering, shaking, stretching, moving,* and *vocalizing.* They are divided into two basic categories: floor exercises (lying prone or sitting) and standing exercises. Remember, as you begin the following sequence, you must have enough room so your movements will not be restricted, and you should not wear clothing that will hamper your freedom.

---

**Exercise 2.1**   **FOCUSING**   Sit comfortably on the floor with your hands to your side, your back straight, and your legs crossed. Select a small personal object that you have with you and that you like a great deal (e.g., a watch, a necklace, a key chain, a ring, or a tube of lipstick). Place the object on the floor in front of you, and focus all your attention on this object as you inhale and exhale slowly and deeply for one to two minutes. Allow any thoughts that arise to play across your consciousness, and then simply return your awareness to the object in front of you. At the end of this exercise you should feel more peaceful and calmer.

---

**Exercise 2.2**   **MEDITATING**   Lie down on the floor. Allow your arms to rest at your side. Extend your legs straight out along the floor away from your head and allow them to roll outward in a comfortable position. Pick a point on the ceiling, making that your focal point during this exercise. Concentrate on your breathing. Inhale through your nose and exhale through your mouth. After you regulate your breathing, begin to vocalize an elongated [a] sound as you exhale. Continue this breathing pattern until instructed to do otherwise. Notice the movement of your chest and abdomen. Try to suppress all other thoughts, feelings, and sensations. If you feel your attention wandering, simply refocus on your breathing.

Now as you breathe in, channel your attention to different parts of your body (i.e., right leg, left leg, abdomen, chest, right arm, left arm). Take your time. Once you have completed this sequence, say the word "peace" as you inhale. As you exhale, say the word, "calm" aloud. Extend the pronunciation of the word so that it lasts the entire exhalation. "c – a – a – a – a – l – l – l – l – m – m – m – m." Repeating these words as you breathe will help you to concentrate. Now return to breathing without speaking. Remember to breathe in through your nose and out through your mouth.

Meditation is focused on your breath for a good reason: breath is life. Now raise your right hand and arm, holding it in an elevated position for fifteen seconds. Notice if your forearm feels tight and tense or if the muscles are soft and pliable. Let your hand and arm drop to the ground and relax. Notice what happens to the muscles in your arms and hands as they transcend from a state of tension to relaxation. Repeat this process of elevation and relaxation with other parts of your body (i.e., left arm, pelvis, right leg, left leg, and head).

---

**Exercise 2.3**   **TENSING AND RELEASING**   Throughout each phase of relaxation exercises, you should frequently check yourself against excess tension. Most of us have tensions of which we are not aware, and relieving them is an ever-present problem, in life as well as on the stage. We go about our daily activities—walking, sitting, driving, even lying down—using more than the required energy. We should develop a habit of frequently checking ourselves in whatever we are doing to discover what muscles are unnecessarily tense and then proceed to relax them. We may often find we are holding onto a pencil as if it would jump out of our fingers, or we are walking with tense shoulders or standing with our knees locked, talking with a tight jaw, or reading with a frown.

Routinely checking for tensions and relieving them yields several benefits. Although it may be impossible, onstage or off, to keep an overabundance of tension from occurring, this habit will help induce a state of general relaxation. Our goal is to eliminate excess tensions at will—a capacity of great value to actors, who are always subject to nervous strain. Perhaps most important, finding tension helps actors discover their own nervous mannerisms. Different people reveal tensions in different ways, some by contracted muscles, others by random movements. Among the most common movements are shaking the head, pursing the lips, frowning, snapping the fingers, raising the shoulders. Make an inventory of your personal signs of tension, and focus on ridding yourself of them.

To release excess tension, we begin by creating it deliberately and then letting it go. As each area is named below, isolate and tense the muscles associated with that part of your body for approximately fifteen seconds, while keeping the rest of your body relaxed. On the instructor's command, release the tension with a vocalized and elongated [a]. Feel the muscular movement as tension is released. We will work our way down the body from your head to your toes.

Tense all your facial muscles inward toward the center of your face. Hold for fifteen seconds and release. Press your tongue against the roof of your mouth. Hold for fifteen seconds and release. Now work your way down your body in this order: neck, shoulders, right arm, right hand, left arm, left hand, upper chest and back, abdomen and lower back, groin and buttocks, right leg, left leg—your entire body. Once you have completed the sequence, repeat the entire exercise again, but this time hold the tension in each area for only three seconds, remembering to keep everything free of tension until its turn in the sequence.

---

**Exercise 2.4**    **CENTERING**    While still on your back from the previous exercise, make yourself as long as possible. After one minute, make yourself as short as possible, compressing your vertebrae as much as you can. Again after one minute, make yourself as wide as possible, flattening your body and stretching as far as you can from side to side. Now, make yourself as narrow as possible without decreasing your length.

Once completed, roll to your side, in a tucked position, and then over so your face and stomach are facing the floor. With your feet on the ground, uncoil into a standing position by aligning (or stacking) your vertebrae one at a time, with your head being the last part to uncurl. From this standing position, gently lift from the lower part of your spine, again making yourself as tall as possible. Drop the upper half of your body forward like a rag doll. Your hands will probably brush against the floor. Let your knees bend slightly for balance and support. Locate the excess tension and gently move that part of your upper body, allowing the tension to drip out of your skin. Alleviate the tension in your face by making a "motor boat" sound. Don't be afraid to drool on the floor. Now, gently sway from side to side three or four times and then rise to a standing position by again aligning (or stacking) your vertebrae one at a time. Drop from the waist and repeat the entire sequence.

---

**Exercise 2.5**    **SHAKING**    While standing in place, simply "shake" the tension out of the following areas of your body: wrists, right elbow, right arm, left elbow, left arm, right leg, left leg.

---

**Exercise 2.6**    **STRETCHING**    Stretching prepares our bodies for physical activity. While it lowers blood pressure and improves blood flow to the heart, for the actor (and athletes), stretching increases muscle temperature, making them more pliable and adaptable to changes from the body's habitual use. The following is a sequence of stretching exercises that flow logically from one to the next, beginning in a supine position on the floor, then sitting upright, and finally from a standing position.

**A.** Stretch and Yawn

Lie on your back comfortably on the floor, and stretch your entire body. Extend your limbs, drop your jaw, and yawn. Repeat and encourage a "real" yawn. Let the natural vocalized sound empty out of your body.

**B.** Spinal Stretch (Shoulder Press)

Place your arms at your sides. Relax the small of your back, and stretch your legs out parallel to each other. Now lift your legs and hips by making a tripod with your elbows on the floor. Extend your legs toward the ceiling, making sure your toes are pointed. Hold for fifteen seconds. Continue this movement, keeping your legs straight, until your toes touch the floor above your head. After fifteen seconds, bend your knees, bringing them to your ears. Take a deep breath. Straighten your legs and again extend to a vertical position with your toes pointing toward the ceiling. Slowly roll your body back down using your spine until you are again lying flat on the floor. Take another deep breath, and repeat the entire sequence.

**C.** Posterior Stretch

Bend your right leg and place both hands around the underside of your right knee. Pull the knee toward your left shoulder, keeping your head, shoulders, and right leg relaxed. Hold for fifteen seconds and repeat. This time, however, pull both your right knee and ankle toward your left shoulder. Repeat the entire sequence with your left knee and ankle.

**D.** Lower Back Stretch (Diagonal Twist)

Straighten your legs and place your arms straight out from your body. Raise your right leg and rotate it over to the left at a ninety-degree angle and touch the floor with your right foot. Rotate your upper torso the other direction, looking to the right. Be certain your right hip is pointed up to the ceiling. Hold for fifteen seconds, and repeat with the left leg. Once completed, repeat the entire sequence two additional times.

**E.** Front of Trunk Stretch (The Cobra)

Roll onto your stomach, and bring your hands to the sides of your shoulders and ease your chest off the floor, keeping your hips firmly pressed onto the ground. Hold for fifteen seconds and repeat.

**F.** Lower Back Stretch (The Cat)

Assume a position on your hands and knees (like a cat) and then arch your back toward the ceiling. After fifteen seconds, press your spine toward the ground.

Now, sit back on your heels, and reach forward with your arms. Once you have completed the three-part sequence, repeat two additional times.

**G.** Middle Eastern Prayer Stretch

Begin in a tucked position with your knees, face, and arms resting comfortably on the floor. Inhale to the count of four as you rise to a kneeling position, sitting on your lower legs with your arms at your sides. Exhale to the count of four as you put your hands on the floor behind you and push forward and up as far as you can with your pelvis. Inhale to the count of four as you return to the sitting position. Then, exhale to the count of four as you return to the original Middle Eastern Prayer position (i.e., tucked with knees, face, and arms on the floor). Repeat the sequence once using four counts for each movement and then repeat the sequence twice using two counts for each movement.

**H.** Groin Stretch

Sit with tall posture, and ease your feet toward your body, bringing the soles together and allowing your knees to come up and out to the side. Resting your hands on your lower legs or ankles, ease both knees toward the ground. Hold for fifteen seconds and repeat.

**I.** Hamstring Stretch

Start with your legs stretched in front of you, and place the sole of your left foot alongside your right knee. Allow your left leg to lie relaxed on the ground, and bend forward, keeping your back straight. Hold for fifteen seconds, and repeat with your other leg.

**J.** Lower Spine Stretch

From a squatting position on the floor, give yourself a wide base by placing your feet wider than shoulder width apart. Roll up your spine—one vertebra at a time—to a standing position and reach for the ceiling. Hold for fifteen seconds. Bending at the waist and keeping your spine straight (known as "flat back"), reach forward, making certain to keep your head up and looking forward. Hold for fifteen seconds before relaxing the spine and hanging from the waist down to the ground ("rag doll position"). Repeat the sequence.

**K.** Chest Stretch

Standing tall with your wide base and knees slightly bent, hold your arms out to the side parallel with the ground and the palms of your hands facing forward. Clasp your hands together behind your back and gently lift. Hold for fifteen seconds, and return to the original position. Repeat.

**L.** Shoulder Stretch

Place your right arm parallel with the ground across the front of your chest. Bend your left arm up and use the left forearm to ease the right arm closer to your chest. Hold for fifteen seconds, and repeat with left arm.

**M.** Shoulder and Triceps Stretch (The Back Scratch)

Keeping your wide base, fully extend both arms above your head. Drop your right hand and swing your left hand around your back to grab your right elbow. Hold for fifteen seconds, and repeat with left hand.

**N.** Side Stretch

From your wide base position, again hold your arms out to your side parallel with the ground and the palms of your hands facing forward. Keeping your arms straight, take your left arm up and over your head, reaching to the right. Take your right arm across your chest and reach to the left. Hold for fifteen seconds, and repeat to the other side. Repeat sequence.

---

**Exercise 2.7    MOVING**

**A.** Walk/Run/Freeze

Everybody in class begins by walking. Do not perform this action for anybody else's benefit. Do not "act," and avoid walking in a circle. Note the way you carry yourself, the way your feet touch the ground, the way you move your arms. Where is your center? Do you lead with your chest? Your head? Your pelvis? Change directions. Modify your stride. See yourself in relation to everyone in the room. Throughout this sequence, you may interact with others as you walk. Have fun. When the impulse arises, run. Run fast (but in control). Now you are either walking or running. Follow some others in the class. Note the distinct way they carry themselves, and adapt your movement to theirs. Do not enlarge upon or mock their movement; instead, note the subtle differences. Break away in a different direction. Don't plan these actions. Be impulsive. Be erratic. Sometimes you are walking; sometimes you are running; sometimes you are following; sometimes you are not. Continue this pattern for a while noting your body's changes. Freeze. Do not move a muscle or look about the room. Note your position, your carriage. Where is your center? Resume moving. Sometimes you are walking; sometimes you are running; sometimes you are frozen; sometimes you are following; sometimes you are not.

**B.** Run/Freeze

Everyone in the room run at the same time. Freeze at the same time. There are no leaders. There are no followers. Everyone must work together.

After a few minutes and upon the orders of your instructor, stand face to face with a single partner. Move at the same time; freeze at the same time. You do not have to mirror your partner. Your movements will be distinct with regards to both form and tempo-rhythm. But you must start and stop at exactly the same time. Vary the lengths of time you move and freeze. Explore various movements, using your entire body. Again, be erratic. No one is leading; no one is following.

Again at the discretion of your instructor, change partners. Stand face to face and move at different times. Partner A moves while Partner B remains frozen. Partner A continues to move until Partner B interrupts him with her movement. Partner A freezes while Partner B moves. Partner B continues to move until Partner A interrupts her. This pattern continues until you are instructed to stop. Your movements should not be empty forms, but rather they should reflect your state of mind.

**C.** Shaping/Reshaping

Again, change partners, and determine Partner A and Partner B. A makes an abstract shape (like a statue). B makes a different shape and places it in relation to A's shape. Once B has assumed a shape, A steps out of the original shape and reshapes in relation to B's shape, etc. Fill the negative space without touching. Move slowly and smoothly. Think creatively using your whole body. As you do this, consider the following suggestions with regard to your shapes.

- circular
- angular
- spacious
- twisted
- complex
- arched

Now consider the following images, and design your shapes/reshapes accordingly.

- a gentle breeze
- lightning
- falling leaves
- an erupting volcano
- melting ice
- rain
- mud
- a river
- an ice storm

**D.** Walking with Purpose (Justifying Your Actions)

Everybody in the class begins walking again. As you did in Exercise 2.7A, avoid walking in circles. Note your carriage, your feet, your arms, your center. Now begin to walk with specific purpose. Walk (or crawl) as if you were:

- a baby learning to walk
- a teenager approaching another teenager of the opposite sex
- an elderly person crossing a busy intersection
- a trapper on snowshoes
- a native balancing a can of water on your head
- a burglar hugging the sides of the buildings in a dark alley
- a hunter stalking a deer
- a fashion model on the runway
- a soldier crawling on your stomach under gunfire
- a drum major or majorette

**E.** Point to Point

All should stop wherever they are in the room. You are now at Point A. Do not move until you have determined Point B. This point should not be arbitrary or "in space." It should be a specific destination. Once Point B is determined, take the shortest, logical path to that spot. After you have arrived at Point B, determine Point C. Cross to that point, and so on. Continue this exercise, moving point to point, with the following variations.

Cross with different tempo-rhythms. Be specific and justify your actions. For example, you are late for an important meeting or you are an elementary student who has been sent to the principal's office.

Cross with the intent of completing a specific activity. For example, you cross to the dictionary to look up a specific word or you cross to your backpack to retrieve your hairbrush and brush your hair.

---

### Exercise 2.8  VOCALIZING

A. Massage your face with the palm of your hands and fingertips. Apply some pressure, paying particular attention to your jaw, your nasal-labial folds (your "laugh-lines"), and your forehead.

B. Vocalize the sound "hummmmmmmmm" five times.

C. Shake your face back and forth. Your cheeks and lips should be loose.

D. Wet your lips and stretch your mouth open as wide as possible.

E. Make the sound of a motorboat—first without sound, then with monotone sound, and finally with sound that moves up and down in pitch.

F. Stick out your tongue as far as you can. With your tongue, touch the tip of your nose, your cheek on the right side, your chin, your cheek on the left side, etc.

G. Anchor your tongue behind your bottom front teeth, and pulsate your tongue with a sigh, "aaaaaahhhhhh."

H. Make the sound of a drum roll—first without sound, then with monotone sound, and finally with sound that moves up and down in pitch.

I. Repeat the sound [k] five times, projecting it to the back wall of your classroom or performance space.

J. Repeat the sound [g] five times.

K. Alternate between [k] and [g] five times.

L. Repeat the sound [p] five times.

M. Repeat the sound [b] five times.

N. Alternate between [p] and [b] five times.

O. Vocalize "hummmmmm maaaaaahhhhhh" five times, raising your pitch each subsequent time.

P. Again, make the sound of a motor boat.

Q. Vocalize "me me me me me me me me maaaaaahhhhhh" five times.

R. Again, massage your face with your palms and fingertips.

**S.** Vocalize "me me me me may may may maaaaaahhhhhh" five times, making certain to drop the jaw as you say "maaaaaahhhhhh."

**T.** Repeat "me me me me may may may may maaaaaahhhhhh" five additional times, only now add an upward inflection at the end of the phrase.

**U.** Repeat the following tongue twisters three to five times each.

    **i.** Red leather, yellow leather

    **ii.** Synonym, cinnamon, aluminum, linoleum

    **iii.** You know New York. You need New York. You know you need unique New York.

    **iv.** A proper cup of coffee in a copper coffee cup

    **v.** Whether the weather be cold, or whether the weather be hot, we'll weather the weather whatever the weather, whether we like it or not.

    **vi.** Peter Piper picked a peck of pickled peppers. A peck of pickled peppers did Peter Piper pick. If Peter Piper picked a peck of pickled peppers, how many pickled peppers did Peter Piper pick?

    **vii.** Father fries fish in a fish fryer.

    **viii.** She sells seashells by the seashore.

    **ix.** A big black bug bit a big black bear and made the big black bear bleed blood.

    **x.** Sixty-six sick chicks

    **xi.** Does this shop stock short socks with spots?

    **xii.** He thrust three thousand thistles through the thick of his thumb.

    **xiii.** Rubber baby buggy bumpers

    **xiv.** I slit a sheet. A sheet I slit. And on that slitted sheet I sit.

## Terms and People to Know

**centering**    A term synonymous with proper alignment and good posture. Rather than posture that is stiff or artificially frozen, centering involves the correct alignment of our vertebrae that is our body's natural position.

**creative state**    A concentrated state of relaxation in which actors can attain their utmost capacity for accomplishing any activity.

**resonance**    An opening of the oral cavities amplifying the vocal sound and giving it strength, tone, timbre, and personal quality.

**Strasberg, Lee (1901–1982)**    One of the founders of the Group Theatre and later the Actors Studio and developer of what came to be known as Method Acting, an internal approach based on the early teaching of Stanislavski emphasizing affective memory, which is explored in Chapter 7.

## CHAPTER 3

# Discovering Physical Actions

*"An actor becomes an actor when he masters the choice of actions."*

–Constantin Stanislavski

The discovery of actions is the first step in the physicalization of any character. Although your ultimate goal is truthful inner emotions, they cannot be obtained directly. In and of themselves, feelings are shapeless and vague. They are an end result. Therefore, you do not consider them at this point. Instead, you must focus on honest behavior. Remember that in Chapter 1 we stated that you must create a character who "behaves logically in imaginary circumstances." Truth comes from within, but only your physical body can communicate your thoughts and feelings. Thus, the discovery of physical actions will serve as a launching pad for the beginning of your technique training.

At the end of Chapter 1, we gave you a hypothetical situation of having been cast as one of the star-crossed lovers in *Romeo and Juliet*. Suppose you are playing Juliet. Imagine arriving at your first rehearsal, both nervous and energized about the task that lies before you. You are about to embark upon a journey of creating a uniquely original interpretation of this girl living in another dimension. You may understand what is expected of you in the end, but where do you begin? How do you give life to Juliet's soul through your art? How do you discover her specific sequence of truthful actions that occur throughout each scene? Where do you find her physical form? You begin with a careful study of the play's **given circumstances,** the unchangeable facts found in the text; they provide you with the basic raw material for creating your character's external form.

Arriving at this first rehearsal, you no doubt have read the script more carefully than you have ever read anything before. Shakespeare's words should have fueled your imagination, but now you face the problem of materializing Juliet's thoughts and feelings, of discovering her physical actions. The given circumstances found in the text provide you with much material to begin this process. From the script, you (the actor) know that "you" (the character) are a girl of thirteen.* "Your" mother and nurse confirm this in Act I, Scene iii. "Come Lammas Eve at night shall she be fourteen." This is an unchangeable fact. "You" discover that "your" parents have arranged for "you" to marry a young count, Paris, who is kinsman of the Prince. There is no reason to doubt the accuracy of this information either. "You" know "you" are an only child. "Your" father verifies this when he says "That God had lent us but this only child. . . ." "You" know "you" are a Capulet, and "you" come to realize that "you" have fallen in love with one of "your" family's mortal enemies. "'Tis but thy name that is my enemy." All these facts, these given circumstances, are undeniable and unchanging.

Like many scripts, however, scores of details in the given circumstances in *Romeo and Juliet* are subject to interpretation. For example, Lady Capulet describes Paris as a young man "writ with beauty's pen." This is not factual information, it is merely "your" mother's perception of him. "Your" opinion of him may be quite the opposite. "You" may consider him to be arrogant with sharp features and void of humor. Similarly, certain details about your character may be only suggested or inferred. As an actor, you must make decisions about your portrayal by using Juliet's own words, as well as things that are said to or about her. You have many blanks to fill. For example, "you" know "you" come from a wealthy household. The lines infer that "you" have received a proper education—unlike most Italian girls living during the Renaissance. You can also deduce that "you" consider "yourself" to be a romantic who dreams of an idyllic love. Your decisions about Juliet's education and dreams of love are inferred in her lines as she first meets Romeo, "You kiss by th' book." From this small clue, you can surmise that "you" have never kissed a man. "You" have dreamed of love. "You" have read about it in the books, but "you" have never experienced it. In a later scene, "your" father, in a fit of rage, shouts that "you" are not fit to marry "so worthy a gentleman"

---

*When creating a role, you should always think in first person. If you speak of your character as "he," you will automatically be distancing yourself from him and his actions. Thus, when discussing your character, you should always speak from his or her point of view by referring to yourself as "I." Anytime the authors of this book speak from the character's point of view, we use forms of "you," always placing quotation marks around the word.

as Paris. He calls you a "disobedient wretch" and refers to you as "a whining mammet." Lord Capulet's lines are part of the given circumstances, but they are delivered in an emotional tirade. They are subjective and delivered from his point of view at this particularly vulnerable moment. As the actor portraying Juliet, you must decide what information extracted from the dialogue is true and what is false, exaggerated, or twisted by someone else's subjective opinion.

As in real life, not all characters speak the truth. Like us, they look at their world subjectively. They have a unique point of view about every issue and every other person in the play. They bring with them certain beliefs, values, and prejudices. It is your responsibility to discover the truth as perceived by your character. Once you have firmly established your character's point of view regarding "the facts" and understood their implications, you will be ready to augment the circumstances with material drawn from your own imagination. The latter aspect is significant, for it is the technique from which actors place their distinctive interpretation on the role.

Creating a unique point of view is one of the most exhilarating facets of acting. Unfortunately, this excitement can seduce actors into rushing into that phase of their work before they have sufficiently completed their study of the script. Your character's behavior must always be firmly grounded in the perceived circumstances. "Let each actor give an honest reply to the question of what physical action he would undertake, how he would act (not feel, there should for heaven's sake be no question of feelings at this point) in the given circumstances created by the playwright," wrote Stanislavski in his book, *Creating a Role*. "When these physical actions have been clearly defined, all that remains for the actor to do is to execute them."

Your search for the given circumstances begins in the script, with a study of the dramatic elements of character, plot, place, and time. In most instances, the playwright uses these facts to tell you about your character. You must carefully study your character's words, her every action. Where and when do these physical actions occur? At a later point in the rehearsal process, the given circumstances will also include directorial choices, stage business, costumes, and scenic environment; but mastering these elements is an aspect of acting that will be discussed in a subsequent chapter. For now, let us focus on answering four questions: Who? What? Where? When?

Each of these four Ws (we will add an essential fifth in the next chapter) asks questions to which you must find specific answers either in the text or in your imagination. Until these answers are clear, your acting, from simple exercises to complex characterizations, will be at best confusing and at worst meaningless. The answers to the W questions generate physical actions, and these actions, when clearly performed, communicate the circumstances of the play to the audience.

Your acceptance of the role of Juliet has committed you to act in the given circumstances of the Shakespeare's play. She is a specific character created by a master dramatist. You will be expected to play her to the fullest extent that your

**Figure 3.1** Ty Hewitt (*left*) as Burton, Adam D. Wasserman as Larry, and Stacie Beth Green as Anna in a scene from the University of Missouri–Kansas City's production of *Burn This*. Directed by Mark Robbins, scenic design by Ivan Chagas, costume design by Jonathan Knipscher, lighting design by Temishia Johnson. Never embark on an acting assignment until you have thoroughly investigated the four Ws. Also note the shared positions and focal points in the composition of the actors in this scene.

experience and imagination enable you to understand the playwright's direction. You have no choice, of course, but to play her with your own body, your own voice. You must use your own past experiences and imagination to deliver appropriate live responses. It follows, then, that in seeking to discover the physical life of young Juliet, you must always find a logical sequence of actions you can understand, that you can *believe* are *necessary*. Again, the vital question is, "What would I do *if I were this character* in these circumstances?" To ask only "What would I (the actor) do in these circumstances?" inevitably means that you play only yourself rather than the young woman drawn by Shakespeare.

In creating a role, you must use the four Ws to trigger your imagination, and by opening night, these given circumstances will be rooted in your psyche. You will not have to think about these questions, "you" will simply know who "you" are, where "you" are, and when this sequence of actions (the what) are taking place. At this point, you will only consider the **moment before** (where "you" have been and what has occurred) and "your" reason for entering this new space. Well before you arrive at this point, however, you must answer each of the four major questions and all the subsidiary questions precisely and fully.

It is not sufficient for an actor in Act I, Scene i of Neil Simon's *Biloxi Blues* to answer the "Where?" question with "in a train." A more satisfactory initial response would be, "an overcrowded and stifling coach of an old train, pressed into service because of World War II." The actors playing Jerry and Peter in *The Zoo Story* cannot sufficiently stimulate their imaginations by thinking of themselves as "in a park." They must concentrate on being "in Central Park, near 75th Street and Fifth Avenue in New York, about nine blocks north of the Central Park Zoo." As a young actor, however, you may never have experienced a long trip in a railroad car or visited Central Park. Nevertheless, it is still your responsibility to make the "Where?" as truthful and specific as possible. You have your whole life from which to draw, and you have no doubt experienced congested school bus trips that reeked from junk food, foot odor, and other bodily emissions. You have enjoyed many excursions to a local park. You probably have vivid memories of playing with your dog or throwing a Frisbee®. You know the trees, the landscape, and the specific details of your favorite outdoor hideaway. You certainly have at least some understanding of life in a large city. By transferring these life experiences—added to proper analysis and research—you will have the ability to create a stage environment that is equally specific and detailed.

The questions "What?" and "When?" demand the same specificity. What has happened previously? What has occurred the precise moment before? What is happening in the play right now? What are your character's expectations? What is the year? The season? The day? The weather? At what time does "your" selected life begin? More importantly, how do the conditions discovered in the "When?" and "Where?" affect the "What?"

The "Who?" question must not merely trigger the preconceived—and usually stereotypical—notions of a lawyer, a cheerleader, or a prince, because these terms stand for an infinite variety of people. All lawyers are not the same any more than individual members of a cheerleading squad are the same. Prince Hamlet of tenth century Denmark is vastly different from Prince Harry of early fifteenth century England. "Who am I?" demands thorough investigation using all your resources. In creating a **character autobiography**—more thoroughly discussed in Part II, Chapter 8, "Creating a Character"—you certainly must record your character's list of experiences, relationships, and achievements. More important, though, you must explore your character's dreams, fears, values, and spirituality. What is "your" present state of being? What are "you" wearing, and how does it affect "your" actions?

Perhaps the most important question you must ask yourself about "Who?" is "How do 'I' perceive myself?" Again, remember that actors cannot judge their characters if they are to wear their clothing and behave truthfully in the given circumstances. Prostitutes do not necessarily consider themselves amoral. On the contrary, they may regard themselves as extremely decent and honest people—although industrious and streetwise—who are stuck in extraordinary circumstances and must do what they can to survive. A mass murderer can justify his every action. Although we may consider Adolph Hitler to be one of the most evil men in history, Hitler professed himself to be the spiritual savior, the purifier of his race. He may have perceived himself as a charismatic leader, who had the vision and means to accomplish his political and honorable goals. Judging characters—no matter how different they are from you—will only stifle the creative process. Actors who cannot or refuse to drop their own point of view and moral sensitivities regarding the character's actions and beliefs will create nothing more than a hollow stereotype. Actors who will only look at their characters from the outside will never have the ability to fully invest in truthful actions.

Without specific and detailed responses to all four Ws leading to plausible, consistent behavior, you—as well as the audience—will never *believe* in your character's reality. However, the four Ws are not always equally important in every scene. Sometimes, for instance, logical actions growing out of "Who?" dominate the moment. For example, at the beginning of *A Streetcar Named Desire*, when Blanche sneaks a drink before Stella comes home, she needs to dispose of the glass. An appropriate physical action selected by the actor will speak volumes about Blanche's character. In the original Broadway production, Jessica Tandy, standing in front of the kitchen sink, ignored the seemingly logical choice of rinsing out the glass. Rather, she shook it vigorously and replaced it in the cabinet. In this way, the preliminary picture the audience had probably formed of a delicate but fading southern belle was cracked, if not shattered. As you perform the exercises at the end of this chapter, try altering which of the W questions is dominant in the scene. Notice how each selection will offer a different range of physical choices.

Exploring your character's physical actions and building on your own live responses are important problems to be considered in later chapters. We are also postponing for the moment a thorough discussion of the actor's use of emotion, complying with Stanislavski's warning that "there should be no question of feelings at this point."

For now, we will simply state that emotions, of course, play a critical role in acting; however, they are unpredictable. You cannot act an emotion, nor can you call forth an emotional response at will. You must learn to begin with tangible and controllable physical actions. You cannot play happiness any more than you can play anger; however, you can at every performance carry out a series of actions whenever you will to do so. What is more, because physical actions and internal emotion are inextricably linked, performing the needed actions in the given circumstances may bring forth the desired feeling. We will speak of this in greater detail at the beginning of the next chapter. But whether or not the physical actions generate an emotional response, the careful playing of them will realize the intention of the scene and accomplish the actor's primary responsibility. Success is not to be judged by whether emotion is aroused in the actor.

## Committing Yourself to Action

The above reference to the actor's *will* introduces you to one of your most valuable inner resources. So important is your **will,** or full commitment to your actions onstage, that it became the cornerstone of the teaching of one of the greatest twentieth-century American acting teachers, **Sanford Meisner.** He believed that the foundation of acting is the "reality of doing." Meisner's "reality of doing" is our will, our commitment to actions. In life, we don't pretend to get dressed in the morning. We actually put on our shirts, our pants, and our socks. We really tie our shoelaces. The stage is a secondary reality, a mirror to nature. However, you must invest as fully in your stage actions as you do in life. At the beginning of his acting classes, Meisner invariably asked his students to solve in their head a multiplication problem. "What is nine hundred thirty-one times eighteen?" His students sat in silence. Some of them pretended to concentrate while others attempted to answer the question. No one solved the problem. The correct answer is 16,758. The answer, however, is not important. What is important is your will to work out the problem.[1] In attempting to solve your simple and complex problems onstage, you must always search for solutions that are subject to your will. You must find appropriate actions to which you can fully commit and that can be repeated and kept under control at every rehearsal and performance.

The will to action is one of your most powerful inner motive forces, both on the stage and off. Creativity is directly related to your complete investment in the physical life of your character. The strength of your desire to "do fully" determines how interesting your performance will be to yourself and, to a large extent, how remarkable it will be to your audience. Your commitment to your actions is effective only as long as those actions are directed toward logical activity, supported by the given circumstances, and meaningful to the character. Your activity must also be capable of motivating strong desire. There is no place either on the stage or in the rehearsal room for half-heartedness or indifference. Actors who pretend to drink, pretend to read a letter, pretend to smoke, pretend to kiss will never arrive at "true emotions" onstage. Their actions will simply be false indications of the truth. You must learn to commit yourself without reservation to the purposeful acts of your character. Doing so, you will find that this personal commitment is one of the principal generators of feeling.

© 2003 Utah Shakespearean Festival. Photo by Karl Hugh.

**Figure 3.2**   Anne Newhall (*left*) as Billie Dawn and Craig Spidle as Harry
Brock in *Born Yesterday,* 2003. Note the determination of will by both
actors in this scene; also notice that through the arranged composition,
the woman receives primary focus, while the man is in a power position.

Unfortunately, a dedication to strong will does not in itself sufficiently guar-
antee believability. You must also recognize that, through lack of knowledge or
experience or imagination, you can fully commit to inappropriate speech patterns
or illogical character choices that are unsupported by the given circumstances.
The result will be a performance that is at odds with the play. For example, if you
were born and raised in Massachusetts and have been cast as Annelle in Robert

Harling's *Steel Magnolias*, it is illogical to maintain your strong New England dialect, ignoring the small town, Louisianan speech of your character. You must find both her obvious accent and subtle variations of language. Conversely, the playwright, Arthur Miller, does not specify a city or state for *All My Sons*, but he very clearly asserts in the text that the action takes place approximately seven hundred miles from New York City.

MOTHER: Why did he invite her here?

KELLER: Why does that bother you?

MOTHER: She's been in New York three and a half years, why all of a sudden . . . ?

KELLER: Well, maybe . . . maybe he just wanted to see her . . .

MOTHER: Nobody comes seven hundred miles "just to see."[2]

From the textual references and the type of successful business built by Joe Keller, we can safely deduce that the action takes place close to a smaller urban area. Therefore, your production may be set in Cincinnati, Indianapolis, Louisville, Charlotte, or another smaller city close to this seven-hundred-mile radius. If you are an actor who was raised in Dallas, it is irrational to ignore the dialectical differences in locale between Dallas and any of the aforementioned cities.

Strong commitment to proper action must not be confined to performance. You must practice this wholeheartedly in every classroom exercise. You must give your total being to your actions during every moment of every rehearsal. Such commitment is an important part of all creative talent.

---

**Exercise 3.1**   **DISCOVERING ACTIONS**   To illustrate what is meant by "exploring your inner resources" and "discovering physical actions," in Chapter 1 we talked about playing a young Russian princess or Romeo or Juliet. But these problems, involving knowledge of foreign customs or an understanding of what you would do in a scene of emotional crisis, are too complex for beginning practice, so we shall start with a simpler exercise.

In the first act of *The Boys Next Door,* by Tom Griffin, the mentally challenged Lucien, dressed in a pair of worn pajamas and carrying a mop and a flashlight, cautiously enters the living room area of his apartment and calls for his roommates, Arnold and Norman, to tell them that he has trapped a rat under the toilet. Following some nervous banter about what to do with the rodent, the three men devise "an airtight plan" to "blind" the rat by turning off the lights. After that, Arnold instructs Lucien to shut the door—without letting him "know where you are." Thus, the rat will be forever ensnared in the lavatory. They extinguish the lights, but before Lucien can close the door, the rat escapes the bathroom and scurries into the kitchen area. Confusion ensues, and they capture the rat with a pillow. Lucien, wild with excitement, pounds the cushion with his fists. They cautiously lift the pillow to "check him out." Once they determine he is dead, Lucien guardedly lifts the rat by the tail and carries him into the bathroom, where he flushes him down the toilet.

Here is an acting problem providing an opportunity to explore your inner resources for the purpose of finding the logical sequence of actions demanded by the given circumstances. If you had never been spooked by the emergence of an unexpected intruder (e.g., a mouse, squirrel, bird, or cockroach) in your home, it would be impossible for you to solve this problem until you had enlarged your experience. Fortunately, however, most everyone can identify with the irrational fear of having to apprehend such uninvited intruders, so it is relatively easy for you to find in your own experience what you would do if you were Lucien in this situation. This is a simple but very real acting problem.

In this exercise, you are playing the role of Lucien. Ignore the existence of "your" roommates and the context of the scene. Likewise, disregard the sex and mental capacity of your character and work on a sequence of actions until you can truly *believe* everything "you" do. Here, as in all succeeding exercises, choose your actions so they constitute a definite dramatic structure. This means they should have a *beginning* (acquainting the audience with the problem); *middle* (developing the problem); and *end* (resolving the problem). Each of these three structural elements should be played clearly and precisely. In the early exercises the structure will be simple. Construct your sequence of actions as follows:

**The Beginning:** "Your" approach to the bathroom door in order to trap the rat.

**The Middle:** The rat's escape and "your" subsequent chase, capture, and ultimate killing of the rat beneath a pillow.

**The End:** The lifting of the rat by the tail and exiting with him into the bathroom.

Plays are filled with situations like this one that require you to perform in such a way that you convince the audience you believe the actions you must undertake.

## Believing Your Actions

Several times already, beginning with the title of this book, we have referred to "believing your actions" or "creating a character in whom you can believe." You must believe what you are doing. Your fundamental responsibility to the audience is to induce their belief in your actions. Thus, the objective of the above exercise is not to pretend you are wild with excitement; rather, it is to make yourself *believe your sequence of selected actions* as "you" try to capture the rat. Acting is literally a matter of make-believe, fueled by an attitude almost identical to that which comes naturally to children.

Children have the innate ability to create for themselves a set of circumstances very similar to those given to the actor by the dramatist. During play, a little girl may take on the persona of her Barbie® doll in various situations; a boy may pretend he is camping under the dining room table. With very little prompting, children have the ability to fully believe in their reality as a king, princess, soldier, fairy, Superman, or even a dog. They instinctively behave in whatever fashion their experience or imagination leads them to think is true to the imposed conditions.

The pleasure children receive from the game is in direct proportion to their ability to believe their actions. As the game wears thin and their belief decreases, they invent new circumstances to stimulate further action. One child may propose: "Let's make believe the king wasn't really hurt when he fell off his horse but was only pretending. He did it so the prince would feel sorry for him and help him fight the Black Knight." A whole new sequence of actions is justified, allowing the child and his playmates to continue the game with renewed belief.

Of course, the throne is actually their parents' dining chair. The king's crown is from a fast-food restaurant. The swords are plastic. When the game is over, the precious crown that has been guarded so carefully is kicked to one side of the living room floor. The children never think these things are real, yet while the game is on they treat these "**props**" as if they were genuine.

It is the same for the actor. During the day King Lear's robes hang limply on a hook in the dressing room, and the imperial crown lies unguarded on the prop table. But when the performance begins, if the actor playing Lear is to convince the audience he is every inch a king, he must believe in the circumstances given him by Shakespeare, by the director, and by the designers as thoroughly as he believes in the actual world around him. "No half-belief," as Michael Redgrave said. "Belief . . . does not begin and end by an intellectual process, but . . . is so deep-rooted that it fires each movement, echoes in each silence, and penetrates beyond 'the threshold of the subconscious,' where it becomes creative."[3]

We do not suggest the actor subject himself to a kind of hallucination that blurs his view of the surrounding reality and induces him to accept the pieces of glass in the crown as diamonds. The actor playing Lear knows that the life of the character he is playing lives only in the imagination, and, like the children, he knows that the crown and robes are not really adorned with priceless jewels. He knows, in short, that he is not actually King Lear. He is an actor, so toward all these things he says: "I will act as *if* they were real." And this conviction in the truth of his actions enables him to believe also in the *truth* (not the *reality*) of the costume.

Remember, only reality exists. As we stated in the first chapter, you cannot help but believe in the truth of reality. With the help of the "magic if," however, you can suspend your disbelief and enter into your character's world with more passion than you believe in your own reality. *If* is a word that can transform our thoughts. *If* allows us to transport ourselves into any situation. "If 'I' were in love. . . ." "If 'I' won the lottery. . . ." "If 'I' were on death row. . . ." "If I were a tenth-century prince and my mother married my uncle not two months after the

Photo by Kenn Stilson.

**Figure 3.3**    Lisa Curtis and Stephen Fister in Southeast Missouri State University's production of *Picasso at the Lapin Agile.* Directed by Robert W. Dillon, Jr.; scenic design by Dennis C. Seyer; costume design by Rhonda C. Weller-Stilson; lighting and sound design by Philip Nacy. The simplest physical actions will induce the greatest feelings of belief. Also look at the simple give and take positions of these two actors, which give the female character focus and power.

death of 'my' father." The word *if* is incredibly powerful. *If* gives us a sense of certainty about our new world. If the actor playing Lear loses his sense of truth, it will not be because the crown is not real but because he cannot believe his own actions in relation to it.

Learn this Stanislavski axiom well: *Concentration on your most simple physical actions will induce the greatest feelings of belief, and the sum total of your small actions are of vast significance to the whole play.*

Once you learn to believe in the truth of your actions, sustaining that belief is a difficult and ever-present problem. You must work in front of an audience, surrounded by the inevitable distractions of a theatrical production. You must be able to summon your belief on cue whenever the moment to enter the stage arises. The slightest doubt as to the rightness or truth of what you or the other actors are doing is likely to upset you immediately. An actor playing Lear who treats his crown like the leather with hot-glued costume jewelry it really is can destroy the belief of everyone onstage, just as a cynical child can obliterate the game's magic by protesting they can't fight with "plastic." You may renew a wavering belief, just as the child does, by discovering new circumstances that will excite new actions.

## Incorporating Improvisational Technique

All live theatre integrates a certain degree of **improvisation,** the spontaneous invention of lines and business without fixed text or actions. Actors lose their train of thought; entrances are missed; and electronic devices fail. This is the Murphy's Law of theatre. There are no second chances onstage. Just you and your partners stand metaphorically naked in front of an audience. This is why we say theatre is both exhilarating and dangerous. Improvisational skills help you walk this tightrope without a safety net in performance.

The ability to create through improvisational choices also plays a vital role in rehearsals. Throughout the process of creation, it is your job to make strong choices. Once your character becomes rooted in your subconscious, rehearsals involve decision making. Every time you work a scene, you are playing your character's objectives through an investigation of tactical choices while working against obstacles. (This is the primary focus of the next chapter and the core of all subsequent exercises.)

Improvisation as a method of learning, rehearsing, and performing has dominated actor training during the past several decades. Much of the theory underpinning this approach grows out of the research on games and play conducted by psychologists, anthropologists, sociologists, and theatrical pioneers like Viola Spolin. The charm and indeed the value of the method lie in its ability to tap into your natural propensity to pretend, to make believe, to create, and to perform in a game of the imagination.

Improvisational technique training enhances your natural instincts as an actor. As in life, you are reacting to ever-changing external stimuli onstage. Your performance and the production, although painstakingly rehearsed, changes slightly each night. A new audience, with different views, moods, and expectations, fill the seats. You know who "you" are, but each time you walk onto the stage your manner of delivering your lines and actions varies to some extent. No two kisses are identical. The way in which you physically touch your partner tonight is different than last night. The way he looks at you is modified to meet tonight's changing circumstances. Every line and action incorporates minor adjustments with each new performance. The literal connection between you, your partners, and the audience is as ephemeral as life. In portraying a role, you may think you know what is to come. You know your cues; you know your next line. You have rehearsed and performed the play countless times. Again, theatrical reality is planned. As in life, however, you—both as an actor and a character—never *really* know what will happen next. Therefore, while onstage you must have the ability to adapt to changing conditions. This is where improvisation plays a vital role in your training.

Life is unstructured and transient. As we go through each day, we rely on our intellect and intuition, our natural impulses in response to stimuli. In reality, everything happens for the first time because it *is* the first time. Similarly, great actors onstage never lose their ability to give an honest and spontaneous reaction to familiar stimuli. With strong improvisational skills, you will never lose the ability to approach each thought and action as *if* it were happening for the first time. This is our illusion. This is our greatest freedom. What better objective for a student who would learn the art of the actor?

Improvisational exercises retain the quality of a game because their performance situation is not controlled by a playwright's words or a director's movement scheme. You are given the bare parameters of a situation and are left to perform the actions suggested by your physical involvement in the moment. Do not be fooled, however, for improvisation requires you to develop the given circumstances prior to and as the scene unfolds. Like everything related to acting, an improvisation must provide you with precise objectives that you must decide to accomplish in a specific way.

It is important for you to develop a sense of personal freedom and self-expression during improvisational exercises. There is no right or wrong way to perform your actions. However, before you begin the improvisation, try to bring yourself into the psychophysical state in the circumstances you have built. Do not attempt to be anyone but yourself in these initial improvisations, although you will be yourself in different circumstances: a parent, a child, an athlete, a politician. Each improvisation must have a beginning, middle, and end, and it is sometimes easier if you begin the scene with an entrance and end with an exit. Some improvisations—particularly those executed by the solo performer—should be performed without the need to speak. Do not attempt to explain your actions to your audience through indicated or false dialogue, and do not pretend to talk to a nonexistent person at this early stage in your training. But keep in mind that people do sometimes sing to themselves or speak aloud in fragmented ways—sighs, grunts, partial sentences, or expletives—when the situation requires them to do so. Finally, do not choose any actions that cannot be played fully in your acting classroom, such as opening or closing doors or windows that do not exist. In fact, avoid pantomimed actions altogether. Use only real objects and bestow upon them the physical and psychological properties that will help you to believe in their reality. Your instructor will serve as the master of the game. You will bring your own insight, imagination, and experience to performing the actions; because they are your own, they cannot be known until you discover them and create them for your audience.

---

**Exercise 3.2**   **IMPROVISING SIMPLE TASKS**   As an introduction to improvisation, perform an imaginary scene using one of the words from the list below as the basis of your actions. Remember, the scene must adhere to the instructions explained in the above paragraphs. Play yourself in a solitary situation, but ask yourself the four W questions, just as you would if you were preparing a role from a play. Your instructor will help provide the given circumstances of the scene.

**Dressing** (e.g., for bed, for a special occasion, for work)

**Waiting** (e.g., at a dangerous subway stop, at home, at the airport, in a ticket line)

**Searching** (e.g., for a lost object, a telephone number, a word in the dictionary)

**Sitting outdoors** (e.g., at the beach, in the woods, in the park)

**Reading** (e.g., a textbook, a "Dear John" letter, a romance novel)

**Packing** (e.g., to go on vacation, to move to a new home, to run away)

**Hiding** (e.g., from a stranger, from a friend)

**Stealing** (e.g., in a department store, in a friend's home)

**Exercising** (e.g., in a gym, at the beach, at home)

**Any other simple task**

---

# Making a Score of Physical Actions

Early in your training, you need to master a dependable method of working that will not only guide your study but yield practical results. Some would-be actors have a notion that practical effort, especially if it involves the use of pencil and paper, will dampen spontaneity and hamper creativity. This notion is ill founded. Inspiration comes from conscious technical effort; talent that cannot be nourished by hard, no-nonsense work has little chance of succeeding. Writing down thoughts stimulates further thinking, and practice carried on in the imagination can provide a solid theoretical foundation for a method of working that will sustain you throughout your career.

You now know how to discover the physical actions for your character in a given scene. Once you have done so (and this does require pencil and paper), you should list your actions in order. Your list (and don't be afraid to number them) should form a sequence that is logical and appropriate for the character in the situation, and each action should be such that you are psychologically and physically capable of carrying it out. Your list for the following exercises should be relatively short and not excessively detailed, as it will not be practical unless you can keep it easily in mind. It should, on the other hand, be complete, with no gaps that make it difficult for you to go from one action to the next. Your imagination, stimulated by the given circumstances, will provide the necessary strong desire to accomplish the sequence.

Making this list is the first step in a practical technique that Stanislavski called "**scoring.**" It is just a beginning, because much of the remainder of this book is devoted to finding ways of expanding and deepening your score. When completed, your score becomes a comprehensive working design of your role and will include your physical and psychological actions, your major and minor objectives, images, subtext, and line readings. Scoring a role provides three advantages:

1. The preparation of it forces you to dig deeply into the play and into yourself.

2. Adding to it during rehearsal keeps you alert to the stimulation of the director and the other actors.

3. The existence of the score makes it possible for you to review your creative effort whenever the need arises.

Your score begins with a simple list of actions. You will practice deriving such lists when you get to the problems in Exercise 3.3. The following is an example:

Set in the urban wasteland of North Philadelphia, *Orphans*, by Lyle Kessler, follows the plight of two brothers clinging desperately to the notion of family. Treat, a rage-filled petty thief, supports himself and his younger brother Phillip by stealing wallets and jewelry. Phillip, agoraphobic and profoundly naive, spends his days in their cluttered old row house watching television, eating mayonnaise out of the jar and hiding in a closet filled with his long-dead mother's coats. In the opening sequence of the play, Treat, out of breath, enters from outside. He blocks the door and looks out the window down the street to see if he has been followed. Relaxing, he snaps his fingers, surveys the living room, empties his pockets, and then searches for Phillip.

## The Beginning: "Ollie Ollie Oxen Free"

1. Quickly enter from outside.

2. Lean against inside of door to catch breath.

3. Laugh.

**4.** Look out the window down the street.

**5.** Place board against underside of doorknob to serve as a lock.

**6.** Snap fingers and survey the living room.

### The Middle: "Inspecting the Booty"

**1.** Cross to sofa.

**2.** Empty pockets of bracelets, wallets, rings, watches, etc. on coffee table.

**3.** Sit.

**4.** Inspect most expensive piece of jewelry.

**5.** See empty mayonnaise jar.

**6.** Take out butter knife and discard on table.

**7.** Pick up old biscuit on coffee table and shove in mouth.

**8.** Cross to trash can and discard empty jar.

**9.** Hear noise.

### The End: "Hide and Seek"

**1.** Cross toward closet.

**2.** Bang on wall, calling for brother.

**3.** Slowly open door, peering through collection of mother's coats on hangers.

**4.** Pick up stuffed animal.

**5.** Examine the room.

**6.** Quickly cross to pile of boxes, clothes, magazines, etc., and knock them over.

**7.** Cross back to window and look out to see if Phillip is outside.

**8.** Hear breathing.

**9.** Slowly turn and see Phillip hiding behind pile on stairwell.

Just as in Exercise 3.2, this score has been divided into structural units—a beginning, a middle, and an end—that will give the exercise form, clarity, and dramatic interest. Also, each of the units has been given a name suggestive of the essential quality and the basic reason for the series of actions. In this case, the titles reflect children's games. Choosing an appropriate name for each part of the structure is an extremely helpful technique, as it unifies the actions and helps you understand the proper attitude. It also helps establish suitable relationships with the objects you are handling and with other characters in the exercise or scene.

Although the parts of the score should be closely related, progressing logically and inevitably from one to the other, you must clearly make a *transition* from one part to the next. Clear transitions bring each unit of the score to a definite terminal point and start the new unit with a firmly positive attack, a new impulse manifesting itself in movement, gesture, or speech. Terminal points and new attacks make the structure evident and give both you and the audience a sense that the play is moving forward.

The beginning, middle, and end of a score of physical actions are not arbitrary but represent distinct components of the overall action. For example, the routine of the beginning must come to a complete end (terminal point) before the action of the middle can commence. The conclusion of an action like "snapping fingers and surveying the living room" results in an instant of stasis, a momentary vacuum, a transition from which comes a strong impulse for new action—crossing to the sofa to examine the loot. Recognizing the terminal point of an action is essential to building a score of actions, and pushing off or attacking a new task gives actors an opportunity to reinforce their belief in the human actions they are reproducing.

A sequence of individual actions can be distinguished further because each action will be influenced by the speed or pace of its environment (*tempo*) and by the internal performance pattern of the character (*rhythm*). Environmental influences are almost limitless, but some predominant sources of tempo are the prevailing mood, the weather, and other external circumstances, and even (or often especially) such artistic considerations as the placement of the action within a scene. The major sources of rhythm are within the character, and deciding on their rhythmic range is a consequential choice for the actor.

Life rhythms are extraordinarily important. The widely popular stage production *Stomp* is based primarily on our daily routines and rhythms. As in life, you must have a clear understanding of and feeling for your character's internal rhythms. "All human activity follows some rhythmic pattern, which can be felt by the actor and expressed physically," writes Mel Gordon in *The Stanislavsky Technique: Russia.* "Every stage movement should be conceived in Rhythm. Also, each character has a private Rhythm. Finding the character's Rhythm is an essential key to discovering his personality."[4]

Once a character's rhythm is discovered, combining it with the proper tempo is a subtle process, yet one at which experienced actors often seem to be intuitively right. When actors correctly sense what their characters are saying and doing onstage, correct tempo-rhythms are likely to come without conscious effort. In learning a technique, however, it is usually necessary to make a *conscious* effort before mastery of the technique produces *unconscious* results.

Because the two are so closely related, Stanislavski used the term **tempo-rhythm** to designate the combined rhythmic flow and the speed of execution of the physical action (including speech) in a given scene. Tempo-rhythms have a natural appeal to both actor and audience—an almost magical power to affect one's inner mood. This power is, of course, most evident in music. Recall the different moods created by your responses to swing music, rap, ragtime, R & B, and country music. Indeed, the popularity of rock is primarily a result of the effect of its pervasive tempo-rhythm.

**Figure 3.4**   John Glover and Elizabeth Norment in a scene from Edward Albee's *The Goat, or, Who is Sylvia?,* produced at the Philadelphia Theatre Company. Directed by Tim Vasen, scenic design by Todd Rosenthal, costume design by Murell Horton, lighting design by Ann G. Wrightson. By working off each other, actors establish the tempo-rhythm of a scene. Also note that although these actors share the composition equally, Mr. Glover is in the position of power.

In the exercise from *Orphans,* make clear transitions between the units by using the technique of terminal points and new attacks. Then, experiment until you find an effective and distinct tempo-rhythm for each action. Be conscious of how it changes as you move from the actions of one unit to those of the next. The tempo-rhythm may even change within a single passage. For example, in the sequence from *Orphans,* Treat's initial tempo-rhythm will be dominated by a combination of the rhythm the actor chooses for his character as it is affected by the tempo of the circumstances of the scene—he fears he may have been followed. If Treat were to see anyone as he looks out the window, the tempo-rhythm would change even if the activity he was performing had not been completed. A major change in the external circumstance will produce a major change in the tempo-rhythm.

Tempo-rhythm is applied ordinarily to the basic flow and speed of execution in each individual unit rather than to whole scenes of a play. In a sense, a scene's various tempo-rhythms add up to its overall pace. Scenes tend to have a pace that remains constant. The term *pace* refers to the speed at which the actors speak their lines, pick up their cues, and perform their actions.

To **pick up cues** does not imply that actors should race through a passage or scene. Usually, a director asks actors to pick up their cues to avoid the continual "line-pause-line" syndrome so common among new actors. In real life our communication with each other has a flow, and our silences have a significance that a dramatist can only hint at in transferring the spoken word to the written page. Actors then translate the playwright's words back into the sounds and silences of real speech.

Let's take a look at a second score of actions taken from Brian Friel's *Dancing at Lughnasa*. Rose, a simple-minded young woman, left the house several hours ago with her older sister to pick berries. Feigning illness, she informed her sister that she wished to return home to rest. However, she slipped away to secretly rendezvous with a young man. In this scene, Rose returns home from her encounter carrying a red poppy. She is wearing her good shoes and skirt, but they have been soiled and wrinkled. Lethargically crossing through the family's garden, she sees her sister's cans of fruit. After a moment, she decides to sample the contents before entering the house to confront her worried family. Study both this example and the one from *Orphans* until you can understand and apply the technique of scoring to your own work.

### The Beginning: "Dreams"

1. Slowly, lethargically enter yard.
2. Stop.
3. Turn back to look at trail leading to house.
4. Smile in quiet reflection.
5. Upon hearing a bird, look into a tree.
6. Smell the red poppy.
7. Gently place flower in front pocket of dress.

### The Middle: "Defiance"

1. Resume march toward the house.
2. See cans of fruit.
3. Stop beside them.
4. Check to see if anyone is watching.
5. Place hand in jar and thrust handful of berries into mouth.
6. Wipe mouth with dress sleeve and back of hand.

### The End: "Womanhood"

1. Look once again at trail.
2. Notice stained fingers.
3. Hear noise inside house.
4. Turn and notice movement through window.

**5.** Wipe hands on dress.

**6.** Calmly move toward front door in quiet determination.

---

**Exercise 3.3**    **SCORING FROM SCENARIOS**   Make and perform scores for several of the problems suggested below. Use pencil and paper: *write them out.* Remember that a score is a sequence of physical actions constituting logical and appropriate behavior in particular circumstances. Make the circumstances specific; find definite answers to the questions of *who, what, where,* and *when.* Choose actions that will communicate your meaning to an audience; that is, do not develop a habit of acting only for your own benefit. Your score should designate the beginning, the middle, and the end, and each of these units should have a suitable name.

After you have made the score, plan a simple arrangement of exits, windows, furniture, and whatever you need for the action, but let your imagination create as much detail in the environment as possible. Note that this detail provides a rich source for discovering physical actions. Give yourself actual or substitute objects (magazines, coffee cups, and so forth); do not try to pantomime nonexistent props. As you are working by yourself in this exercise, do not invent unnecessary dialogue. Use speech or sound only as necessary to call out or to release inner responses. Do not try to feel emotion. Do not try to be dramatic: simplicity is one of the first (and one of the hardest) things to learn. All of these "do nots" should make you aware that actors always work within a set of prescribed limitations. Only after boundaries have been established can freedom be achieved.

Note the difference between this carefully planned improvisation and the spontaneous exercise suggested before. Perform each score many times. Technique is developed through repetition, and each repetition should stimulate your imagination to greater belief. It is not necessary in these exercises to realize all the circumstances of the play; rather, the situations described should stimulate you to provide circumstances from your imagination.

**A.** In *Barefoot in the Park,* by Neil Simon, Corie, an energetic, young newlywed, enters an unfurnished apartment holding a bouquet of flowers. She looks around the room and sighs. After examining the room, she fills a paint can with water for the flowers, throwing the wrapping on the floor. She searches for an appropriate place to put the arrangement.

**B.** In Harold Pinter's *The Caretaker,* Mick, a young man, sits alone on a bed. He looks at each object in the sparsely decorated room before he stares at the ceiling and at a hanging bucket collecting rainwater from a crack in the ceiling. He sits still for a long moment before hearing a bang at the door and muffled voices. Mick turns to look at the door and quietly moves toward it.

**C.** On a sultry summer evening, Maggie, in *Cat on a Hot Tin Roof,* by Tennessee Williams, charges into her bedroom from the supper table to assess the damage one of her nephews has done with a hot buttered biscuit to her pretty dress. She opens the curtains to allow more light in the room and decides to change her dress.

**D.** In *Coastal Disturbances,* by Tina Howe, it is August, and Leo, a lifeguard, gets ready for a day's work by doing his stretching exercises standing in the sand by his lifeguard's chair. Holly Dancer, a pretty young woman, comes to the beach. The pace of Leo's exercises varies as he tries to attract her attention.

**E.** In David Henry Hwang's *The Dance and the Railroad,* Lone, a twenty-year-old Chinese railroad worker, sits alone on a rock on top of a mountain. He rotates his head so that it twirls his ponytail like a fan. He then jumps to the ground and practices opera steps.

**F.** In *Desdemona: A Play about a Handkerchief,* by Paula Vogel, Emilia, an attendant to Desdemona and scullery maid, has been ordered to peel potatoes. As she pares the potatoes, she vents her resentment by gouging out eyes, and stripping the skin from a potato as if flaying a certain mistress (Desdemona) alive. She then stops to contemplate a proposition offered to her by her mistress that would allow her to escape her husband and live a life of luxury. She begins to energetically, resolutely, and obediently slice the potatoes.

**G.** In August Wilson's *Fences,* Corey, a young Marine corporal, enters his recently deceased father's yard carrying a duffel bag. He studies his surroundings before seeing Raynell, his father's illegitimate daughter. Keeping the posture of a military man, he slowly crosses to the sister he has never known.

**H.** In *Losing Time,* by John Hopkins, a young single woman living alone returns home just after having been mugged and raped while outside.

**I.** In *Lu Ann Hampton Laverty Oberlander,* by Preston Jones, the teenaged Lu Ann is left alone in the living room of their modest, small-town Texas home after her mother leaves for work. She turns on the radio, dances to the country-and-western tunes it plays, sneaks a smoke from a cigarette her mother has discarded, and then has to greet her brother and a stranger who arrive unexpectedly.

**J.** In *Purlie Victorious,* by Ossie Davis, Purlie has involved Lutiebelle, a backwoods serving girl, in a scheme in which she will try to pass herself off as Purlie's educated and sophisticated Cousin Bee. After Lutiebelle examines the beautiful clothes Purlie has bought for her to wear—slips, hats, shoes, nylon stockings—she picks up her own humble belongings and tries to escape.

**K.** In *Request Concert,* by Franz Zavier Kroetz, a woman comes home from work and goes about the specific and mundane details of her household chores. She seems to be "putting her house in order." At the end, she commits suicide. (This scene could also be played by a male.)

**L.** In *Summer and Smoke,* by Tennessee Williams, Alma is an intelligent, tensely sensitive girl who has developed an abnormally reserved attitude toward young men. On an autumn evening she walks in the park, realizing that her prudishness has been responsible for her losing a brilliant young doctor with whom she has been deeply in love for a long time. She drinks from the fountain and quiets her nerves by taking a relaxation pill. When an unknown young man appears, she decides to make up for her past mistakes by attempting to attract his attention.

**M.** In *When You Comin' Back, Red Ryder?,* by Mark Medoff, nineteen-year-old Red is alone finishing his night shift at a truck-stop restaurant in an out-of-the-way New Mexico town. He plays the jukebox, smokes, and reads a newspaper, but prepares to make Angel feel bad for being late when she comes to relieve him.

---

## Terms and People to Know

**character autobiography**   A method by which actors explore their character's world by asking questions such as "Who am I?" "What are my circumstances?" "What are my relationships?" and "What do I want?" The autobiography should be written in first person from the character's point of view.

**cheat**   A term used without any derogatory meaning when an actor plays in a more open position, or performs an action more openly than complete realism would permit.

**cue**   An impulse derived from another person's actions onstage that motivates a verbal or physical response. A cue may come at the end of another person's speech or action, but many times this impulse occurs before the other actor has completed her speech or action.

**exit**   To leave the stage; also, an opening in the setting through which actors may exit.

**fourth side**   In both interior and exterior settings, the imaginary side(s) of the room or environment that is undefined and left to the imagination of the actor.

**given circumstances**   The unchangeable facts that affect the playing of the scene; the who, what, when, and where of a scene.

**improvisation**   Spontaneous invention of lines and stage business (movements and actions) without a fixed text.

**Meisner, Sanford (1905–1997)**   One of America's great acting teachers, who sprang from the Group Theatre of the 1930s. His focus on "the reality of doing" spawned acting exercises widely used in current teaching.

**moment before**   Just prior to entering the stage, the consideration of where "you" have been, what has just occurred, and "your" reason for entering this new space.

**positions, onstage**

    **body**   When one actor is turned either open (full front), one-quarter out, profile, three-quarter back, or closed (full back)

    **shared**   When two actors are both open to the same degree, allowing the audience to see them equally well.

    **give and take**   When two actors are not equally *open,* the one who receives a greater emphasis is said to *take* the scene. The other is said to *give* the scene.

    **upstaging**   When one actor takes a position that forces the second actor to face upstage or away from the audience.

**properties**   Tangible onstage objects, properties or "props" are divided into several categories: hand, personal, costume, and stage.

**score of physical actions**   A list of the character's motivated movements, forming a sequence that is logical and appropriate for the situation and is capable of being carried out.

**stage areas, proscenium or thrust**

BACKSTAGE

| Up-Right | Up-Right-Center | Up-Center | Up-Left-Center | Up-Left |
|:---:|:---:|:---:|:---:|:---:|
| UR | URC | UC | ULC | UL |
| Right | Right-Center | Center | Left-Center | Left |
| R | RC | C | LC | L |
| Down-Right | Down-Right-Center | Down-Center | Down-Left-Center | Down-Left |
| DR | DRC | DC | DLC | DL |

AUDIENCE

**stage directions**

    **downstage**   Toward the audience.

    **upstage**   Away from the audience.

    **stage right**   The actor's right as he stands on stage facing the audience.

**stage left**   The actor's left.

**below**   Synonymous with "downstage of."

**above**   Synonymous with "upstage of."

**in**   Toward the center of the stage.

**out**   Away from center.

**stage movement**

**cross**   Movement from one area to another. When noting a cross in your script, the standard abbreviation is X.

**counter**   A movement in the opposite direction in *adjustment* to the *cross* of another actor.

**adjustment**   An actor's physical alteration to accommodate a new position by a fellow actor to be in a position beneficial for the audience's viewing.

**cover**   The movement of another actor into a position between you and the audience, thus obstructing you from view; also, a term used to define the speech or action invented by an actor to keep the audience from detecting a mistake.

**stages, types of**

**alternative**   Also known as "environmental" or "found," alternative theatre spaces can be any area not traditionally used as a theatre, and it can have any actor-audience configuration.

**arena**   Also referred to as "in-the-round," arena stages have audience members seated on all sides.

**proscenium**   Stage in which the audience sits on one side; a proscenium arch usually separates the acting area from the auditorium. This is still the most common type of stage in the twenty-first century.

**stadium**   Stage with the audience sitting on two opposite sides with the action taking place in between.

**thrust**   Also known as three-quarter thrust, this common type of stage has the audience positioned on three sides of the acting area. Thrust stages sometimes have proscenium arches and a fly system in the upstage portion of the acting area.

**tempo-rhythm**   The combined rhythmic flow and the speed of execution of the physical action (including speech) in a given scene.

**will**   Full commitment to your actions on stage.

## CHAPTER 4

# Defining Simple Objectives

*"All that concerns the actor is to create the artistic action."*

–Constantin Stanislavski

Throughout his career, Stanislavski sought a deeper understanding of the mystery of inspiration onstage. Great actors, he observed, had the uncanny ability to present an inspired performance each and every night. But Stanislavski did not understand the source of their inspiration. How do great actors reach into the depths of their souls to play a role that demands extreme anguish, hate, or joy when they know that everything around them is a lie? The truthful communication of emotions is the actor's ultimate goal, for feelings lie at the core of theatre's existence. Yet actors cannot "play" emotions, which are ambiguous and uncontrollable. So how do brilliant performers apparently conjure them at will? While working with his Moscow Art Theatre company throughout the early part of the twentieth century, Stanislavski tried to get his actors to add humanity to their creations by revealing truthful feelings onstage. His early attempts were extraordinarily original and progressive, but, for Stanislavski, each experiment ended in utter disappointment. His actors' emotions, when forced by conscious will, seemed hollow and untruthful, false indications of reality. Undaunted, Stanislavski made it his mission to create a system that would allow any proficient actor to exert control over unwilling emotions. He set out to develop a method that would allow the actor to consciously and repeatedly uncover the source of his own creativity, the part of his being from where inspiration springs and passions are genuine. All this, he came to believe, could be attained by way of logical organic actions focused on simple objectives.

Although it is unclear whether Stanislavski had any direct contact with the famous Russian scientist Ivan Pavlov, their experiments investigating the connection between internal experience and its external expression (conditioned response) coincided with one another. Both Stanislavski and Pavlov came to the conclusion that the body and soul are so closely attached that they stimulate and influence each other. Before that point in time, many scientists believed that the body and soul were separate entities with minimal effect on one another. These two men, however, demonstrated through scientific means that every feeling, every thought, every decision, every mental process is transmitted through the body and manifests itself through external expression. Their proven discoveries became a law of mental and physical unity within the central nervous system. Human behavior, in this new light, becomes a continuous, uninterrupted *psychophysical* process. Through this **psychophysical union** of body and mind, the actor can perform truthful physical actions, inevitably provoking appropriate emotional responses. By performing a score of physical actions, the actor can obtain logical emotions, thus giving him a better chance of achieving his ultimate goal of inner truth.

The discovery of a character's appropriate physical actions is a key component in uncovering a conscious means (actions) to the subconscious (thoughts and emotions). Beginning in 1935, Stanislavski began to refer to his new approach as the **Method of Physical Actions**—a breakthrough in acting training and his gift to all future actors. Stanislavski considered the expression "method of physical actions" conventional. "They are psychophysical actions, he used to say, but we call them physical to avoid philosophical debate," wrote Vasili O. Toporkov. "Physical actions are concrete and material, they are easier to perceive and define; but they are closely connected with a person's typical attitudes and feelings."[1] Thus, when an actor performs a purely physical act, he inevitably introduces elements of the emotional and psychic into the process of creation.

Stanislavski's Method of Physical Actions could be modified, even personalized, to fit every actor's changing needs and circumstances. It transcended time and place, thus assuring its creative power in the twenty-first century and preventing it from degenerating into sterile conventions relevant only to his life and times. According to numerous reports, Stanislavski feared and fought against the stagnation of his discovery above all things. Like the very nature of theatre itself, his system was a living thing that must be adapted to various cultures in an ever-changing world.

At this point, however, we must define the difference between **physical action** and **physical movement.** Physical action—which may also be verbal—has purpose. It exists within the play's given circumstances and has a point. While movement may be simple and devoid of impulse, action is stimulated by motive. Therefore, the question "What?" cannot exist without a parallel question, "Why?" According to Sonia Moore, "If you fulfill only the physical side of an action, it will be dead, and if you are interested only in the inner side, it will be equally dead. You are learning to involve your psychophysical process."[2]

Through Stanislavski's Method of Physical Actions, we learn that the process of life itself may be reversed onstage. In life, an external stimulus triggers an appropriate internal feeling that manifests itself in external expression. Onstage, the actor responds to a stimulus through external expression (action) that triggers truthful internal feeling.

**Life**

**(Reality)**

Stimulus → Internal Feeling → External Expression (Action)

**Stage**

**(Secondary Reality)**

Stimulus → External Expression (Action) → Internal Feeling

Therefore, the Method of Physical Actions is the sum total of the relationship between your psychological and physical being—the psychophysical *union.* The stage is not a place of reality; otherwise, the actors playing Romeo and Juliet would actually have to kill themselves at the end of the play. The tragedy does not really occur; it is a secondary reality. However, playing the appropriate physical actions through the eyes of the character within the world of the play allows an actor to experience true emotion onstage without artificial means. Therefore, as a result of the psychophysical union, emotion is approached indirectly through the discovery of physical actions.

In Chapter 3, we learned that you begin your task of believing by making a score of appropriate physical actions and learning to perform them honestly. We have just learned that it is counterproductive for you to be concerned about how either you or the character "feels." Even in scenes of tragedy, you must concern yourself with *actions* rather than *feelings*. The question never is, "How would I feel if I were this character in these circumstances?" but rather, "What would 'I' do?" You should now know how to make a score of actions as the very first interpretative step in performing any role. You know each action must follow another in a logical sequence. They must be truthful, and you must believe each action is what you would do *if* you were the character in the given situation. Now we will learn how to make actions purposeful.

All stage events must have purpose; they must serve some end beyond the accomplishment of unmotivated movement. Moment by moment, the intent or meaning or significance of the performance, both for the actor and the audience, rarely lies in the action itself but in the purpose for which it is done. Even melodramatic actions such as loading a gun or mixing poison are not in themselves dramatic. We must know why, toward whom the lethal activity is directed. Clearly played for the right reasons, any number of simple, everyday actions—packing a suitcase, moving furniture, lying down on the floor—may be dramatic.

So, to the four Ws discussed in Chapter 3 we have now added a fifth: *Why?* Answering this question gives you a reason to carry out your sequence of physical actions. You can learn no lesson of greater significance. *Any action performed without a compelling reason holds no dramatic interest for the audience.*

Again, to discover "Why?" you look first in the dramatist's text, the place where all analysis begins. A careful reading should provide explicit reasons for your score of physical actions. If not, or if these reasons are unclear, you should follow the same procedure you followed with the other Ws. You turn next to what is *implied* by the text. (During this step the director usually becomes the chief interpreter for a particular production.) Finally, you solidify your decisions and personalize them by drawing on your own insight and imagination.

Knowing how to make action purposeful is among the most valuable of all acting techniques. It allows you to believe more strongly in what you are doing as the character. It gives you a reason for being on the stage and thus relieves your tension. Finally, it provides a principal means of conveying or communicating your character's story to the audience.

In this text we shall call a character's purpose for carrying out a sequence of physical actions the **simple objective,** or *objective* for short. Others call it different names: intention, goal, motivation, desire, impulse, or intended victory. Stanislavski himself called it *zadacha*, which translates as *problem*, while Uta Hagen stated it as a question—"What are you fighting for?" "It has been called many things in many books and some people don't call it anything; but it is a process that is going on, if they are really acting," wrote **Robert Lewis.** "I myself don't care if you call it spinach, if you know what it is, and do it, because it is one of the most important elements in acting."[3]

"Spinach" might prove confusing, but *objective* is a term commonly used by actors and directors. By definition, an objective is "a determination to act in a certain way or to do a certain thing." So let's agree that *action* will mean the sequence of physical actions, the *what,* and that *objective* will mean the reason for doing them, the *why.* Put simply, objective is what you want, what you are fighting to accomplish through your actions.

**Figure 4.1**  Cara Rawlings, Jonathan Becker, Megan Carboni, and Matt Shofner in a scene from Virginia Commonwealth University's production of *Big Love*. Directed by Gary C. Hopper, scenic design by Ron Keller, costume design by Elizabeth Weiss Hopper, lighting design by Andy Waters. Physical action, such as the dance in this scene, has purpose and helps communicate the character's simple objective.

# Stating the Objective

Return to the exercises in Chapter 3, and extend them by carrying out your actions to satisfy a clearly stated, simple objective. This important step forces you to dig again into the circumstances. Once you have found the objective by examining both what the playwright gives you and your own experience, it is important for you to state it in a form that compels you to execute a sequence of simple but psychologically motivated actions.

Here is the way it might work in the problem from *Orphans*. In Chapter 3, we made a score of physical actions and separated them into structural units, so now we will add this circumstance, discovered by studying the script: When Treat enters his home, he is out of breath from having been chased by one of his recent burglary victims. He blocks the door and looks out the window down the street to see if he has lost his pursuer. Once he realizes the "coast is clear," he laughs, snaps his fingers, and crosses to the coffee table to survey his newly acquired property. In addition to the score of physical actions, we now have a psychologically motivated objective. Treat is apprehensive and exhilarated by the experience. Stealing is necessary for his brother's and his survival, but he also revels in the game. At the top of the scene, we state his objective as "I must secure my home turf before enjoying my winnings with my brother."

Stating and playing simple objectives in the problems from this exercise will be relatively easy. Mastering this early work will pave the way later for understanding the complex problem of *units of action* and *super-objectives*.

---

**Exercise 4.1   REFINING YOUR SCORE**

**A.** Improvise the score of actions from *Orphans* with the objective "I must secure my home turf before enjoying my winnings with my brother." Keep the objective closely in mind throughout the presentation, and let your imagination work!

**B.** Carry out the same actions, but modify your simple objective to "I must secure my home turf before teaching my brother a lesson about survival." Hold firmly to this slightly more menacing objective, even as the action turns from the pursuer to finding "your" brother. Use your imagination to justify this objective.

---

Let's look at two more examples of determining actions and objectives from a script. In *When You Comin' Back, Red Ryder?* by Mark Medoff, the setting is a diner in the desert of New Mexico in the late sixties or early seventies. Stephen/Red is a nineteen-year-old who wishes to escape the mundane world and become as famous as his movie hero. Angel, the waitress, is a few years older and accepts her life. She has a crush on Stephen and wants him to stay. In the opening scene, the conversation is about coffee, their names, and coupons, but Stephen/Red's objective is "I want to steer Angel's attention away from me," and Angel's is "I must force Stephen to pay some attention to me." This scene has many actions to be played, including reading a newspaper, drinking coffee, and eating a donut.

*The Crucible,* by Arthur Miller, deals with the famous witchcraft trials in Salem, Massachusetts, in 1692. The theme is the frightening effects of injustice and the misuse of authority. John Proctor, about thirty years of age, is a hard-working farmer of independent spirit. His wife Elizabeth, also about thirty, has discovered that John had an adulterous affair with Abigail, a girl who worked for them and has since been dismissed. Abigail is one of the children bringing charges of witchcraft against innocent people, including Elizabeth. Earlier, Abigail admitted to John that their allegations are not true. Elizabeth's Puritan ethic has magnified her husband's single infidelity into a situation of major proportions. At the opening of Act II, her objective is "I must compel John to go to Salem to expose and denounce Abigail." John's is: "To restore normality to my house, I must satisfy my wife's wishes."

## Incorporating Action Verbs

To make your character's actions personal and compelling, note carefully the way a simple objective is stated: "I wish . . . ," "I want to . . . ," or "I must . . . ," followed by an **action verb.** Common verbs such as running, leaving, reading, fighting, or kissing may all be classified as action verbs in the grammatical sense; however, these verbs are dramatically *static,* an end in themselves. For you, the actor, action verbs must motivate a sequence of smaller actions. "To provoke," "to seduce," "to belittle," "to protect" are examples of action verbs that stir the imagination and give rise to subsequent simple actions. You must even avoid the use of more complex **static verbs.** Take, for example, the word "power." To say "I wish for power" is too general. If you phrase it as a question, "What must I do to obtain power?" it will move you more toward purposeful activity; however, the word "power" still remains too large and relatively inert. You cannot execute "your" need for power at once. Try playing a scene in which you wish for power in general. Stanislavski believed you must have something more concrete, real, nearer, more possible to do. Your chosen verbs must give you motivation for a succession of selected actions. This discussion may sound trivial to the beginning actor, but learning to identify the proper action verb is a necessary and learned skill.

Once you possess the ability to articulate a good action verb, you instinctively surge forward with appropriate subsequent actions. Think always in terms of what you must *do* by way of action verbs, not in terms of what you want to *be.*

Example 1

+ Poorly phrased: "I am jealous of my colleague's recent accomplishments."

+ Well phrased: "I must belittle my colleague's accomplishments to make myself look better."

Example 2

+ Poorly phrased: "I am frustrated by my friend's dispute."

+ Well phrased: "I wish to negotiate a truce between my friends."

Jealousy and frustration are states of being and cannot drive forward an objective, whereas "to belittle" and "to negotiate" stimulate specific activity.

You cannot summon an emotion at will, a point Stanislavski realized from the very beginning of his investigation into the subconscious. True emotions arise involuntarily in reaction to external and internal stimuli. Any attempt to consciously summon an artificial state of being will result in nothing more than indicated and meaningless movement, an external parody or cliché of a generalized emotion. Certainly, your state of being affects your choices as well as the tempo and rhythm of your selected actions, but emotions are the result. This is one of the most common mistakes made by young actors, attempting to act by *being* rather than *doing*. If you attempt to concentrate upon *being* drunk, *being* angry, *being* happy, *being* sad, or *being* afraid, you will certainly fail. Concern yourself, just as you do in reality, with what you would do in each situation, not with what you would be or how you would feel. Remember, through the Method of Physical Actions and as a result of the psychophysical union, the emotion will be there if the actions are carried out to the fullest extent of your will.

---

**Exercise 4.2**   **DOING VERSUS BEING**   Upon your instructor's direction, perform the following sequence, allowing thirty to sixty seconds for each of the commands. Standing before the class, try to act excited. Now attempt to play anger. Make an effort to look sexy. Now try to relax. After a few minutes of this, most likely you will become frustrated or confused by the above directions. Now sit on a chair or sofa, and take off your shoes and socks. Rub your feet.

Acting excited, playing anger, looking sexy, and then trying to relax without a specific sequence of actions is almost impossible. When instructed to act excited, did you stand on your toes and artificially throw your arms in the air while spinning about? How do you relax in front of an audience who is watching your every move? You cannot simply *be* in a vacuum. Relaxation results from purposeful activity. You need to create a set of circumstances that justifies your feelings and then perform specific actions under these invented circumstances. The moment you were instructed to perform a specific sequence of actions—sitting down, taking off your shoes and socks, and rubbing your feet—relaxation followed. Your nervousness over *being* any of the aforementioned states probably disappeared. Rather than focusing on the audience and how you appeared to those watching you, you concentrated on your actions; thus, you "got out of your own head" and out of the realm of self-consciousness.

*Being* is a passive concept. Compare being excited versus the act of opening an unexpected gift. Weigh the idea of being angry versus shredding a piece of paper and stomping the fragments into a trashcan. Try to imagine being sexy versus mixing the perfect cocktail and then putting on your favorite CD. You can act the second half of the above phrases. On the other hand, if you are playing a state of being, your energy is directed inward toward your emotional center rather than outward toward acting in the dramatic situation. When you are angry, your mind does not focus on being angry. Rather, you are concerned with the cause—the person or thing that has made you angry—and you may deal with the cause in any number of ways. You may overlook it. You may seek release from your anger in some act of physical violence—shredding the paper and stomping on the fragments. You may plan some dreadful revenge. But certainly you are not saying to yourself, "I must be angry." You *do* something about it. When you are frightened, you do not *want* to be afraid. Instead, you want to dispel your fear in some way. You may want to escape or to seek comfort from someone. You may want to calm your fears by turning your attention to something else. You may want to investigate the source of peril. As an actor, you must always place an emphasis on concrete details. Never try to act in general and never attempt to convey a feeling such as love or hate in some vague, nebulous manner. In life, we express emotions in terms of specifics: a nervous man smokes a cigarette while fidgeting with his lighter; an angry woman slams the door on her fiancé and pulls a handkerchief from her purse to wipe her eyes; an anxious teenage girl quickly closes the window blinds and sits on the sofa clutching a pillow. Actors must find equally specific activities; otherwise, they will simply be feigning a generalized emotion.

You cannot act a state of being, an emotion, or a condition. If an unknowing director tells you "In this scene, you are really angry. I want you to play the anger," you will undoubtedly respond with, "Okay, but how do I do that? What do you want me to do?" This type of vague direction will simply leave you stuck scratching your head. What is anger, anyway? For that matter, what is happiness? What is depression? People have their own interpretation of these states of being, and we are never simply one particular emotion. At any given moment, we may be happy with our lives but anxious about a forthcoming presentation. At the same time, we are frustrated with our family and yet concerned about our child's health. You may be a bit intoxicated from the wine you had at dinner, angry with the driver who cut in front of you on the freeway, and overjoyed about your recent promotion. States of being are subjective and inconsistent, and they vary greatly depending upon the circumstances. Trying to play a state of being will only lead you into stereotyped movements and gestures (e.g., clenching your fists to show your anger, putting your hand to your forehead to show you are being thoughtful, or contorting the muscles of your face to show your pain).

Burning your hand may *be* painful. But you want to *alleviate* the pain by applying salve, butter, cold water, or some other remedy. When an actor such as Al Pacino is pointed out in a crowd, you may *be* curious. But you want to *secure a position* where you can *see* and perhaps *get* his autograph. To be in pain or to be curious is not actable. But to relieve pain or to satisfy curiosity is. You can easily carry out the actions of applying a remedy to your burned hand or of working your way into a favorable position.

---

**Exercise 4.3**   **ACTION FROM AN EMOTIONAL STATE**   To realize more fully the importance of *doing* rather than *being* and of stating your simple objective with an active verb, work carefully on the following problem. Choose a word from the list below, and make it the basis for a series of actions. Do not let this instruction lead you into a trap. As you study the list, you should now realize that you cannot act any of these words. Each is an end result, an effect. You must imagine a circumstance providing a reason for the *action that will produce the effect*. Then forget the effect, and concentrate on carrying out the actions. For example, the following circumstance would provide an action for the word *cautious*: *You have just escaped from a war prison. In darkness, starved and exhausted, you are making your way across an area filled with booby traps. You find a knapsack that might contain rations.* State your objective as "I must work my way through the area without triggering a trap."

The following circumstance would provide an action for the word *spiteful*: *You have not been getting along with your roommate. You resent your roommate continually asking to borrow money to satisfy an extravagant taste for clothes. You return home to find that your roommate has "borrowed" money that you were saving to buy a present for your fiancé. You take several articles of your roommate's new clothing, cut off all the buttons, and put them in the box where your roommate keeps coins.* State your objective as "I must teach my roommate a lesson for being so selfish."

Now, look over the list and select a word. Devise appropriate circumstances. Make a score of your actions. State your simple objective. Structure your score, and name each of the three units. Carry it out in an imaginative sequence of actions. Observe the instructions given for the exercises in Chapter 3.

| | | |
|---|---|---|
| breathless | embarrassed | jealous |
| awkward | distracted | sickly |
| bewildered | bashful | grouchy |
| coarse | excited | panicky |
| drunken | frantic | tantalizing |
| genteel | exhausted | spiteful |
| maudlin | nervous | dazed |
| cautious | infuriated | ruthless |
| lethargic | terrified | jovial |
| violent | condescending | detached |

Note: The above list is taken from playwrights' directions to actors in a single volume of modern American plays. They illustrate how dramatists (and often directors) ask for effects. Actors must be able to think of effects in terms of actions and objectives. A frequent comment to actors from directors is "Don't play the effect [even though he may have just asked for it], play the action!"

---

**Exercise 4.4**     **EVERYDAY ACTIONS**     Choose one of the following "everyday" actions. Create circumstances, and provide an objective you can attack with unfeigned interest and excitement. Take, for example, polishing silver: You are in an antique shop in a foreign country. You discover among many dusty articles a blackened silver bowl that you think is the work of Benvenuto Cellini. Beneath the tarnish may be revealing marks. If you are right, the proprietor obviously does not suspect its origin. State your simple objective as "I must remove the tarnish from this bowl without attracting the proprietor's attention."

For another example, consider "walking five steps": You are in the hospital with a serious illness. You are very weak and short of breath. You are under strict doctor's orders to stay in bed. You decide to test your strength by walking a short distance to a chair. You reach the chair exhausted but convinced you are beginning to recover. State your intention as "I must regain the strength in my legs if I am ever to return to full health."

Now it is your turn. To solve the problem suggested by one of these "everyday actions," you need specific circumstances, a properly stated objective, a score of physical actions, and imagination. Execute all physical actions precisely, clearly, and with complete commitment. Avoid any activity that requires pantomime. Take your time. Give your actions form.

+ reading a newspaper
+ looking through a window
+ opening a door
+ hunting for a lost object
+ writing a letter
+ lying down on the floor
+ applying or removing makeup
+ arranging furniture
+ getting dressed or undressed

+ drinking alcohol or a soft drink
+ examining a photograph
+ wrapping or unwrapping a package
+ crawling on your hands and knees
+ packing a suitcase
+ walking five steps
+ examining a bundle of clothes
+ waiting for someone
+ stretching

Plays are filled with simple actions for which actors must find objectives that stimulate their imagination and make the actions communicate the playwright's meaning.

# Working Against Obstacles

**Obstacles** are the foundation on which great dramas and comedies are built. Most plays center on a single character's overall objective, but there is no drama without something standing in the way of his achieving his goal. In every play, there is always something that the leading character wants but cannot have due to numerous obstacles, and the character's subsequent actions come about through his desire to overcome these barriers. Every moment you are onstage, "you" face at least one opposing objective. This opposition, whether stated or implied, creates conflict; it heightens the reality. For example, perhaps you are playing a character in a long-standing relationship, and "you" want to "take it to the next level." "You" decide to tell "your" girlfriend that "you" love her, but "you" are afraid. Perhaps "you" fear rejection. What if she doesn't share the same feelings? The moment "you" say "I love you," she might suggest that "maybe we should see other people."

Now assume you have created a character involved in a physically and emotionally abusive relationship. Fearing for "your" own mental health and perhaps even "your" life, "you" make the decision to leave "your" husband. In this scene, "you" intend to ask "your" husband for a divorce, but "you" find it incredibly difficult to do. Inexplicably, "you" still love him, although "you" fear him. "You" cannot imagine life without him. How will "you" survive financially? Maybe "your" religion doesn't recognize divorce. Perhaps he has threatened to kill "you" in the past. What about the well-being of "your" children?

The interest in a play or scene lies in the possibilities it offers you to gain an objective against odds—odds sometimes so great that the struggle ends in defeat, either glorious or ignoble. The greater the obstacle, the more engaging the action will be to the audience. On the other hand, plays without conflict have little interest for either actor or audience. Conflict is basic to dramatic structure, as it is fundamental to life. The degree to which your character overcomes her obstacles is the measure of her success in achieving her goal. And once your character achieves one simple objective, another is born, complete with a different set of barriers. This is the basis for drama, and the best scripts have the most interesting and complex obstacles.

---

**Exercise 4.5**    **OPPOSING OBJECTIVES**  The following improvisation requires two people, one male and one female. A young high school couple living in a small rural community has been in a relatively long-term and stable relationship. Right after graduation, the young man, who struggled with his grades throughout high school, plans to enter into his family's construction business, a fairly successful company he will someday inherit. The young woman, on the other hand, comes from a poor family. However, she excels academically and, unbeknownst to him, she has received a large scholarship to a prestigious university that will cover tuition, room, and board. It is late evening following their senior prom. They are alone in a car at "Lookout Point." The young man's objective is to tell his girlfriend for the first time that he is *in love* with her. He then intends to ask for her hand in marriage. The young woman really *likes* him, but her objective is tell her boyfriend about her plans to leave this small town, go to college, and pursue her dream. For many weeks, she has deliberated her problem. Now that prom is over, she decides that tonight is the night to break up with him.

---

As you formulate each simple objective, ask "What is the *obstacle?*" or "What stands in my way of accomplishing my goal?" With no obstacle, there is no problem—no scene—no play! The obstacle, like the objective, may be internal or external. Internal obstacles always grow from the character's own personality and experience; external obstacles come from all other sources, such as family, societal expectations, religion, politics, nature, laws—even such natural phenomena as the weather and the time of day.

Obstacles may also be either physical or psychological, and frequently they are so closely related that it is not possible, or desirable, to separate them. For example, Patrick Myers's stunning play, *K2,* is a psychological drama of two characters in search of survival while physically stranded on the side of the world's second highest peak. Taylor Brooks and Harold "H" Jamieson are old friends, polar opposites temperamentally, who share a mutual, obsessive passion for the challenge of the climb. On a recent vacation, a planned 10-day trip on Mount McKinley, they barely escaped with their lives after an overhead jet created an avalanche. Regardless of the fact that two in their party died, the pair decides to scale K2, "the toughest mountain in the world" because "half of the people who go there don't come back." After a successful climb to the 28,250 foot summit, they begin their descent. At 27,000 feet, "H" falls on a sheet of ice and breaks his leg. When the play begins, they are stranded on a dangerous shelf, scared, with no rope, tent or oxygen and just one can of chicken soup between them. There are many physical obstacles they must overcome: the mountain itself, the icy ledge to which they cling, the altitude and consequent lack of oxygen, the shortage of food and equipment, the blizzard weather conditions, and the broken leg. However, the physical obstacles, daunting as they are, do not sustain the play. This is a psychological drama of survival—man against mountain. The mental obstructions facing these two men give the play texture, depth, and meaning. The physical and psychological are interrelated, but the conflict of one man's acceptance of the mountain and its death sentence versus the other's dogged determination to endure provides the greatest drama.

Onstage, as in life, your psychological objectives and obstacles stimulate your selected actions. Climbing a mountain is much more than just the act of overcoming the impending physical obstacles. Once exhaustion sets in and the men face the other tangible impediments, the story becomes about will, mind over matter. A woman's recent accomplishment of navigating the globe on a one-person sailing vessel took great physical endurance, but overcoming the resulting psychological hurdles proved the real victory. In sports, a winner's motivation is nearly always psychological. A ball player does not want simply to outscore the opponent; rather, he is motivated by a desire to win, to bring honor and prestige to himself and to the team. Professional golfers require years of physical technique training. They must also have extraordinary hand-eye coordination, but golf is a mental sport requiring Zen-like coordination of mind and body. The act of physically conquering something, whether it is on the athletic field or in your everyday life, holds no dramatic interest without psychological barriers.

From the above illustrations, we suggest you consider three important points. First, psychological objectives and obstacles can stimulate your imagination more strongly than physical objectives and obstacles can. Second, you must make a personal commitment to overcome the obstacle(s) and accomplish your objective. As we have seen with the Method of Physical Actions, this commitment generates true emotion. Third, you must feel the challenge physically as well as intellectually. A runner does not win a race by *wishing* to, *thinking* about strategy, or *feeling* victorious. Goals are achieved through purposeful *action*.

You must pay particular attention to the importance of obstacles. Your psychophysical actions, if they are to have any dramatic interest, must be performed to overcome an obstruction that exerts a strong force against the accomplishment of your simple objectives. You must not be indifferent to this opposition. Dispassion toward the challenge of overcoming obstacles, too common among student actors, will inevitably render a performance ineffective. An even more basic error occurs when actors fail to clearly identify their obstacles. Until you define your complications, you cannot discover what means the dramatist has provided, either directly or by implication, for overcoming them. You will then be deprived of the only true and defensible stimulus for drawing additional strategies from your imagination.

# Employing Strategy

According to the military definition, **strategy** is "the art and science of employing armed strength to meet the enemy in combat." Although conflict between the character and the obstacle is not always open warfare, you would do well to conceive your whole performance as a strategic plan to overcome the forces working against your character. You are searching for the most interesting and provocative way to reveal your character by your line of attack. You must find a way to satisfy your character's needs. To what extent are "you" willing to manipulate the world to get what "you" want? Employing strategy means exploring

© 2003 Utah Shakespearean Festival. Photo by Karl Hugh.

**Figure 4.2**    A. Bryan Humphrey (*left*) as Pantalone and Richard Kinter as Dr. Lombardi in *The Servant of Two Masters,* 2003. Once a simple objective is defined, each actor must plan a strategy to overcome the forces working against them.

active choices in rehearsal. Learn what strategy works best for "you," and make the stakes as great as possible.

Plays are about important moments in people's lives. You must ask yourself the degree of importance. What are the consequences if "I" don't get what I want? What lengths am "I" willing to go to obtain "my" objective? A barren young woman may be so desperate to have a child that she is willing to break into someone's home to kidnap another woman's baby. Her need is so great that she is willing to risk getting caught and possibly going to jail, thus sacrificing her own freedom. A love-struck young man may be so desperate to gain the affection of a girl that he is willing to make a fool of himself in a public place in order to demonstrate his feelings. As an actor, you must know to what depths "you" are willing to go to get what "you" want. The stakes must be significant enough to make an impression on the audience, making us feel and care for your character. We must feel we are watching a life being lived in front of us. Not only must you know the stakes, but you must make us feel the importance of your actions.

The depths of your character's desire affect every strategic decision you make. We are guided by our desires; they are the involuntary urges our bodies feel to perform an action. Desire is your character's emotional drive, a craving or ache to fulfill "your" real wants and wishes. The subject of a play generally centers around someone's intense desire for such things as love, power, revenge, fame, glory, truth, spirituality, sexual pleasures, or self-preservation. How far are "you" willing to go to achieve "your" objectives? Would "you" sacrifice "your" pride and self-respect? Would "you" kill someone? Would "you" die? Would "you" steal, cheat, lie, or ruin someone else's life?

Always attempt to simplify the conflict by finding your character's elemental need; do not try to complicate it. For example, a year ago "your" husband took out a large life insurance policy on "you," and recently "you" began hearing rumors that he has been having an affair with "your" best friend. Last week, "you" wrecked "your" car after someone cut the brake lines. "You" now have a frantic need to discover the truth about "your" husband. Are the rumors true? Is "your" life in danger, or were these events merely coincidental? If this sounds melodramatic, remember that such material is the stuff of which drama is made. The content of Shakespeare's plays in the hands of a hack writer yields soap operas, and the Greek tragedies become second-rate horror movies. "Good drama, of whatever kind, has but one mainspring—the human being reduced by ineluctable process to a state of desperation," wrote British critic Kenneth Tynan. "Desperate are the cornered giants of Sophocles; desperate, too, as they huddle in their summer-houses, the becalmed gentry of Chekhov; and the husband of French farce, with a wife in one bedroom and a mistress in another, is he not, though we smile at his agony, definably desperate?"[4] Carrying out your planned strategy must come from your character's objective as a "desperate quest" to overcome any obstacles.

## Adapting to Changing Circumstances

While onstage, you must constantly remain in the state of "I am," playing each moment as if it were occurring for the first time—what the nineteenth-century actor William Gillette referred to as "the illusion of the first time." As in life, your characters cannot be clairvoyant. They cannot *know* the future. Someone once asked the legendary twentieth-century actor Sir Laurence Olivier how he remembered all his lines in *Hamlet*. He responded with "I don't. I simply remember the next one." Colleagues of great actors such as Gillette and Olivier report that they always seemed surprised by the events of the play. They lived in the present. While onstage, even though you *know* the next line and have performed your character's actions countless times, you cannot truly *know* what will happen next. Attempting to anticipate another person's actions will only result in your delivering indicated movements with artificial effects. Therefore, you too must play each scene moment by moment, remaining in the present.

The state of "I am" does not mean that your character does not think ahead or speculate about the future. In fact, everything you do in the present is conditioned by your **expectations** about the future, and what actually happens is never fully what you expected to occur. The famous acting teacher Uta Hagen wrote, "When the actor anticipates what he will see, hear, and feel and what the others will be doing (because he has seen, heard, and felt them doing the same thing since the early days of rehearsal), it is because he has failed to include the logical expectations that condition his actions, or merely paid them lip service."[5]

**Adaptation,** on the other hand, is synonymous with perhaps the most vital question you must ask yourself while onstage. You have answered the five Ws and you have devised a strategy, and now adaptation obliges you to answer the essential sixth question, "How?" Of this query, Stanislavski once said, "*Adaptations* are our 'paints.'" and "Your first duty is to adapt yourself to your partner." As an actor, you must understand that an action (*What?*) is incomplete unless you fully incorporate answers to "Why?" and "How?" *What* you are doing? *Why* you are doing it? *How* do you accomplish your goal?

Adaptations depend on ever-changing given circumstances. Each time you walk onto the stage, it *is* for the first time; you (and your character) have expectations, but you cannot know. Theatre is a living art; therefore, you will have to make adjustments to your strategy. There are dozens of ways to break up with your fiancée, burn a letter, fire an employee, or seduce a person to whom you are attracted. Exploration of "How?" is one of most important and satisfying parts of both rehearsals and performances. The more proficient you are at strategizing and then adapting to changing circumstances, the fresher your creation remains. The richer your imagination, the more choices you have. The more choices you explore in rehearsal, the more interesting your final product.

As you are exploring the various means with which to achieve your objective, your partner will have counteractions, thus creating unforeseen obstacles. There must be dramatic conflicts onstage; otherwise theatre would be amazingly dull. Stanislavski wrote:

> Every feeling you express, as you express it, requires an intangible form of adjustment all its own. All types of communication—for example, communication in a group or with an, imaginary, present, or absent object—require adjustments peculiar to each. We use all of our five senses and all the elements of our inner and outer makeup to communicate. We send out rays and receive them, we use our eyes, facial expression, voice and intonation, our hands, fingers, our whole bodies, and in every case we make whatever corresponding adjustments are necessary.[6]

In life, we must all have the ability to adapt to changing circumstances. Those who cannot adapt will never get across the street alive, much less manage the more subtle interpersonal challenges they face. We deal with people both logically and psychologically, and the kind of adaptation we make—whether it is bold, delicate, daring, or cautious—is important to our success. Each day brings an infinite number of situations requiring a wide range of adjustments. Your situation is the same onstage. Your performance must always be conceived in relation to other characters who either help or hinder you in accomplishing your objectives, and you must consider these other characters in planning your actions. You have the ability to adapt and sometimes to abandon your plans as you are confronted with the unexpected. You watch and listen and remain ready to adjust what you do and say to the needs of the moment.

Stage action often seems dull because a realistic sense of adjustment has disappeared in the actor's struggle to remember and repeat lines and movement. A technique that allows for adaptation to the needs of the moment is a necessity in the actor's training. When performing actions onstage, you must concentrate on your actions and how you expect them to affect the behavior of the other performers. You must also focus on other actors' counteractions, their adaptations to your employed strategy. For the audience, the focus, then, is on what happens *between* the performers, for that is where theatre happens.

## Improvising Group Scenes

Many people still think that Stanislavski discussed his productions for months before allowing his actors to explore the physical environment. This may have been true before he developed the Method of Physical Actions, but as soon as Stanislavski discovered the psychophysical process of human behavior, he sent actors onstage after they had read the play and briefly discussed the plot and characters. According to Sonia Moore, "Stanislavski realized that the discussions at the table artificially divided the actor's physical and psychological behavior. 'I think that you have done enough work now to begin moving, improvising on the stage.'"[7]

You may obtain further practice in adaptation through exercises involving group improvisation, a further extension of the exercises you have already been doing. Improvising with a group necessitates more complicated and interesting problems, bringing you closer to your ultimate aim of a shared performance. You will begin, as always, with the given circumstances out of which you must create an active, attractive, and truthful objective. You will face an added complication because you cannot know what you will need to do until you know what the others are doing. As they play their objectives, they will create obstacles for you. Because the final definition of the scene will depend on your actions and counteractions with the other performers, you will need to be ready to adjust moment by moment. And again, the actions you adjust must be truthful and logical; you must believe they are what you would really do if you were the character in the circumstances. As you begin to sense your effect on the actions of the other performers and as you adjust your actions to the obstacles they present, you are on your way toward learning one of the most important lessons of the theatre: acting is communal, and successful performance depends utterly on the stimulation you receive from and give to your fellow actors.

Set a time limit—at the beginning, ten to fifteen minutes for a group exercise. After it is over, the work should be carefully analyzed (preferably by a competent observer) so that you are aware of the points at which you have or have not behaved logically and truthfully and at which your adjustments have fallen short of what could have been expected. You can help yourself and sometimes help others by recalling when you succeeded in making real contact, when your actions seemed true and spontaneous and when they did not. The analysis should not be concerned with whether the scene would be entertaining or exciting to an audience. Improvisation is a means, not an end, and you will defeat its purpose if you think about results other than truthful behavior. Your first attempts may be frustratingly unfruitful, for group improvisation is a technique that takes time to learn. But it is time well spent, and it is essential to your training.

---

**Exercise 4.6**    **NOT ON SPEAKING TERMS**    This exercise concerns two people who are not on speaking terms. Talk over the given circumstances with your partner. Define your objectives. Know your obstacles. Create a central conflict. Understand your relationship. Determine the five Ws. The point of this and all improvisations, however, is an investigation of the sixth question, "How?" In fact, the exploration of *strategy* and *adaptations* is the most important part of rehearsals for a scripted scene or play. For this first exercise in group improvisation, however, do not speak or pantomime. There should be no need to talk. As soon as there is an organic need to speak, the improvisation is complete.

---

**Exercise 4.7**    **WAITING**    This exercise involves a group of people sitting at a bus station. Know who you are and where you are going. Although we establish immediate relationships with everyone with whom we come in contact, there again should be no reason to speak to one another in this exercise. You may also perform this exercise with the following settings:

+ riding in an elevator
+ waiting in line
+ relaxing in a park

+ lounging on the beach
+ sitting in a doctor's office
+ sitting in detention in high school

---

**Exercise 4.8**    **GIBBERISH**    Next, we will set circumstances that permit communication through psychologically motivated physical actions and expressive sounds—*without the* *use of dialogue.* The first scene of Romeo and Juliet, in which the servants of the rival houses of Capulet and Montague confront each other in the public square, suggests the situation. Because the two families are ancient enemies, the servants feel compelled to challenge each other whenever they meet, although they may have forgotten (or perhaps never knew) the cause of the age-old hatred. The servants are uneducated, not dangerously armed, and not overly courageous. Their purpose is to insult and perpetrate minor physical assaults. In this exercise your group must accomplish the objective through physical actions (including gesture and facial expression) and vocalized sounds—no articulated words. The servants of one house should create obstacles for the others. Actors should strive to play their objectives as fully as possible. Remember, though, that the actions must always be logical and appropriate within the given circumstances. The scene should not become chaotic. Each action must be purposefully performed. The circumstances prescribe a number of obstacles to a realization of the objective: the natural timidity of the characters, the need for self-protection, and the need for a degree of furtiveness because these encounters in the public streets have been forbidden by law.

Let the beginning consist of the meeting in the street and some cautious advances by one or two of the servants, followed by hasty retreats. Let the middle develop the confrontation, as some of the servants, exhorted by others, become bolder in their actions and ultimately involve the whole group. Let the end consist of the arrival of someone of authority who breaks up the quarrel.

The group could decide to set the scene in circumstances other than those of Verona in the Italian Renaissance. In *West Side Story,* a modern musical based on *Romeo and Juliet,* the enemies were not "two houses both alike in dignity" but rival street gangs in New York. It would be valuable to work on the same situation in different sets of circumstances.

**Exercise: 4.9   ALIENS**   The next situation is taken from *Tales of the Lost Formicans,* by Constance Congdon. Similar to the above exercise with *Romeo and Juliet,* the group should communicate only through psychologically motivated physical actions and expressive sounds—alien language. The actor playing Jerry, a human, should not speak. In this scene, Aliens are gathered around Jerry, taking notes, while he lies unconscious on a bench. Jerry wakes up and opens his mouth to scream but can't make a sound. To calm his nerves, the Aliens massage his jaw and stroke him like children petting a dog. They proceed with the examination—it should satirize a field examination of a wild animal—all with the air of dispassionate scientists. For example, one Alien finds various objects in Jerry's pockets and holds them up for other Aliens to see. They all laugh rhythmically. Once the examination is complete, the Aliens tag Jerry's ear, zap him unconscious and exit.[8]

The value of group improvisation lies in your learning to make real contact with other actors, to heed what they do and say, to adapt the playing of your objective to the need of the moment, and to work freely and logically within the imaginary circumstances. What you learn should carry over into everything you do because all good acting is to some degree improvisational. Even a scene that has been "set" demands constant adjustment—a living connection with fellow players. The choices you make in the adjustments must be credible and appropriate. Behaving logically within the circumstances is the beginning of truthful acting. Avoid choices that are sensational, that are calculated solely for dramatic effect, or that mindlessly repeat what you have seen other actors do or even what you have done in the past. Verbal group improvisation is best when your imagination leads you truthfully into spontaneous adjustments.

Verbal improvisation is decidedly different from nonverbal improvisation in that it requires the actors to create their own dialogue. You should always remember that words and physical actions are synonymous. Just as you do not perform a physical action until the circumstances demand you to do so, you must not speak until the situation mandates it. Like all physical actions, verbal action is a means of expressing inner life. As you add dialogue to a scene, you must carefully consider your character's inner life and "your" relationship to the other people and circumstances. Although the dialogue is not scripted, your words, your inflections, your syntax, your inner objects, your silences will directly affect your partner, and ultimately the audience, at least as much as your external physical actions. Just as you do in life, you are attempting to influence the actions, images, and emotions of others through words in your fictitious improvisational scenes.

As in life, you must listen with full attention. You must respond to the other character's words through your psychophysical being. If your partner onstage is attempting to cheer you up through her verbal and physical actions, she is looking into your eyes for continual feedback. She is watching your movements and gestures and interpreting your projected mood. Whatever your objectives, your partner must have counteractions to create obstacles. As with scripted scenes, you and your partners must create communion onstage. There must also be communion between the actors and audience, and the audience must completely *suspend their disbelief* for the entirety of the scene. In short, you must believe in your character, your given circumstances, your relationships, and your every action. Otherwise, your improvisation will fall short of its intended goal.

A final word of caution with your verbal improvisations. Do not try to impress your classmates with your quick wit! Contrary to some people's belief, verbal improvisation is not the same as comedy improvisation such as you would see on the television show, *Whose Line Is It Anyway?* or onstage with Second City or The Groundlings. Verbal improvisation must complement your formal acting technique training. These improvisations, more often than not, will be dramatic in nature. Your characters, situations, and actions must be completely three

**Figure 4.3**   Sara Clark, Claire Whiteside, and Kite Wilkinson in The University of Oklahoma's production of *Much Ado About Nothing*. Directed by Judith Midyett Pender, scenic design by Michael D. Fain, costume design by Aaron Turner, lighting design by Frank Soto. Training in improvisation helps actors to make creative choices and to work spontaneously off the actions of their partners.

dimensional. By pandering to the audience and by attempting to transform every improvisation into a comedy sketch, you will succeed in creating only the shell of a human being.

**Exercise 4.10**   **BUILDING A SITUATION**   These first verbal improvisations involve two people. Build the situation. Think of the analogous emotion that you have experienced in life. When you are onstage, think of the physical behavior that will be expressive of what you have built in your mind. The partial objectives listed below are intended for one of the actors; however, the partner must create his or her own objective and counteractions.

| | | |
|---|---|---|
| to humiliate | to deceive | to persuade |
| to enlighten | to challenge | to seduce |
| to encourage | to motivate | to con |
| to provoke | to tempt | to coerce |

Come up with additional action verbs that motivate immediate simple actions.

**Exercise 4.11  GROUP IMPROVISATIONS FROM SCENARIOS**   The following situations provide opportunities for verbal group improvisations. In each case additional circumstances must be supplied from either the play or the imaginations of the actors. All characters must clearly understand their objectives and attempt to realize them through actions appropriate to the circumstances.

**A.** In *Big River*, by William Hauptman and Roger Miller, Huck Finn follows Tom Sawyer to a cave on the side of a hill, with walls "of clay—damp, sweaty, and cold as a corpse." Tom lights a candle as they enter the cave. Ben Rogers, Jo Harper, Dick, and Simon are already there. Their intention at this gathering is to start a gang of robbers, Tom Sawyer's Gang. They discuss their mission to rob and murder before swearing an oath of secrecy, punishable by death to the families of the boys who tell the secrets. (This improvisation can be performed by men and women of any ethnicity.)

**B.** In Tony Kushner's *A Bright Room Called Day*, five friends have gathered in Agnes's apartment in Berlin in 1932. They have been celebrating the New Year. As the scene progresses, their conversation turns to Hitler and the war.

**C.** In *Fences*, by August Wilson, Troy Maxon tells his wife, Rose, that he is going to have a baby by another woman. Soon after he breaks the news, Gabe, Troy's brain-damaged brother, enters talking about various things. The two try to talk in between Gabe's babbling until Rose suggests that he go inside to make himself a sandwich. After he enters into the house, Troy and Rose continue their discussion.

**D.** In *Five Women Wearing the Same Dress*, by Alan Ball, four mostly unwilling bridesmaids lounge in a bedroom while the sounds of a rather raucous wedding reception can be heard outside. Frances, the youngest and most naive of the lot, sits in front of a vanity, while Trisha and Georgeanne sit by her side performing a makeover. Trisha applies makeup; Georgeanne prepares to apply nail polish. Mindy is seated on the edge of the bed, holding a plate of food. All except Frances have made themselves comfortable; most have cocktails and are at various levels of inebriation.

**E.** In Frank Loesser's *Guys and Dolls*, a group of gamblers convene in a New York City sewer for a high-rolling, illegal crap game. The group comprises gentlemen gangsters and shysters, who have chosen this spot to avoid detection from the law. The men enter into the space, greet one another (while sizing each other up), remove their jackets and hats, count their money, prepare strategies, and jockey for position around the central area.

**F.** In *Catholic School Girls*, by Casey Kurtti, four first-grade girls—Elizabeth, Colleen, Wanda, and Maria Theresa—enter into the classroom. They are dressed in white uniform blouses, blue ties, white cotton slips, knee socks, and brown oxford shoes. They are carrying their uniform jumpers. They each stand by a student desk and begin to dress. They look around the classroom and at each other as they dress. Then Elizabeth raises her skirt to pull her blouse down neatly. All follow suit, straightening their blouses. When they are finished, Elizabeth shouts that she is ready. On this first day of school, the girls await the arrival of their teacher.

**G.** In Eugène Ionesco's dark, absurdist comedy, *The Lesson,* a mild-mannered professor and his newest female student prepare for her first lesson in his home. At the beginning of the scene, she is quite shy but then becomes progressively agitated and whiny as the scene goes on. She complains periodically of a toothache that also worsens as the action unfolds. As her pain increases, so does the intensity of the professor's lecture. Finally, he works himself up into a state of frenzy bordering on hysteria. At the peak of his fervor, he pulls out a knife and stabs the girl repeatedly. Following the murder, he becomes immediately frightened and contrite. He confesses his latest crime to the housekeeper, who is not at all happy with his actions, treating him as a bad child.

**H.** In *The Rainmaker,* by N. Richard Nash, H. C. Curry and his two sons go to town to try to get the deputy sheriff, File, to pay a call on Lizzie (H. C.'s daughter), who is nearing that time when she will be thought of as an "old maid." They try to work the invitation into their conversation without being obvious about it.

**I.** In *A Soldier's Play,* by Charles Fuller, a group of black soldiers return to their barracks after a baseball game. They are carrying their equipment, and they engage in the exuberant, loud, locker-room banter of young men in the army. A sergeant unexpectedly enters, and the raucousness of their conversation abruptly abates. (Actors of diverse racial and ethnic backgrounds could play this improvisation.)

---

**Exercise 4.12  NON-CONTENT SCENES**   Thus far, we have introduced numerous acting exercises with selected bits of given circumstances, yet the dialogue was left to improvisation. **Non-content scenes** are also improvisational, as they are an excellent way to introduce specific dialogue into predetermined and yet unprepared scenarios. We refer to them as "non-content" because although there is explicit dialogue, there is no fixed plot or characterizations. Non-content scenes can be quickly memorized—usually in less than ten minutes.

Working in a classroom situation, the instructor will divide the class into pairs and assign the following dialogue.

A: No

B: Please

A: I can't

B: Watch

A: I'm trying

B: Look

A: This makes me nervous

B: That's it

A: Help

B: Wow

A: You owe me big time

Each pair of actors will decide who will memorize character A's lines and who will memorize B's. Lines should be memorized by working aloud together. During memorization, you should refrain from interpreting the lines; at this point the script is to be learned simply by rote.

Once memorized, the instructor will switch pairings so that each "A" will be coupled with a "B" with whom they have not rehearsed or spoken the assigned dialogue. Working with one group at a time, the instructor will then assign one of the following scenarios upon which to build the improvisational scene.

**A.** You have been invited to a formal, but you don't know how to dance. Your sister (or brother) is trying to teach you a few basic moves.

**B.** You are seriously ill with the flu, but you have a second callback with a major Broadway producer in one hour. Your friend (or significant other) comes over to help you get dressed and ready for the audition.

**C.** You and a fellow student break into a professor's office to look for an exam you are to take in the morning.

**D.** On the battlefield, you try to rescue one of your fellow soldiers, but you must stay beneath the gunfire while crossing to safety.

**E.** It is the evening before Halloween, and you have been asked to find a place for a party. You and a friend break into a vacant house that is reportedly haunted.

**F.** You have developed intimate feelings with a long-time friend. While helping him (or her) with his homework, you attempt to share your feelings. (You may replace homework with any other activity.)

**G.** While doing the dishes, you lose your wedding ring down the drain. You and your spouse try to retrieve the ring.

**H.** While hiking in the woods, your friend falls and twists his (or her) ankle. You must stabilize the injury before helping him back to camp.

**I.** You and a friend are at a sorority (or fraternity) party. You both desperately wish to become members of this group. You have both been drinking, but your friend has had a few too many. Outside the house, you try to sober up your friend before returning to the party.

**J.** Any other scenario given to you by your instructor.

Since the dialogue in a non-content scene has no specific meaning, you must build upon the given circumstances using your assigned scenario as a basis for your improvisation. The lines, however, are completely open to interpretation. Thus, you are serving as the playwright by creating who, what, when, where, why, and how. As this is an exercise in subtext, you are not allowed to change the actual text in any way. In other words, there should be no adlibbing. No person may deliver two lines in a row, and you may not switch characters in the middle of a scene. Additionally, you cannot speak any line until it is completely logical for your character to do so.

Non-content scenes are action-centered, and each participant should have a clearly defined objective while working against major obstacles. Remember, the action may begin well before the first line is spoken, and what occurs between the lines is as important as the subtext of the lines themselves. Non-content exercises force you to make defined and actable choices, but you must avoid the trap of always making obvious choices. Consider alternative line readings. Playing the opposite of the obvious will make your scene infinitely more interesting. It is incumbent upon you to work off your partner and to fully commit to each of your selected actions. This exercise is the perfect way to master the previously presented techniques without having to fully analyze an entire script. Non-content scenes may be performed multiple times with various combinations of partners.

Below is another sequence of dialogue that may be substituted with the above non-content scenarios.

A: Excuse me

B: Don't

A: I have to

B: I don't understand

A: This is your fault

B: I need you

A: After what you did

B: Let me try

A: Is it real

B: Yes . . . No

A: Fine

# Terms and People to Know

**action**   Either physical or verbal, action happens in and is dictated by circumstances. Not to be confused with *physical movement* (a mechanical act), action has purpose and is motivated by the character's *simple objective*.

**action verb**    Word that motivates a sequence of smaller actions. "To provoke," "to seduce," "to belittle," "to protect" are examples of action verbs that stir the actor's imagination and give rise to subsequent actions.

**adaptation**    The ability to adjust and sometimes abandon the present plan of actions when confronted with the unexpected.

**adjustment**    The technique that allows actors to hold fast to the reality of their roles while altering objectives or actions to fit the changing circumstances of the scene.

**commenting**    A technique by which actors "distance" themselves from their roles, continually pointing out the significance of each action in relation to the total meaning of what the characters are doing and saying.

**expectation**    Without knowing what will transpire, the character's continuous state of anticipating what will happen next.

**justification**    A validation of and strong belief in every action that an actor makes for the character in pursuit of each *simple objective*.

**Lewis, Robert (1909–1997)**    American director, producer, writer, and actor, Lewis was an original member of the Group Theatre during 1931–41 and later founded the Actors Studio Theatre. His publications remain some of the most accessible interpretations of Stanislavski's theories ever written.

**Method of Physical Actions**    The heart of the Stanislavski System, it is the actor's logical sequence of actions that leads to the stirring of emotions, thoughts, imagination—all the psychic forces.

**non-content scene**    Improvisational scene for two actors with specific yet simple dialogue with no predetermined scenario.

**objective, simple**    A character's quest at any given moment, expressed and pursued by use of an *action verb* that motivates a sequence of simple actions (e.g., to provoke, to belittle, to seduce). A simple objective is the best known translation of Stanislavski's term *zadacha* (problem).

**obstacle**    A physical or psychological obstruction that hinders the character from completing an *action*. Obstacles provide conflict and heighten the dramatic effect.

**physical movement**    A physical act stripped of any context or meaning.

**psychophysical union**    The inseparable connection between internal experience and its external expression. Every mental process is immediately transmitted through the body in visual expression.

**static verb**    Words that do not motivate an immediate sequence of simple actions. Examples of static verbs include: run, sit, jump, hit, and read. Although action verbs in the grammatical sense, these words lack progression and are an end in themselves.

**strategy**    The overall plan of attack to overcome opposing forces.

**System Acting**    Stanislavski's technique training that permits the actor to create a character through primary focus on the play's given circumstances.

## CHAPTER 5

# Developing Your Powers of Observation

*"A true artist is inspired by everything that takes place around him."*

–Constantin Stanislavski

Great actors have the uncanny, chameleon-like ability to observe lives and adapt their own bodies and minds to fit every new character that springs forth from their imaginations. They know that every portrayal is highly unique. Every creation is physically, vocally, and psychologically different. Each character materializes from some untapped source within an actor and differs from any other individual he or she has ever brought to life.

Look at the phenomenal range and development of the two-time Academy Award–winning actor Tom Hanks, beginning with his work on the television series *Bosom Buddies* and in his early films such as *Splash, Bachelor Party,* and *The Money Pit,* followed by his explosion as one of the greatest and most malleable actors in the world today. Hanks' ability to observe diverse people and cultures is extraordinary, and the wide range of characters he created in *Big, A League of Their Own, Sleepless in Seattle, Philadelphia, Forrest Gump, Apollo 13, Saving Private Ryan, Cast Away, Ladykillers,* and *The Terminal* are extraordinarily diverse.

Another Academy Award–winning actor, Chris Cooper spent much of his youth on his father's cattle ranch; therefore, it is not surprising that he found fame in playing cowboys, ranchers, and other hardworking men. He undoubtedly drew upon his childhood observations in such movies as *Lonesome Dove, The Horse Whisperer, Seabiscuit,* and *October Sky.* However, Cooper demonstrated the depth of his versatility in such movies as *American Beauty, The Patriot, The Bourne Identity,* and particularly in his portrayal of an eccentric, sad, poetic, and toothless orchid hunter in the Florida Everglades in *Adaptation.*

Each character created by such actors as Tom Hanks and Chris Cooper has distinctive internal thoughts, images, desires, impulses, fears, prejudices, and points of view. Even the greatest actors may create characters that have some external similarities, but through imagination and the power of observation, these actors develop for each character a singular method of expressing behavior through speech, movement, and gesture.

As an actor, each of your portrayals must be a singular creation derived from three sources: the given circumstances as interpreted from the script and the surrounding production, your imagination, and your **personal history,** including everything you have experienced, felt, read, or observed in life or fiction. For each character, you must touch a different wellspring from within your lifetime of observations. You are your own instrument. Unlike the pianist and the painter, you have only your own body and spirit. You are the creator, the material, and the instrument all in one. Therefore, you must develop your ability to *see.* You must expand your ability to absorb mental images to be used on stage or screen at a later time.

One of the most important parts of your acting training is the observation of life itself. You must be a student of life, a person who can remain objective while observing the subjective actions of others. You must develop your skills of observing both the ordinary and the unusual in your everyday life. Our senses are so intensely bombarded by our all-inclusive surroundings in the modern world that we tend to take most things for granted. We do not *really* look at people's faces, hear their voices, listen to sounds, or even taste the food for which we have paid dearly in an expensive restaurant. Emily in *Our Town,* by Thornton Wilder, movingly expresses this indifference. Returning from the dead to relive a childhood experience, she sees people going insensitively about their everyday tasks. She says of her family at breakfast: "They don't even take time to look at one another." You must learn to observe familiar things as if you had never seen them before, and you must retain the experience. Through remembered observation, you will build a stockpile of materials from which you can construct performances. But more important, you will enrich your life, and an enriched life will increase your chances of being an insightful actor.

Just as you "surf the net" for data to be downloaded onto your computer, so must you build your mind's capacity to take in mental images. Just as you add additional memory into your computer to increase its capacity, so must you expand your power to store your observations. Once these memories have been added into your "storage," you must develop the ability to objectively recall them when necessary onstage. The power of observation will make you sensitive to humanity and to the art of creating a new human being living in an imagined world. The ability to see facilitates your adjustments to any business you may be required to perform in a role. When an actor *really* observes another person's behavior, it opens his eyes "to the full extent in appreciation of different personalities and values in people and works of art . . . it enriches his inner life by full and extensive consumption of everything in outward life," wrote Richard Boleslavsky. "The actor who has his gift of observation dulled and inactive will appear in worn-out dress on a gala occasion. As a rule, I believe that inspiration is the result of hard work, but the only thing which can stimulate inspiration in an actor is constant and keen observation every day of his life."[1]

Observations produce **inner images** that reside in your subconscious. They are the mental pictures that flash across your mind as you speak. You must have the capability to recall at will your inner images, as this will enable you to transform scripted dialogue and onstage objects from something cold, intellectual and rational into something that is "warmly felt." Developing your ability to contact your inner images relates directly with your ability to observe and retain the life around you.

As an actor, you cannot withdraw yourself from life, for your work onstage must reflect real people. To become an artistic recluse goes against every principle of your technique training. As a student of life, you must observe the behavior of others, remain abreast of contemporary events, read biographies and political and cultural histories. Study movies, television, photography, art, literature, psychology, sports, languages, and even the culinary arts. Nothing is outside your realm as an actor. Observe the world by traveling. When you are experiencing another culture, observe their customs and behaviors without judgment. Search for beauty. "For the good and the beautiful, Stanislavski points out, exalts the mind and evokes a man's best feelings, leaving indelible traces on his emotional and other memories."[2] Stanislavski encouraged his actors to study nature, both the beautiful and the ugly. Try to put into words what you see, and learn from your observations. You cannot be an actor (or any artist) without the ability to *really see.*

Stanislavski said that "Life excites [the true artist] and becomes the object of his study and his passion; he eagerly observes all he sees and tries to imprint it on his memory not as a statistician, but as an artist, not only in his notebook, but also in his heart. It is, in short, impossible to work in art in a detached way. We must possess a certain degree of inner warmth; we must have sensuous attention. That does not mean, however, that we must renounce our reason, for it is possible to reason warmly, and not coldly."[3]

The technique of observation begins with a conscious effort to develop fuller awareness of happenings around us, a fine-tuned sensitivity to what we see, hear, taste, feel, and smell. Uta Hagen tells a story of an argument between Albert Basserman's director and a designer about producing the special effect of an actual rainstorm onstage. After a brief discussion, Basserman interrupted with, "Pardon me, but when I enter, it will rain!" According to report, when Basserman entered, it did rain—without special effects.[4]

Observation is both intellectual and sensory. The mind tells us the uses of things, classifies them, analyzes them in any one of a number of ways, and permits us to retain them in memory. Recognizing that a flower is a carnation and not a buttercup and is red and not yellow is an intellectual response. However, we perceive the flower through our senses. Experiencing a carnation is not just knowing about it. It is seeing its color, smelling its fragrance, holding it, touching it. Fortunately our memory can retain sensory as well as intellectual experience, and sensory perception is the bedrock of the technique of observation. You must have the capacity to recall not only your knowledge of the carnation but also the way it affected your senses.

The more extreme your sensory experience, the easier it will be to recall onstage. At some point in your life, you have surely stubbed your toe, burned your finger, or cut yourself on a sharp object. But how do you recall everyday experiences? While onstage, how do you deal with putting on mascara with a brush that has no makeup on it? How do you drink tea as if it were brandy, get drunk on a non-alcoholic beverage, burn your tongue on food that is room temperature, or nick your face with a bladeless razor? How do you make yourself believe you are hot and sweaty while onstage in a cold theatre, nauseated due to illness that does not exist, or, like Basserman, make it rain on a dry stage? The more sensitive you are to the real world, the more intensely you will respond to the stimulus that induces these everyday sensory experiences.

As an actor you must have the dexterity to produce a natural behavioral response in order to arrive at the essence of the experience. Just as you cannot "play" an emotion, you cannot entirely produce a sensory experience simply by thinking about it or isolating it from subsequent behavior. There are two ways in which you may make your onstage sensory experiences truthful to yourself and to your audience.

First, you may give the quality of one object to the quality of another object. For example, you may drink water as if it were vodka. A cold stove may be treated as if it were hot, and a dry mascara brush may be treated as if the bristles were wet with makeup. Playwrights often require physical objects that actors cannot actually use onstage. Real firearms, drugs, and alcohol obviously do not belong onstage, for they pose a genuine danger to the actor or alter the actor's mode of thinking. Drinking beer onstage is not a morality question but rather a question of foolishness. The theatre has no room for anything that poses a threat

**Figure 5.1**    Timothy Davenport (*foreground*) and Jennifer Tosatto in Missouri State University's production of *Marvels!* Directed by Jay E. Raphael, scenic design by Robert Little, costume design by Lou Bird, lighting design by Bee Bee Lee. Although the theatre is probably a comfortable 68 degrees, the actor in this scene must play the condition of cold.

or affects your ability to think or act with clarity. Even such everyday objects as eye makeup, onions, and hot irons are precarious items for the actor to use while performing before hundreds of people. In the same regard, valuable antiques, jewelry, authentic paintings, and any object of extreme value should not be onstage. The actor must find similar, less dangerous or expensive objects and bestow upon them the essential qualities of the actual item.

Second, to discover truthful environmental and human conditions, such as heat, rain, sleet, drunkenness, anxiety, and exhaustion, you must determine their precise cause and their particular effect on a specific part of the body. From there, you must find the correct physical adjustment necessary to overcome the condition. If, for example, you arrive at your "imaginary" beach and try to "feel" the intense heat of the sun by simply thinking about it, you will find it almost impossible to believe your reality. You can, however, believe an appropriate set of physical actions that result from the imagined conditions that surround you.

---

**Exercise 5.1**    **PLAYING A CONDITION**    Perform the sequence of actions listed in the simple score below. Instead of isolating the condition of heat, simply concentrate on the activities.

### The Beginning: "Hot, Hot, Hot"

1. Carrying a bag and a cooler walk quickly to selected spot on "sandy beach"
2. Set down bag and cooler
3. Take towel from bag
4. Spread towel onto sand
5. Hop onto towel as quickly as possible
6. Wipe sand off bottom of feet

### The Middle: "Taking It In"

1. Notice ship off in distance
2. Squint
3. Shield eyes and look up at glaring sun
4. Rummage through bag for sunglasses
5. Put on sunglasses and look again at ship
6. Grab cold beverage from cooler
7. Open can and take long drink

### The End: "Nirvana"

1. Sit on towel
2. Find suntan lotion in bag
3. Apply lotion while watching seagulls dance overhead
4. Find book and small pillow in bag
5. Take another long drink
6. Place pillow at end of towel
7. Lie back and begin reading

Your belief in the condition of heat results from your belief in your score of physical actions.

---

To believe your stage life, including the most trivial sensory conditions, you must either substitute the qualities of one object for that of another or perform the logical sequence of physical actions necessary to alleviate the imagined conditions. Only then can you produce the sensation at will.[5] To believe you are drinking a steaming cup of coffee when in fact it is room temperature, you perhaps stir it with a spoon and blow across the brim before carefully picking up the "hot" cup with your fingertips and taking a sip. Onstage exhaustion may perhaps be achieved by kicking off your shoes, putting on your slippers, pouring a drink, reclining on the sofa, turning on the television, sipping your drink, and shutting your eyes. What do you do to alleviate the environmental condition of rain? What is the sequence of actions you undertake to alleviate the human condition of grogginess when waking up from a deep sleep? What do you do to lessen the condition caused by a pungent odor, a sour lemon, a bitter pill, a dark room, or a slippery surface? Just as the Method of Physical Actions allows you to discover true emotion, an appropriate sequence of physical actions allows you to actually believe in the sensory experience.

---

**Exercise 5.2    THREE OBJECTS**

**A.** Create a scenario using three objects that cannot or should not appear onstage. Substitute similar objects and give them the essential qualities of the actual items. Provide for yourself given circumstances. Establish your objective and obstacle(s). Score your actions and title your units. Remember, the sensory experiences are not the primary purpose of the scene but simply part of the given circumstances. You may use the objects listed below or create your own.

| **Object used onstage:** | **Given the qualities of:** |
| --- | --- |
| + inexpensive vase or glass | + a valuable antique |
| + cold iron | + a hot iron |
| + toy pistol or rifle | + a real pistol or rifle |
| + rubber or plastic knife | + a sharp knife |
| + doll | + a newborn baby |
| + empty jar and dry mascara brush | + liquid mascara |
| + a print | + a valuable oil painting |
| + clove cigarettes | + marijuana |
| + plastic or cardboard crown | + a real crown |
| + empty jar and dry fingernail brush | + actual nail polish |
| + costume jewelry | + valuable jewelry |
| + rope | + a snake |

| **Object used onstage:** | **Given the qualities of:** |
|---|---|

| Object used onstage: | Given the qualities of: |
|---|---|
| ✦ razor with no blade | ✦ a bladed razor |
| ✦ tea | ✦ hot coffee or brandy |
| ✦ candy | ✦ medicine |
| ✦ apple | ✦ an onion |
| ✦ silk flower | ✦ a rose |
| ✦ water | ✦ vodka or acid |
| ✦ canned peaches | ✦ oysters or eggs |

**Exercise 5.3    ADJUSTING TO CONDITIONS**

**A.** Adapt your score of physical actions from the above exercise with one or more imaginary conditions. The manner in which you react to or attempt to remedy your condition is part of your adaptations to achieving your objective. You may use the environmental or human conditions listed below or create your own.

| **Environmental Condition** | **Human Condition** |
|---|---|
| ✦ summer evening | ✦ drunkenness |
| ✦ winter morning before daylight | ✦ nausea |
| ✦ sweltering summer afternoon | ✦ exhaustion |
| ✦ rainy day | ✦ high (drug induced) |
| ✦ snowy winter day | ✦ stress |
| ✦ crisp spring morning | ✦ depression |
| ✦ windy fall afternoon | ✦ headache |
| ✦ autumn evening | ✦ starvation |
| ✦ bright winter day | ✦ upset stomach |
| ✦ spring evening | ✦ vertigo |
| ✦ winter ice storm | ✦ broken bone |

**B.** Perform the same sequence of actions, but add the element of time. As an actor, you must always have a specific idea about how much time you have and how much time the specific sequence of actions will take. Notice how the tempo-rhythm of the scene changes with the amount of time you have to complete your objective.

Increasing your awareness of what goes on around you and developing your **sense memory** are your first steps toward developing your powers of observation. Once you have command of observation techniques, you will find that they provide you with three essential kinds of information that can be used as raw material for building a character. They are:

1. Characteristics of *human behavior* (manners of moving, speaking, gesturing, and so forth) that may be reproduced precisely on the stage

2. Other *human situations* that, when filtered through your imagination, may be adapted for use on the stage

3. *Abstract qualities* of animals, plants, and inanimate objects that can help stimulate your imagination about how characters *might* look or behave on the stage

In a description of her working methods, Helen Hayes gave examples of these uses of observation. After defining acting talent as "a peculiarly alert awareness of other people," she continued:

> When I was preparing for my role of the duchess in Anouilh's *Time Remembered,* I had some difficulty capturing the spirit of the role, until . . . I heard some music written by Giles Farnaby for the virginal—you know, one of those sixteenth-century instruments. . . . That old duchess, I told myself, is like the music, light, dainty, period, pompous, tinkling. And, poor me, I'd been playing her like a bass drum. I had one scene in *Victoria Regina* that I played like one of my poodles. . . . I had a poodle that used to just sit, and he'd look almost intoxicated when I'd say, "Oh, Turvey, you are the most beautiful dog" . . . and believe me every night for a thousand and some performances of that play, I saw that poodle.[6]

## Observing People

"Always and forever, when you are on the stage, you must play yourself," wrote Stanislavski. "But it will be in an infinite variety of combinations of objectives and given circumstances which you have prepared for your part, and which have been smelted in the furnace of your emotion memory."[7] The impartial observation of other people is most certainly an important part of actor training; however, this skill is most useful when you learn something about yourself in the process. The simple manifestation of external gestures and movement serves no purpose unless you discover that you have behaved in a similar fashion under different circumstances. You cannot get away from yourself onstage without it leading to *indicated* actions. Therefore, as you observe others, you must find a way to identify with their actions within your own person.

Tom Hanks, for example, drew upon his own childhood experiences in creating the role of Josh Baskin in the feature film, *Big.* After expressing his wish to be "big" to an unplugged electric carnival fortuneteller, young Josh physically passed over pre-adolescence and emerged as an adult. "When I was 13 . . . I was younger than my years," Hanks told a reporter of his approach to creating Baskin.

> I could still play really well. I can remember things that I loved to do, the way you could have toy soldiers or a plane, and you could sit on the couch for hours and have incredible adventures. And I remember being clueless. I remember adults talking to me and just going, "Yeah, right," but not knowing what they were talking about. . . . I remember being 13 and being all elbows and knees. . . . The girls had already grown up. I started the role with the point of view of a newborn giraffe. They have spindly heads that look geeky when they run.[8]

In addition to remembering his own childhood, Hanks spent countless hours making careful observations of David Moscow, the twelve-year-old boy who played Josh as a child. He also studied his own children, who were then ten and six years old. "I tried to get a sense from them of play for the sake of play, of having cars on the carpet and having this great time where you make up your own story, your own little world."[9]

When Hanks later created the title role in *Forrest Gump,* he again drew upon his own personal history, but he was concerned that he needed to speak with a southern dialect. He managed the accent by observing and adopting the vocal patterns of Michael Humphrey, the eight-year-old Mississippi boy cast in the film as young Forrest. He took great pains to research his role. For six months, he even spent a substantial amount of time observing patients at a psychiatric hospital in Los Angeles to help him prepare to create the character of Forrest Gump.

"Developing a characterization is not merely a matter of putting on makeup and a costume and stuffing Kleenex in your mouth," wrote the late Marlon Brando of his development of Don Corleone in *The Godfather.* "That's what actors used to do, and then called it a characterization. In acting everything comes out of what you are or some aspect of who you are. Everything is part of your experience." Brando had an innate ability to absorb the world around him and incorporate his observations into his characters. "I thought it would be interesting to play a gangster . . . who wasn't like those bad guys Edward G. Robinson played, but who was a kind of hero, a man to be respected." Because of Corleone's power, Brando decided to play him as a gentle man who was quite the opposite of Al Capone, who thrashed people with baseball bats. "I saw him as a man of substance, tradition, dignity, refinement, a man of unerring instinct who just happened to live in a violent world and who had to protect himself and his family in this environment." *The Godfather* was filmed in the seventies, and Brando, throughout the initial creative process, observed the real Mafia. In his autobiography, he reported on a "war" in Little Italy between members of a group called the Black Hand, who were extorting money from immigrants. Some paid for their safety, while others, just like Don Corleone, fought back. He also drew from the government. "There were not many things you could say about the Mafia that you couldn't say about other elements in the United States. Was there much difference between mob murders and Operation Phoenix, the CIA's assassination program in Vietnam?" From these observations, he created a character who was modeled after a CEO of a multinational corporation, a high-ranking government official of the day, or one of the CIA representatives who dealt in drugs in the Golden Triangle while torturing people for information. Nothing was personal.[10]

There are countless other examples of observations used as sources of inspiration for characters. In creating the role of Marcela Howard in *Seabiscuit,* Elizabeth Banks was heavily influenced by the actual Mrs. Howard, the second wife of Seabiscuit's owner, Charles Howard. Tobey Maguire certainly studied the real Johnny "Red" Pollard when creating his role in *Seabiscuit.* Leonardo DiCaprio observed hours of film footage of the real Howard Hughes when creating a younger version of the man in *The Aviator,* just as Kevin Kline studied the actual Cole Porter for nine months before creating his character in *De-Lovely.* Michelle Pfeiffer drew upon her own mother in developing the relationship between the beautiful, free-spirited poet, Ingrid Magnussen, and her fifteen year old daughter, Astrid, in *White Oleander.*

When creating the role of the thief Linus Caldwell in *Ocean's Twelve,* Matt Damon rode the Paris subway in an attempt to observe pickpockets in action. Virginia Madsen, who created the role of Maya in the film *Sideways,* spent a lot of time observing the California wine country and the people of Santa Ynez prior to shooting. Ron Eldard went on many "ride-alongs" with real policemen in preparing for his role as Lester in *House of Sand and Fog.* According to Russell Crowe in numerous interviews, he got ready for the role of Captain Jack Aubrey in *Master and Commander: The Far Side of the World* by spending three months learning to sail before shooting began on the film.

---

### Exercise 5.4    OBSERVATION NOTEBOOK

**A.** Each day during the next week, make a special effort to use your powers of observation. Start an observation notebook. Carefully note mannerisms, gestures, and ways of talking, walking, and eating that reveal character traits. Visit a busy railway station, hotel lobby, or some other place where you will have the opportunity to observe people of all ages. Practice reproducing details until you can do them accurately and until you feel you have captured some of the inner quality of the person. Again, remember to look for character traits which you can relate to your own past and present external behavior. Attempt to discover their objectives by observing their physical actions.

**B.** From one of the above observations, prepare a complete character autobiography, answering all the appropriate questions, as discussed in Chapter 3 and more thoroughly in Chapter 8. Score the actions and define your objective and obstacle(s). Rehearse and present a short scene with imagined circumstances leading to action that you believe would be truthful for the character you create from the observed raw material.

**C.** Observe a painting—an original, if you have access to a museum—that reveals character. Re-create with your own body the posture and the facial expression. Make the character move; imagine how he would walk, sit, and use his hands. If it is a period picture, read about the manners and customs of the period. Make him speak. Invent a scene in which you can bring the character to life in a sequence of actions.

**D.** Write down your observations of a room belonging to an acquaintance or, better yet, to someone you are meeting for the first time. Study the furniture. Speculate on the reasons for its choice and its arrangement. Observe the style of the decoration. Are the colors carefully planned or haphazard? Is the room neat or disorderly? What feelings does the room evoke in you? What does it tell you about the person who occupies it?

## Adapting Observations Through the Imagination

A piano has eighty-eight keys. Each one is capable of producing a solitary note. Any person of average intelligence can learn to play the individual notes. Most of us can even learn to put together basic chord combinations. However, it is only through the imagination of an artist that the individual notes and chords can be combined with an infinite variety of tempos and rhythms to create a spectrum of music. **Imagination** is the power of the mind to form an inner image or concept of something that is unreal or not present. As an actor, the building blocks for your imagination are always taken from your own experiences and observations. To stimulate your imagination, you must know how to retain observed behaviors, situations, and abstract qualities. Then you must have the ability to separate and recall your observations before creating a new combination for the stage. Great actors, like great scientists and painters, have enormous imaginations. In Steve Martin's comedy, *Picasso at the Lapin Agile,* young Pablo Picasso tells Albert Einstein, "There is nothing in my way anymore. If I can think it I can draw it." A few moments later, referring to a realistic painting on the wall, they continue their debate on the creative imagination.

PICASSO: . . . I see it as an empty frame with something hideous in it that's waiting to be filled up with something NEW. (*He picks up a pencil and holds it like a foil.*) Advancing out into the unknown, the undrawn, the new thing must be coaxed out of its cave, wrestled with and finally pinned up on the wall like a hide. When I look at Goya, it's like he is reaching his hand through the centuries to tap me on the shoulder. When I paint, I feel like I am reaching my hand forward hundreds of years to touch someone too. . . .

EINSTEIN: I work the same way. *I* make beautiful things with a pencil.

PICASSO: You? You're just a scientist! For me, the shortest distance between two points is *not* a straight line!

EINSTEIN: Likewise.

PICASSO (*still dancing*): Let's see one of your creations. (EINSTEIN *pulls out a pencil.* PICASSO . . . *gets a pencil.* . . . *The others back away as if it were a Western shoot-out.*) Draw!

EINSTEIN: Done! (*They swap drawings.*) It's perfect.

PICASSO: Thank you.

EINSTEIN: I'm talking about mine.

PICASSO: (*He studies it.*) It's a formula.

EINSTEIN: So's yours.

PICASSO: It was a little hastily drawn. . . . Yours is letters.

EINSTEIN: Yours is lines.

PICASSO: My lines mean something.

EINSTEIN: So do mine.

PICASSO: Mine is beautiful.

EINSTEIN: (*Indicates his own drawing.*) Men have swooned on seeing that.

PICASSO: Mine touches the heart.

EINSTEIN: Mine touches the head.

PICASSO: (*Holds his drawing.*) Mine will change the future.[11]

The real Albert Einstein used his imagination by combining phenomena to discover natural laws, while the actual Pablo Picasso fed his imagination by drawing from life the most diverse aspects of it. Both men, through their imaginations, produced favorable conditions through which to express their creativity.

While onstage, your artistic imagination helps you find appropriate actions for your character. Your imagination uncovers the hidden recesses of your subconscious. It helps you to recall and then adapt your observations for the stage. Your observed memories combined with your creative imagination lead you to physical actions and ultimately to truthful emotion. For this reason, your imagination is one of your greatest gifts. Without imagination, there will be no art.

Most adults do not exercise their imaginations. All children have a natural affinity to create. However, as we grow older, we become engrossed in the practical matters of daily existence. We are raised in a culture that suppresses the creative imagination. Ours is a world of "don't." "Don't behave like a child." "Don't show off in public." "Don't raise your voice." "Don't stand out in a crowd." We are a society of conformity. We have strict rules of behavior and customs. We must talk and dress like our friends. We are chastised for being different. Our learned perception of acceptable adult behavior is one of rational, conformist thought and controlled emotions. As an actor, you must reject this idea. You must constantly rekindle your imagination. You must not allow it to lie dormant in the darkest recesses of your mind. It must be exercised. Without it, creativity is not possible. Once your imagination is unleashed, you will rediscover your childlike affinity to develop newly shaped inner images and abstract concepts that are appropriate to your onstage character.

Characters are works of fiction. Theatre is a secondary reality. It is not a slavish imitation of life on the stage, for art demands invention. "The problem of the actor and his creative technique is, therefore, how to transform the fiction of the play into artistic stage reality," writes Stanislavski scholar David Magarshack. "To do that the actor needs imagination." Your imagination is your dearest friend, for it, with the help of the "magic if," combined with the given circumstances and your personal history and observations, gives life to your creations. "An actor who has no imagination, Stanislavski declares, has either to develop it or leave the stage, for otherwise he will be entirely in the hands of the producers who will foist their own imaginations on him, which would be tantamount to his giving up his own creative work and becoming a mere puppet.[12]

---

**Exercise 5.5   SUPPLYING CIRCUMSTANCES FOR OBSERVED BEHAVIOR**   Make careful observations of human behavior. When you see a situation that stimulates your imagination, supply circumstances you can use as the basis for an improvisation. Why, for example, might a sailor in a nightclub be dancing with a child's doll? Why might an old woman selling pencils on the street be reading a report of the New York Stock Exchange? Remember that the purpose of these imaginary circumstances is to provide a reason for action. Action means specific physical objectives that show believable behavior for the person observed. Work out the details carefully.

Rehearse the scene until each part seems right and logical. *Warning:* Do not attempt to substitute a "made-up" situation for the original observation. Without the observed fact, you have no way of knowing whether your imaginary circumstances are true. *Imagination must have a basis in reality.*

---

---

**Exercise 5.6    CREATIVE IMPULSES**

**A.** Creative impulses must be exercised. The instructor will give someone in the class a noun. Ordinary nouns such as *pizza* or *car* will not be used; instead, the instructor will give you a noun with extensive connotations like *religion* or *politics*. Without preparation, you will then stand up and improvise on whatever the word suggests to you. Do not attempt to define the noun with your improvisation; it simply is your immediate reaction to the word. Your response may consist of one or more movements and may or may not include words or sounds. Anything goes, as long as it is short and unplanned. When you finish, you will then give the next person a word, and she will repeat the process.

**B.** Repeat the above exercise, only this time substitute a famous name instead of a noun. The person may be dead or alive, but it must be a person with whom everyone is familiar. You will then stand and improvisationally do something that reveals the essence of the character.

**C.** The instructor will give you a single piece of fabric. You will then stand and create a recognizable character by the way in which you use the material. Don't just wrap the cloth over your head and proclaim yourself to be an Arab woman; rather use the cloth in such a way that the class will know who you are portraying. (Note: This exercise can be repeated with any prop.)

---

# Observing Objects and Animals

The study of plants, animals, and inanimate objects as a means of understanding a character is a third way an actor may use the technique of observation. The process involves **abstraction,** a commonly misunderstood principle. *To abstract* means, literally, "to separate, to take away." The actor applies the principle of abstraction by observing an object for the purpose of taking away from it qualities that will be useful in developing a character.

The qualities of elegance, glitter, and aloofness abstracted from the observation of a crystal chandelier might be important elements in coming to understand some of the characters in Restoration drama or a Noel Coward play. Observing, then abstracting, the comfortableness, the homeliness, and the unpretentiousness of an old leather chair might provide insight into a character of a completely different kind. Cate Blanchett abstracted the qualities of clouds, breezes, and wind while creating Galadriel, the elf queen, in *The Lord of the Rings* trilogy. Her character left no footprints upon the earth.

Russell Crowe's brilliant portrayal of mathematician John Forbes Nash, Jr., in the feature film *A Beautiful Mind,* could be compared to a radiant computer

**Figure 5.2**   Arthur Hanket (*left*) as Charles and Stephanie Erb as Elvira in the Utah Shakespearean Festival's 2004 production of *Blithe Spirit*. Ms. Erb may have abstracted the qualities of a chandelier or a piece of crystal to help her create the role of Elvira.

that develops a virus. Based upon a true story in Cold War America, we see the world through the eyes of Nash. His mind operates on a level that is beyond the comprehension of even the most educated people. Pictures, formulas, codes, and theories flash across his mind at lightning speed; this is reflected in the actor's eyes. However, as the film progresses, a virus infiltrates his computer-like mind, as the prominent mathematician begins to suffer more and more from schizophrenic hallucinations. The virus attacks the data in his brain, causing him to see, hear, and feel "virtual" people. Paranoid about the government, Nash finds hidden meaning in newspapers, magazines, and other documents of no significance. He believes there is a secret conspiracy against him, and he slips into madness until he is rescued by his wife's undying love. If a computer developed feelings, it would have the emotional coldness of Crowe's creation. If it had cognitive reasoning skills and could interpret images, it would be reflected in his eyes. If a damaged computer could walk, it would attempt to move with certainty in many directions simultaneously. If a computer's speech had emotional thought behind it, it would sound like the distant thoughts of Crowe's interpretation of Nash.

**Exercise 5.7** **MOVEMENT ABSTRACTED FROM INANIMATE OBJECTS** Working as a group from the list below, move about your acting studio as if you were a person with the abstracted qualities of:

| | | |
|---|---|---|
| a cloud | a doormat | a tuba |
| a computer | a freight train | a piccolo |
| an eggplant | a superball | a mink stole |
| a chandelier | a whip | a flower |
| an old tennis shoe | a gentle breeze | a stump |
| a sailboat | a bulldozer | an egg |
| a crystal wine glass | a kite | taffy |
| an oak tree | a tornado | ice |
| a knife | a sports car | silk fabric |
| Play-Doh | burlap material | any inanimate object |

Remember that you can observe through all of your senses, not just through sight. Besides considering how the object looks, consider how it feels, how it smells, how heavy it is, and possibly how it tastes. Think of all its characteristic qualities. Remember you will not be trying to make yourself believe you are an eggplant or a crystal wine glass or silk fabric; rather, you are abstracting the essential qualities through your imagination and incorporating them into a person with those characteristics.

People are often compared to animals. We say that a certain young girl is kittenish, that a certain person is as clumsy as a bear, that one man is foxy, another is wolfish, and that still another is a snake in the grass. These comparisons are examples of abstracting an animal's essential qualities and applying them to aspects of human behavior. An actor will find that creating such abstractions from animals is another worthwhile exercise in observation that can provide outstanding raw material for characterizations.

We can easily draw parallels between Tobey McGuire's character in *Spiderman* with that of an arachnid. Halle Berry's portrayal of the title role in *Catwoman* is certainly based on a feline. Remember, however, that Tom Hanks modeled his character, Josh Baskin, in *Big* upon his more subtle abstracted observations of a newborn giraffe with "spindly heads that look geeky when they run." In the motion picture *Seven*, Kevin Spacey played a psychopathic serial killer with extremely subtle abstracted qualities. Like a snake patiently stalking its prey, Spacey demonstrated an amazing ability to simultaneously express spine-chilling villainy, laconic indifference and limitless superiority with merely a few gestures and vocal inflections. Jeff Bridges, who played the Alien in the film *Starman,* considered this

Photo by Buddy Myers.

**Figure 5.3**   Laurie Vlasich Bulaoro in *Berlin to Broadway with Kurt Weill,* produced by Stage West in Ft. Worth, Texas. Directed by Jerry Russell. In addition to physical form, note this actor's animal adaptation and predator-like attitude.

one of his most unique challenges. As a person from outer space, he had nothing on which to base his character. In dealing with the development of the alien who has assumed the body of Jenny Hayden's (Karen Allen) dead husband, Bridges relied on his own studies and observations and, working with director John Carpenter, created a highly intelligent explorer whose physical movement can only be described as birdlike.

A famous, classic example of observing the qualities of animals and applying them to dramatic characters in plays is found in Ben Jonson's *Volpone,* a vicious satire on greed. Each character is appropriately named after some beast of prey.

Volpone, or the Fox, is a rich merchant whose ruling passion is greed. Like his namesake, he is also sly and has hit on a scheme of pretending he is dying so his equally rapacious friends will court his favor with extravagant gifts in the hope of being made his heirs. His friends include Corvino, or Little Crow, who offers Volpone his young wife; Corbaccio, or Old Crow, who sniffs at Volpone's body to make sure he is dead; and Voltore, or the Vulture, who is exactly what his name implies. Slyest of all is Mosca, or the Fly, who turns the tables on Volpone by trying to prove him legally dead. Actors performing these roles would certainly want to find true human behavior that could be abstracted imaginatively from observing the behavior of the animal associated with each character.

An actress preparing for the role of Maggie in *Cat on a Hot Tin Roof,* by Tennessee Williams, might do well to study not the panther but the alley cat. Since Maggie is the "cat" of the title, once again the script provides the starting place for this exploration. Maggie struggles to bring life back into her alcoholic husband with the cunning, persistence, and sensuality of a feline. She has scratched and clawed her way out of poverty, and she is determined to hang on to her marriage, with the tenacity of an alley cat struggling to stay alive in the streets. Hear Maggie purr when it becomes necessary. Her attempts to seduce her husband Brick and flatter Big Daddy are catlike. When Maggie walks, imagine her whole body in motion with feline grace. When she is spiteful, see her claws emerge from their sheath. The actress working on the part will note the human qualities in cats as well as the feline qualities in humans.

*Equus,* by Peter Shaffer, provides yet another subtle example. This play deals with the psychiatric case history of Alan Strang, a seventeen-year-old who has blinded six horses with a metal spike. In the course of the play, the trauma peels away as he relives the experience. Because Alan has a love–hate relationship with horses, the actor might want to observe and catalog the characteristic behavior of these animals as he prepares to play the role. Some potentially usable abstractions might be nervousness; skittishness; restlessness (especially true of a young colt); gracefulness of motion; head carried high, moving from side to side to observe the world; wariness; and rollicking playfulness. Experimenting with these qualities could be a useful springboard when creating the character.

The observation of animals and objects will become an important part of your arsenal of rehearsal techniques. After penetratingly observing an animal, bringing as many of the senses as you can into play, you should attempt to create, in so far as it is humanly possible, the physical and emotional attributes of the animal. If you enter into animal study freely and with an open mind, such stretching of the imagination should then allow you to create a human character who possesses many traits you observed in the animal.

Animal exercises can often put you in touch with feelings and emotions that have heretofore been strange to you. Of course, if animal study is to be useful in developing a specific character in a play, you will need to make certain that the animal traits can be justified by the script. No external characterization tool can substitute for careful study of the given circumstances of the text; therefore, animal improvisations should never be used until after you have selected images and actions for the basic makeup of your character. Once this step has been accomplished, applying the sensations that grow out of the study of pertinent animals and objects can help you discover the unique manner in which your character performs his or her actions.

**Exercise 5.8    MOVEMENT ABSTRACTED FROM ANIMALS**    Working as a group from the list below, move about your acting studio as if you were a person with the abstracted qualities of:

| | | |
|---|---|---|
| a moth | an orangutan | an exotic bird |
| a chicken | a cow | a mouse |
| a gorilla | an elephant | a skunk |
| a lion | a snake | a sparrow |
| a pig | a domestic kitten | a rabbit |
| an otter | a wolf | a squirrel |
| a bear | a prairie dog | a beaver |
| a dog (any breed) | a woodpecker | a horse |
| a tropical fish | a fox | a flamingo |
| a fly | a crow | any other animal |

**Exercise 5.9    CREATING A SCORE FROM ABSTRACTION**    Plan a short individual scene, either with or without lines, in which you develop a score of physical actions for a character with the qualities of an animal or inanimate object. Use your imagination to supply circumstances that would require the person to act in a true and revealing manner. Carrying out these actions will help you to believe you are a person with the same characteristics as your chosen animal or inanimate object.

# Terms and People to Know

**abstraction**    The process of observing an object for the purpose of taking away from it qualities that will be useful in developing a character.

**emotion memory**    A personal emotion that helps an actor find a similar stage emotion.

**imagination** The power of the mind to form an inner image or concept of something that is unreal or not present. Because they are always taken from your own *personal history,* you must know how to retain observed behaviors, situations, and abstract qualities, then have the ability to separate, recall, and adapt them into a new combination for the stage.

**inner images** Specific mental pictures that help an actor to trigger actively traveling thoughts.

**Method Acting** Developed by Lee Strasberg and based on early teachings of Stanislavski, it is an internal approach to acting that gives primary focus to affective memory, which is fully explored in Chapter 7.

**personal history** Everything you have experienced, felt, read, or observed in life or fiction.

**sense memory** The use of past sensations—taste, touch, sound, smell, and sight—as a means to substitute the qualities of one thing for another (e.g., drinking water as if it were vodka or burning your finger on a stove that is not actually lit).

## CHAPTER 6

# Exploring Circles of Attention

*"If the actor is in the center of a pond, the ripples he creates radiate out in an increasing circumference that will eventually embrace the whole pond."*

–Constantin Stanislavski

Most people, under ordinary circumstances, have relatively short attention spans. A few people, however, have the ability to concentrate for long periods of time, sometimes longer than their physical bodies can tolerate. A racecar driver must have the ability to concentrate for hours on end while moving at speeds in excess of two hundred miles per hour with only inches separating his car from his opponent's. Any lapse of concentration means certain failure—or worse. Only after the race is complete can the winning driver physically relax and enjoy his victory. Every actor must have this same basic mental strength, the ability to concentrate for long periods of time while surrounded by infinite distractions. The capacity to concentrate separates great acting from good acting. Onstage, **concentration** is the ability to focus your energy towards a single sequence of actions. These actions may be directed toward an object, oneself, another person, or a group of people—including the audience in certain types of theatre.

As an actor onstage, you cannot put yourself into a trance or wrap yourself in a cocoon against the onslaught of outside disruptions. As you embody your character, you remain aware of the auditorium you can see and the publicness of your performance. You would have to be mentally insane to forget these distracting elements. However, you must not allow the audience to adversely affect your behavior and your carefully selected artistic choices. Great actors are marked by their ability to focus their attention on the actions of their characters. The moment your attention drifts into the audience, you will "get into your own head" and lose control onstage. On the other hand, the instant you withdraw your attention from the audience, you will have power over them. You will compel them to take an active interest in your onstage activities.

Whether in rehearsal or performance, you must surround yourself with what Stanislavski referred to as a **circle of attention.** While focusing on your actions, you are aware of the outer forces; however, you must restrict your circle of attention by "concentrating on what comes within this sphere, and only half consciously seizing on what comes within its aura." You must have control over this imaginary bubble—this ring of concentration. It must be "elastic." You must be able to expand and contract your attention as the theatrical moment necessitates.[1]

Concentration helps you relax by properly channeling your energies toward the accomplishment of a specific goal. It is also the principal means of commanding the audience's attention. The audience must see what you want them to see, hear what you want them to hear during every moment of performance. Otherwise, the spectators' attention may wander casually around the stage or stray to other points in the auditorium. Their minds, like your own, may drift to personal situations that have nothing to do with stage events.

Fortunately, the audience wants to follow the story. Their attention corresponds with your involvement in specific actions. *Attention demands attention.* However, concentration, like the "creative state," is easier to talk about than to do. Too many young actors resemble the fellow described by Stephen Leacock who jumped on his horse and rode off in all directions. Their attention is scattered to all points of the compass. Their minds wander from the stage to the audience to the wings to their next line to an upcoming scene to a past mistake, and so on. They do well to focus ten percent of their attention on anything related to the action, thus dissipating ninety percent of their mental energy.

You can make full use of your talent only by learning to focus your energies. Creativity, whether in rehearsal or during repeated performances, demands complete concentration of both your inner and outer faculties.[2] Successful actors achieve maximum concentration. They find ways to control their attention despite the pressure of the audience, the distraction of backstage activities, and the mechanical demands of the role.

Photo courtesy of Stetson University's Department of Communication Studies and Theater Arts.

**Figure 6.1**   LeRoy Mitchell as C.C. and Jeff Bowen as Buddy in Stetson University's production of *The Diviners*, by Jim Leonard, Jr. Directed by Kenn Stilson. The specific and intense focus of these actors demands the attention of the viewer.

**Exercise 6.1   DISTRACTIONS**   Any activity that requires concentration, especially in the presence of distracting influences, is excellent discipline for actors. People training for the stage need to develop their powers of attention through increasingly complicated exercises. *As with all exercises, however, their value is derived only when they are practiced regularly over a period of time. No exercise has served its purpose until it can be done satisfactorily with a minimum of effort.* Students of Stanislavski suggest the following kinds of activity for improving your ability to concentrate:

**A.** Read expository material in the presence of a group that constantly tries to interrupt and distract. Hold yourself responsible for remembering each detail you have read.

**B.** Solve mathematical problems under the same conditions.

**C.** Present a memorized passage of prose or poetry under the same conditions.

**Exercise 6.2   ADD-A-WORD**

**A.** With a group sitting in a circle, one person says the first noun that comes to mind. The next person repeats the word and adds another word. The third person repeats those two words and adds another, and so on. Use only nouns, for they are easier to remember. Stay in the present. Do not try to think ahead. See in your mind what you have heard; associate the word with the person who said it; and add a noun suggested by the image of the words that preceded it so that a continuous logical story may develop. For example:

+ cigarette
+ cigarette, woman
+ cigarette, woman, nightclub
+ cigarette, woman, nightclub, peanuts, etc.

The process continues around and around the circle until no one is able to repeat the entire series. Anyone who fails is eliminated.

**B.** Under similar circumstances, play a game of numbers. The numbers may be unrelated, or you may progress by having each person add three or seven, eleven or nineteen. The game can become quite challenging.

---

**Exercise 6.3**  **BODY COORDINATION**  Concentrate on coordination of arm movements. With the left arm fully extended, continue making a large circle in the air; with the right arm, continue making a square by extending it straight out from the shoulder, then up, and then to the side. Once coordination is established, reverse the arms, making the circle with the right arm and the square with the left.

---

# Channeling Your Energy

For you, the actor, a circle is the degree of concentration on a single sequence of actions in which all your nerves are brought into focus. Your entire body is working in the same direction, attracting all your powers of observation to itself. All artists must master the power to concentrate. This is particularly true for the actor.

Attention may be either internal or external. The main function of internal attention is to fuel your imagination, whereas external attention helps you to focus your mind on onstage activity, thus distracting you from the horrifying black hole called the proscenium arch. Through exercise, it is absolutely essential that you learn to fix your attention onstage to prevent your mind from drifting into the audience. Through your "sixth sense," you remain aware of their presence, but you must acquire the technique that allows you to focus your attention so firmly on your character's thoughts and actions that the audience no longer has any adverse effects on your behavior. In short, you must learn how to *see* onstage. "For the eye of the actor who knows how to look and see attracts the attention of the spectators, concentrating it on the object they too have to look at," wrote

Stanislavski. "The empty gaze of an actor, on the other hand, merely diverts the attention of the spectators from the stage."

As a means to teach actors to channel their energy while onstage, Stanislavski developed his now famous theory known as "circles of attention." An actor must have a point of attention, and this point must not be in the audience. The more engaging the action, the more it will focus the attention. Stanislavski wrote, "In real life there are always plenty of objects that fix our attention, but conditions in the theatre are different, and interfere with an actor's living normal, so that an effort to fix attention becomes necessary."[3]

Stanislavski demonstrated his point to his students by turning off all the lights in his classroom, leaving it in complete darkness. He then turned on a small lamp, illuminating the center of a table where a number of small objects had been placed. With the students watching, he carefully examined each item. "Make a note immediately of your mood," he said. "It is solitude because you are divided from us by the 'small circle of attention.' During a performance, before an audience of thousands, you can always enclose yourself in this circle like a snail in its shell." It is easy to examine the smallest details of the objects within its circumference, live with the most intimate feelings and desires, carry out the most complicated actions, solve the most difficult problems, and analyze one's feelings and thoughts. In addition, it is possible in such a circle to establish close communication with another person in it, confide to him one's most intimate thoughts, recall the past and dream of the future. Stanislavski described an actor's state of mind in such an imaginary circle of attention as **public solitude.** It is public, he points out, because the whole audience is with the actor all the time, and it is solitude because he is separated from it by his small circle of attention. During a performance the actor can always withdraw himself to his small circle of attention and, as it were, retire into his solitude, like a snail into its shell.

He then expanded the area of illumination but concentrated his attention on performing the same score of actions. He called this the "medium circle of attention." Finally, he flooded the entire classroom with light—the "large circle of attention"—but again focused his attention on the same score of actions.

> When the lights are on you have an entirely different problem. As there is no obvious outline to your circle you are obliged to construct one mentally and not allow yourself to look beyond it. Your attention must now replace the light, holding you within certain limits, and this despite the drawing power of all sorts of objects now visible outside of it.[4]

Although you are aware of the medium and large circles of attention, the small circle of attention allows you to focus ninety percent of your mental energy on the stage action; thus, the audience will more likely follow the story without distraction.

With the widening of this field of awareness, the area of your attention is also widened. This, however, can go on only as long as you can keep your attention

Used by permission of Alice Berry. Photo by Fowler Photography.

**Figure 6.2**   Alice Berry and Jared Logan in a scene from The University of Memphis's production of *All My Sons*. Directed by J. Noble; scenic design by Kim Yeager; costume design by Sandra London; lighting design by Michael DeLorm. Note the sense of communion between these two actors, as the small circle of attention allows them to truthfully portray an intimate moment of public solitude.

fixed within the imaginary circle. The moment the circumference of the circle becomes blurred, you must narrow the circle to the limits of your visual attention. You must acquire an unconscious, mechanical habit of transferring your attention from the smaller to the larger circle without breaking it. You have to remember that the bigger and emptier your large circle, the more compact your middle and small circles must be inside it.[5] *The way to rescue yourself from the most terrible moment of panic onstage is to focus your energy on your score within the small circle of attention.* The more distracted you are by outside forces, the more solitary must your solitude be.

---

**Exercise 6.4    CONCENTRATING ON ACTION**   Much of this book has been devoted to the importance of action. In earlier exercises, you were asked to write down—make a score of—the physical actions you would undertake if you were in the situation of an imaginary character. Actions are tangible and specific for both the actor and the audience, bringing a character to life and revealing the dramatic events of the play. Because actions are never divorced from specific desires, their advantage lies not just in the actions themselves but also in the meaning and feelings they have the power to evoke.

Good dramatists provide ample chances for actors to concentrate their attention on performing physical action. Sometimes the action is to satisfy a simple desire, and sometimes actors must find a logical pattern of action to satisfy their characters' pressing needs. Good actors and directors display great imagination in inventing physical action organic to the character and the situation.

Plan and rehearse a score of physical actions for the following problems. Work on the exercise until you can repeat the score without any feeling of distraction from outside influences—the medium and large circles of attention—and until you are satisfied that every bit of your energy is concentrated on carrying out the action—the small circle of attention. Supply additional circumstances, giving yourself specific details that will lead you to believe your actions.

As always, write out your score, making certain that the scene has a logical beginning, middle, and end. Define your objective and obstacle(s) and perform your score with the greatest possible economy, discarding any details that do not help in achieving your goal.

**A.** You are searching for a lost article that is very important to you.

**B.** After breaking your mother's favorite antique, you attempt to cover your mistake by repairing the damage.

**C.** While folding your fiancée's laundry, you discover an article of clothing that does not belong to either of you.

**D.** Late on a cold winter night, you are standing on a street corner waiting for a bus.

**E.** Sitting alone in a bar, you discreetly attempt to attract the attention of a person you wish to meet.

**F.** Physically ill, you try to study for an important examination.

**G.** You are packing your suitcase in preparation for running away from home.

**H.** While dressing for an important dinner engagement, you discover a stain on your clothing.

**I.** Recovering from a serious illness, you take your first steps.

## Relating to Objects

Although effective acting involves carrying out a sequence of logical and truthful actions, your ultimate goal is not to perform the action itself, but to reveal its significance. The final interest of the audience is not in the events of the play—important as they are—but in the underlying meaning of the characters' relationships.

Consider Goethe's most famous drama, *Faust,* in which the old scholar has sold his soul to the devil in return for a year of restored youth. One of the youthful pleasures he seeks is the seduction of the innocent Marguerite. To help achieve this aim, he leaves a casket of jewels where Marguerite is certain to find them. She does so in the company of Martha, her older and more experienced neighbor. Here is the material for a stunning scene, but it will be meaningful to the audience only if they understand the relationship of the jewels to Marguerite and her neighbor and the effect of Faust's actions on both ladies. The actors involved in this scene have something on which to focus their attention—the jewels. The meaning behind the jewels and both ladies' relationship to the objects will serve to set in motion the actors' creativity as they begin to score the scene. "Imagined circumstances can transform the object itself and heighten the reaction of your emotions to it," wrote Stanislavski. "You must learn to transfigure an object from something which is coldly reasoned or intellectual in quality into something which is warmly *felt.*"[6]

*Faust* offers the actors playing Marguerite and Martha a wonderful opportunity to engage in an intellectual and sensory observation of the jewels. They must experience the color, shape, and brilliance, the feel of them dripping through their hands, and the way they look hung about their necks and from their ears. Since the *prop* jewels will not be real, the actors can—through remembered observation or *sense memory*—give the quality, the beauty and fire of precious stones to the counterfeit jewels.

The actors, however, must not stop there. They must also "transfigure" the jewels into something that is "warmly felt," to make emotional connections between themselves, their characters, and the objects. They (especially Martha) are overcome with the beauty of the stones. They desire them; they covet them. The jewels become a burning temptation, a successful lure in Faust's seduction. In the hands of professional actors, these important objects performs a key dramatic function in the total action of the scene. In both rehearsal and performance, the actors will use their relationship with these objects to trigger their imaginations and to induce believable actions and consequent feelings.

The same object, of course, can evoke a variety of responses, depending on the character and the circumstances. Consider the relationship of a casket of jewels to a hungry beggar. What is the relationship of this object to a wealthy dowager contemplating a purchase? What about a customs inspector or a jewel thief ? Good playwrights and directors are skillful and imaginative in supplying onstage objects that will help the actor find the truth of a scene. Such objects achieve their fullest meaning when, like the jewels in *Faust,* they are both logical and dramatically symbolic.

Think now of the opening scene of Shakespeare's great tragedy, *King Lear.* When the aging monarch literally gives away his kingdom, his action must be clear to the audience, but the real significance lies in the effect of his actions on

**Figure 6.3**   Corliss Preston as Jessica in the Utah Shakespearean Festival's production of *The Merchant of Venice.* Staying within the small circle of attention, the actor in this scene has established a relationship with the ring and turned it into something that is warmly felt.

him and the people surrounding him. Lear's throne, his crown, and the sword of state carried before him all symbolize the kingdom, which is his source of power and which he is now about to give away. The map depicting the newly divided kingdom visually represents the freedom from the cares of state Lear seeks in his old age; it is also a lure that entices his daughters to flatter his vanity by making boundless declarations of love before the assembled court. Shattered by Cordelia's refusal, Lear rashly changes his plan and violently tears the map. The actor who can personalize Lear's relation to these objects—transfigure them into something that is "warmly felt"—will find them to be a dependable stimulus for believable actions and true emotions.

You must also learn to relate to your character's clothing and to the imaginary environment. The character's clothing must be a part of your very existence. You must not treat your clothes as mere costumes that were recently hanging in the dressing room but rather as if your character personally selected them. Your work with your character's clothing will, in fact, communicate directly how your character feels about himself and his surroundings. In the same manner, you must find ways to relate to various aspects of your environment. Like onstage objects, the environment must be logical and symbolic and stimulate action. However, until you define your relationship to your surroundings, it will simply be scenery with no significant meaning. A door, for example, is merely a decoration until you, the actor, use it. Only then will it be given definition in relationship to your character, the play, and the particular scene. All the techniques by which you can instill an object with rich meanings can apply equally to your character's clothing and environment.

Many of the greatest moments in drama supply the actor with an opportunity to use the technique of relating to objects. Continuing with Shakespeare, think of (1) Othello and the candle just before he murders Desdemona: "Put out the light, and then put out the light"; (2) Hamlet and the skull, as he talks about the transitory nature of life: "Alas! poor Yorick. I knew him, Horatio . . ."; (3) Lady Macbeth and her hands, which, in her deranged mind, she believes are covered with the blood of the murdered Duncan: "Out, damned spot! Out, I say!"; and (4) Shylock and the knife he is sharpening on the sole of his shoe to cut out a pound of Antonio's flesh. Shylock's action motivates Bassanio's "Why dost thou whet thy knife so earnestly?"—a gentle reminder from Shakespeare that the actor playing Shylock should be concentrating on his physical action with the object.

---

**Exercise 6.5**    **SCORING A SEQUENCE WITH OBJECTS**    Working alone, score and present a logical sequence of actions that centers on one or more objects. You must supply given circumstances that will provide you with a specific relationship to the object(s). Make sure you have a definite objective and that you work against an obstacle. You should also consider the essential qualities of the object(s) and the human and environmental conditions discussed in Chapter 5. You may base your scenes around the suggested actions listed below or create your own:

| | |
|---|---|
| searching through a box (or drawer) | setting the table |
| counting a large sum of money | attempting to read a poorly drawn map |
| placing a blanket over someone (or a pet) | reading a "Dear John (or Jane)" letter |
| sharpening a knife | trying on clothing |
| reading a will | packing a box or suitcase |
| unwrapping a present | repairing a valuable vase |
| looking at a photograph | interpreting a piece of obscure art |
| taking prescribed medicine (or illegal drugs) | eating distasteful food |
| writing a suicide note | folding your boyfriend's (or girlfriend's) laundry |
| determining the purpose of an unknown utensil | |

---

# Infecting Your Partner

To excite an audience, actors must excite one another. Stanislavski wrote: "Infect your partner! Infect the person you are concentrating on! Insinuate yourself into his very soul, and you will find yourself the more infected for doing so. And if you are infected everyone else will be even more infected."[7] A lion has the power to stalk, attack, and seize its prey without distraction. You must have the same power to seize with your eyes, ears, and senses. As an actor, if you must listen, listen intently. If you are to smell, smell hard. Do not simply gaze at another person, but look into her soul. Infect that person.

"The eye is the mirror of the soul," wrote Stanislavski. "The vacant eye is the mirror of the empty soul."[8] While onstage, your eyes should reflect the deep inner content of your character's soul. Therefore, you must build great inner resources to correspond to the life of a human soul in your characters. Each moment onstage, you must share these spiritual resources with the other actors in the play. This is **communion.** It is like an underground river, which flows continuously under the surface of both words and silences, forming an invisible bond between two human beings. The communion established between actors is the surest source of stimulation, leading to a rewarding theatre experience for the audience.

---

**Exercise 6.6**    **MIRRORS**    Do a sequence of "Mirror Exercises," in which two people stand opposite each other; one makes a movement, while the other mirrors him or her precisely without delay. The effect is that of synchronized swimming, in which partners move at the exact same time.

**A.** At first, do a "Movement Mirror" with abstract, nonrepresentational movements.

**B.** Now change roles by switching who leads and who mirrors.

**C.** Now you are both leaders and both mirrors. Work off your partner, and do not attempt to merely lead or follow.

**D.** Go back to one leader and one mirror, but add realistic physical tasks such as running your fingers through your hair, cleaning your nails, or setting your watch.

**E.** Return to abstract, nonrepresentational movements with one person serving as the leader and the other person mirroring the first person's actions.

**F.** Extend the above exercise into a "Sound and Movement Mirror," in which, along with the movements, the leader utters repetitive but constantly changing nonsensical sounds that are mirrored by the partner.

**G.** Again, change leaders.

**H.** Finally, you are both leaders and both mirrors with your "Sound and Movement Mirror."

---

Onstage relationships may be characterized as the process of conflict between partners. In any given scene, each character is attempting to impose her point of view, her position on the given subject through a sequence of physical actions. Each character will listen and evaluate her opponent's resistance. She will watch his actions, listen to his words and intonations, then decide how to react with a look, a gesture, a word, or a movement that most effectively upholds her position in the conflict. If you are truly engaged in the onstage action, you will not simply wait for your cue to react, but you will have a continuous communion through words and behavior between you and your partner. Even when you are not speaking, you will be engaged in a silent struggle, trying to influence his thoughts and actions.

Conflict produces action. Conflict is always between characters; therefore, your action must always be directed toward your partner. You are trying to persuade, seduce, elevate, destroy, subordinate, or calm his desire, his will. You are trying to change his way of thinking, to alter his actions to meet your desire. Thus, *theatrical action cannot exist without conflict, and conflict cannot exist without communion between partners who are trying to mutually influence each other through words and behavior.* Every moment you are onstage, it is your responsibility to infect your partner, to influence his behavior, and to make him adapt to your point of view. Every person onstage will have unique attitudes toward a subject. *The concepts of action, conflict, and communion are not synonymous, but they are inseparable.* Stanislavski determined that the nature of communion is "an interaction between partners in the process of a struggle on the stage. This means that the actor performs his action in order to elicit from his partner some concrete real behavior, which he needs to attain his own concrete real goal."[9]

Shakespeare's plays, as complex as they are, still center around elemental conflicts of will. *King Lear* begins with Lear's attempt to force his will on his daughters by requiring extravagant declarations of love from them. Othello's tragedy comes from Iago's determination to ruin his contentment, and *The Taming of the Shrew* is a straightforward clash between the robust wills of Katherina and Petruchio. In *The Winter's Tale,* Hermione's honor and life depend on her ability to convince her husband he is wrong in suspecting her of being unfaithful. In Act II, Scene 1 of *Hamlet,* a frightened Ophelia explains to her father a recent encounter with young Prince Hamlet:

> He took me by the wrist and held me hard;
> Then goes he to the length of all his arm,
> And, with his other hand thus o'er his brow,
> He falls to such perusal of my face
> As he would draw it. Long stay'd he so.
> At last, a little shaking of mine arm,
> And thrice his head thus waving up and down,

He rais'd a sigh so piteous and profound
As it did seem to shatter all his bulk
And end his being. That done, he lets me go,
And with his head over his shoulder turn'd
He seem'd to find his way without his eyes,
For out o' doors he went without their help
And to the last bended their light on me.

We sense, in these lines, the wordless communion between Hamlet and Ophelia.

When you engage in communion with your fellow actors by trying to influence their behavior, you will establish an emotional relationship. Both consciously and unconsciously, you will make logical adjustments to each of your partners, and such adjustments depend on an awareness of the other's presence and personality. Often the techniques for relating to objects are equally useful in accomplishing objectives that require you to commune with another person. You use these techniques to "transfigure" your partner into someone who is "warmly felt."

We are frequently faced, both in life and onstage, with the problem of evoking the same responses from two or more people toward whom we have dissimilar relationships. Again, the opening scene of *King Lear* provides a good example. Lear wants to induce his three daughters to shower him with love, but he has a different relationship with each of his offspring. He knows that Goneril is shrewd, cold, ambitious, and willing to do whatever is necessary to gain a share of the kingdom. Regan is a follower who wants what Goneril has and will do what Goneril does. Cordelia, on the other hand, is straightforward and honest; her protestation of love can be assumed to be genuine. Lear's vanity requires a public declaration of love from each of the three, but he uses a different strategy in each case to get it. Toward Goneril, the actor playing Lear may establish a kind of bargaining relationship: tell me you love me, and I'll give you a share of my kingdom. Since Regan's response is so predictable, he might approach her with indifference, perhaps even mingled with contempt. To make the scene have the proper impact, he will most likely seek honest love from Cordelia, for he is depending on her for comfort in the loneliness of his advancing age.

These relationships are merely suggestions. The actor playing Lear establishes relationships that will work for him by (1) probing his imagination for an answer to the question: "If I were King Lear, what would I do in these circumstances to get Goneril, Regan, and Cordelia to behave as I want them to?" and (2) responding honestly to the immediate attempts of the actors playing the daughters to influence his behavior. Spontaneous responses between actors are the principal sources of vitality in any performance.

The process of developing a communion between actors is a technique that aspiring actors should thoroughly explore and practice. Once mastered, this technique allows you to behave toward the other actors as if you believe they are the characters they play and simultaneously to make full use of your sensory and intellectual responses to each as a person. If, for example, the actor playing Lear tries to relate to nothing but a preconceived image of his daughters rather than "working off" his actual partners, he will quite simply be "alone" onstage with other actors. Acting requires **ensemble,** and ensemble requires the equal participation of everyone onstage. Hence the saying, "There are no small roles, only small actors." Just as a lifeline connects mountain climbers to one another as they ascend great heights, actors onstage are connected to their partners by the ensemble. If one person "falls," his partner must "save" him. Attempting to perform alone onstage alongside other people deprives the actor of the stimulation that comes from genuine relationships with fellow performers. The actor playing Lear must respond as fully as he can to the palpable qualities of the others with whom he is playing. If he were to play Lear again with different actresses performing the daughters, his performance would take on a new set of nuances, yet each performance would have equal truth and vitality.

---

**Exercise 6.7**   **THE INVISIBLE ANTENNAE**   Communion is a state of absolute connection with self, the other actors, and the audience. Using no words and limited facial expressions, gestures, and physical actions, create a circumstance in which an engaged couple have quarreled and are not speaking to one another. Seat them as far apart as possible. In the beginning, the young woman pretends not to see him, but she does so in such a way as to attract his attention. He sits motionless, watching her with a pleading gaze, trying to catch her eye so that he might guess her feelings. The young man tries to feel her soul with his invisible antennae, but the angry woman must attempt to withstand his attempts at communication.

---

**Exercise 6.8**   **COMMUNION**   The great acting teacher Sanford Meisner believed the loss of communion onstage to be the biggest problem facing actors. Without this spiritual bond, the scene loses its power and has no chance to connect with the audience. According to Meisner, two actors could theoretically create three-dimensional characters, play the proper actions, discover true emotions, and still fail in the performance. The energy and tension in a scene come as a result of the interaction between characters. Drawing upon Stanislavski's idea of communion and Meisner's famed beginning acting classes at the Neighborhood Playhouse, perform the following sequence of exercises.

**A.** With the entire class, *really* look at one another. Don't pretend to look, but really observe each other. Look at one person's hair, another person's shoes, and yet another person's unsightly blemish. What do you notice? Say what you observe aloud to yourself. Don't worry about "being nice," as there is no place for "nice" onstage. Say what you really notice about the observable physical attributes of the people around you.

**B.** Now stand opposite one of your classmates. Decide who is Partner A and who is Partner B. A turns toward B and says aloud one physical observation about B. For example, A might say, "curly hair." B listens carefully and repeats back what he has heard. Then A repeats back what she has heard; B repeats back what he has heard, and so on. Continue this word repetition exercise until the instructor or observer tells you to stop. Repeat back exactly what you hear, not what you think you are supposed to have heard. Don't anticipate. Don't assume your partner will give you what you expect. For example, if your partner omits a word or accidentally inverts the sentence, do not correct that response. Remember, you should repeat back exactly what you hear. On the other hand, there should be no pauses between phrases. There should be no *thinking* about your response. Also, do not try to be interesting, and do not purposefully do anything with the words. Simply listen and repeat. This exercise is extremely important, for it forces you to listen to one another. It also places your focus outside yourself and onto the other person. Therefore, self-consciousness, a common disease among actors, has little time to develop.

**C.** Now the exercise should evolve into what Meisner called "a truthful point of view." Partner A might say, "You have green eyes." Partner B, who has hazel eyes, may say without pause, "I do *not* have green eyes." or "I have hazel eyes." A says, "You have green eyes," because from her point of view B's eyes are green. B says, "I do not have green eyes," and so on. Let each partner start this exercise five times, leading into repetition. Beware of pausing out of the human need to "be right." Simply respond to what you hear and see from a truthful point of view and with what you know to be true.

**D.** Repeat Exercise C. This time, however, the repetition should evolve into language. For example:

A says, "Your hands are in your lap."

B repeats, "My hands are in my lap."

A says, "Your hands are in your lap."

B repeats, "My hands are in my lap."

A says, "Your hands are in your lap."

B moves his hand to scratch his nose. Now he cannot truthfully say, "My hands are in my lap." Instead it changes to "I scratched my nose."

A then repeats, "You scratched your nose," and so on.

With this change in the repetition comes a remarkable development. Emotion has made an appearance. Sometime during this exercise, laughter may rise. Tears, rage, and scorn may appear. This simple exercise unleashes all kinds of unexpected energy. Keep in mind, however, that neither actor should take the lead by trying to push the dialogue in a particular direction. The repetition should change only when it must.

E. Extend Exercise D by beginning with a personal question. A might ask, "Are you embarrassed by your receding hairline?" B will then allow himself to give an honest emotional reaction—either verbal or physical. A will then describe B's observable behavioral response to her question. There is no repetition at this point. There is only A's question, B's truthful reaction, followed by A's description of what she observed.

F. Now extend Exercise E by allowing it to go into repetition.

A asks, "Are you embarrassed by your receding hairline?"

B reacts by bringing his hand to his head and saying, "I'm not losing my hair!"

A says, "That struck a nerve!"

B responds with "That did not strike a nerve!"

A says, "That struck a nerve!" and so on.

Let your instincts dictate when you must change the repetition. This change must come only from a change in the behavior of your partner. Do not attempt to be outrageous. Do not try to impress your partner. Again, this exercise is about establishing a communion with your partner. *Really* listen and *really* react from a truthful point of view.[10]

---

## Communing with the Audience

At this time, we need to discuss briefly the actor's responsibility to the audience, a matter that we will take up in more detail later. Put simply, you must clearly communicate to the audience everything you do and why you are doing it.

You can make something clear to the audience only if you have made it clear to yourself. Far too many student actors attempt an assignment with vague, general answers to the important "W" questions. As we stated in the opening chapter of this text, you must also infuse the character with an appropriate dimension, energy, and clarity that can communicate the meaning to an audience of a certain size occupying a certain space. If your actions cannot be seen or heard, you will lose your audience's attention. Many young actors get so involved in their actions that they forget to project them to the audience. Inaudible speech and actions are meaningless. To successfully communicate with an audience, even subtle behavior must be performed at a sufficient energy level, which varies with the size of the proscenium arch. Small actions that may be perfectly clear in front of a camera or to an audience in a small experimental theatre may not communicate to an audience in a large proscenium house. Furthermore, student actors who believe that truth is found only in subtlety have a misconception about the nature of human beings. Human behavior is indeed sometimes subtle and understated; however, it is just as apt to be overenthusiastic and raucous. Large actions do not necessarily translate as false indications. Honest human behavior is sometimes

**Figure 6.4**   Mallory Thomas (*left*) and Katharine Baldwin in a scene from The University of Missouri–Columbia's production of *School for Scandal*. Directed by Cheryl Black, scenic design by Jon Drtina, costume design by James M. Miller, lighting design by Dean Packard. The actors in this scene are communing with each other, while the actor looking in the mirror also communes with herself. A strong connection between actors transcends the proscenium and establishes a communion with the audience.

enormous. As long as you behave truthfully in imaginary circumstances, no matter how large your decisions, the audience will believe your actions.

Incidentally, everything the actor does should also be interesting. Attempting to accomplish this requisite, however, can lead the actor into the trap of producing out-of-place and illogical comedy, novelty, or sensationalism for its own sake, rather than for the sake of illuminating the given circumstances. Shakespeare, in Hamlet's advice to the Players, wrote, "o'erstep not the modesty of nature; for anything so overdone is from the purpose of playing. . . ." He later warned, "for there be of them that will themselves laugh, to set on some quantity of barren spectators to laugh too, though in the meantime some necessary question of the play be then to be considered." The actor must recognize that human behavior is inherently interesting and is the heart and soul of communion with the audience. Although the world of the play may be extraordinary, even absurd, audiences expect to see truthful behavior. The way to generate interest in your exercises, as well as when performing a role, is to define the world, make the circumstances specific, and provide conflict via an explicit objective that can be realized only by overcoming a definite obstacle. If you plan carefully and concentrate on each step necessary to carry out your plans, you will have a solid foundation for a performance that will interest an audience.

## Making an Action of Speech

Both in life and on stage, we use words as a means of getting what we want, as a way of realizing our objectives. We use words to ask, beg, demand, plead, explain, persuade, woo, threaten, etc. Full consideration of the particular problems of interpreting lines will be discussed in Part II of this text, but at this point in your training, you need to understand how to incorporate speech in the overall task of performing. A mere reading of the lines, no matter how intelligent or how beautiful, is only a part of your responsibility. No matter how glibly and mellifluously delivered, all dialogue will appear superfluous, unless it is demanded by the action of the play.

Onstage conflict generates dramatic action. Conflict, however, does not necessarily mean open hostility. In life, conflict takes many forms. We smile. We look away. We lie. We talk in hushed tones. Conflict may be camouflaged to the point that others may not be able to detect its presence. We may be in the midst of a heated private debate, yet someone on the outside may perceive our conversation as pleasant and serene. According to Irina and Igor Levin, Stanislavski said that "Immobility of the one sitting on the stage does not define one's passivity. . . . One may be motionless, but, nevertheless, be in genuine action. Often physical immobility is the direct result of an intense action." This expands our definition of stage action to mean something more than movement and physical activity.[11]

Speech is a variant of action. "The artist on the stage must be able to act not only with his hands and feet, but also with his tongue; that is, with words, speech, intonation," wrote Stanislavski. "The word and speech must also act; that is, they must force the other person to understand, see and think just like the speaker does." Later Stanislavski points out directly that "the transmission of one's thought is the same as action" and he ceases to distinguish between "physical" and "verbal" action.[12]

The basic function of stage speech is to help you accomplish your character's goals. You must know the purpose of every word, and you must know how each utterance relates to that purpose. You must have this relationship clearly in mind for every moment of the play, both during rehearsal and in performance. Acting is not only believing, it is also thinking! Concentrating on speaking smoothly or beautifully will interfere with thinking about the action of the play. You must discover a genuine need to use the playwright's words and train yourself to keep your character's thoughts alive as you speak them. You must particularly guard against the abandonment of live thinking during repetitious rehearsals.

In some primitive languages, the word for acting and speaking is the same. "Your" words are important tools for engaging in communion with others on-stage. Simply saying "good morning" has no justification unless you say these words to influence another character in some way or other. The greeting may "infect" the listener with casual indifference, deep love, or intense hate. It may say any one of a dozen things, each intended to evoke a different response.

Communion, however, is two-way influence. You must concentrate not only on *affecting* others but also on *listening* to what is said, resisting or yielding to the desires of the speaker. A special ability to listen is often mentioned as one of the specific skills required of an actor. You must listen and respond to everything said at each rehearsal and performance as if it had never been heard before—Gillette's "illusion of the first time." This illusion is necessary for both you and the audience, no matter how long you have worked on a part—no matter how often you have rehearsed or performed it. For a talented and trained actor, each performance is a new and fresh series of transactions, leading to an appropriate communion between actors and audience.

---

**Exercise 6.9**    **SPEAKING EVERY LINE WITH PURPOSE**    Every line of text in every play must have purpose that will move the dramatic action forward. An actor must produce imaginative physical actions to support each line, and she must concentrate her attention on influencing the behavior of her partner to complete the communion demanded by the scene. Even though each actor will have a single, simple objective for every complete unit of action, she must state the purpose of each line in her own words.

A. In this exercise, two female actors should engage in the following dialogue from David Auburn's Pulitzer Prize–winning play, *Proof.* The actual text is in the left column. In the adjacent to column, the authors of this book have defined a purpose for that line.

*Proof* is a play about a twenty-five-year-old woman (Catherine) who had been taking care of her brilliant mathematician-father for several years until his death, which came after a long bout with mental illness. Now, at the time of his funeral, she must deal with her own volatile emotions; the arrival of her estranged older sister, Claire; and the attentions of Hal, a former student of her father's who hopes to find valuable work in the many notebooks that her father left behind. In the play, Auburn asks the question whether mental illness, as well as mathematical genius, can be passed down from one generation to the next.

This sequence of dialogue takes place the morning after a late-night party in honor of their father. Claire has just suggested to her sister Catherine that she would like her "to move to New York." The simple objective of each character is clear. Claire must convince her younger sister to move to New York with her and her husband so that they may help her regain her mental health and establish a new life. Catherine, on the other hand, must defend her right to stay in their father's house and live her own life.

| **Text** | **Purpose** |
|---|---|
| CATHERINE: I live here. | CATHERINE: I must avoid talking about this. |
| CLAIRE: You could do whatever you want. You could work, you could go to school. | CLAIRE: I must demonstrate the possibilities. |
| CATHERINE: I don't know, Claire. This is pretty major. | CATHERINE: I want time to think. |
| CLAIRE: I realize that. | CLAIRE: I must show my compassion. |
| CATHERINE: I know you mean well. I'm just not sure what I want to do. I mean to be honest you were right yesterday. I do feel a little confused. I'm tired. It's been a pretty weird couple of years. I think I'd like to take some time to figure things out. | CATHERINE: I have to work through this confusion before making any decisions. |
| CLAIRE: You could do that in New York. | CLAIRE: I must make her understand this fact. |
| CATHERINE: And I could do it here. | CATHERINE: I must take a stand. |
| CLAIRE: But it would be much easier for me to get you set up in an apartment in New York, and— | CLAIRE: I must convince her that this will be better for *everyone*. |
| CATHERINE: I don't need an apartment, I'll stay in the house. | CATHERINE: I must defend my decision to stay here while I think. |
| CLAIRE: We're selling the house. (*Beat.*) | CLAIRE: I must force her to see there are no alternatives. |
| CATHERINE: What? | CATHERINE: I want her to say it again. |
| CLAIRE: We—I'm selling it. | CLAIRE: I want her to know this is *my* decision. |
| CATHERINE: *When?* | CATHERINE: I must know how much time. |
| CLAIRE: I'm hoping to do the paperwork this week. I know it seems sudden. | CLAIRE: I wish to appeal to her sense of reason. |
| CATHERINE: No one was here looking at the place, who are you selling it to? | CATHERINE: I must make her prove her lie. |
| CLAIRE: The university. They've wanted the block for years. | CLAIRE: I must show her this is a "done deal." |
| CATHERINE: I *live here.* | CATHERINE: I must defend my rights. |

CLAIRE: Honey, now that Dad's gone it doesn't make sense. It's in bad shape. It costs a fortune to heat. It's time to let it go. Mitch agrees, it's a very smart move. We're lucky, we have a great offer—

CATHERINE: Where am I supposed to live?

CLAIRE: Come to New York.

CATHERINE: I can't believe this.[13]

CLAIRE: I must convince her this is the right thing to do.

CATHERINE: I want to appeal to her sympathy.

CLAIRE: I must convince her to come now.

CATHERINE: I must show her that I am disgusted by her idea.

Of course, in developing a role completely, you may be certain of the action of each line only after you understand the desires that motivate all of your character's behavior. We will also engage in understanding your character's objective more fully in Part II, which considers the actor in relation to the play. At this time, you should continue to work on small scenes without assuming the responsibility of finding their total meaning in relationship to the rest of the play.

**B.** This time, do the same exercise as illustrated above with any appropriate sequence of dialogue from the play of your choice.

---

**Exercise 6.10   KEY LINE IMPROVISATION**   Working with one partner, select one of the following scenarios as the basis for an improvisation. When preparing a role for scene study, it is absolutely necessary to read and thoroughly analyze the entire script. (This will be discussed in depth in Part II of this text.) For this improvisational exercise, however, we do not expect that you will be familiar with the play. Although you are not creating a score of physical actions, you will need a few minutes of preparation. Before you begin the improvisation, you and your partner must create the given circumstances—the who, what, when, where, and why. The "how" will be determined as you present the improvisation. Use your imagination, and don't worry about making wrong decisions with regard to the play as a whole. This is an improvisation from an unfamiliar script. You are only beholden to the generalized scenario and the specific key lines. Once you have established your relationship and the circumstances, focus on playing your objective. You do not know what offensive actions your partner will attempt or what defenses he or she will use against your attacks. Therefore, it is up to you to infect your partner and adapt to the changing circumstances. This give-and-take is the essence of a lively stage performance.

**A.** In *A Lie of the Mind*, by Sam Shepard, Jake is trying to explain to his brother, Frankie, why he beat his wife for her indiscretions. He thinks she may be dead. Their key lines are:

FRANKIE: But you didn't really kill her, did ya?

JAKE: I'm no dummy. Doesn't take much to put it together. Woman starts dressin' more and more skimpy every time she goes out. . . .

**B.** In *Boy's Life,* by Howard Korder, Jack, a self-assured young man in his late twenties, is sitting on a bench opposite a playground in a city park smoking pot and pretending to watch his six-year-old son, Jason. Maggie, wearing running attire, has stopped to catch her breath before continuing in the organized race against apartheid. Attempting a seduction, Jack stands and crosses to her. Their key lines are:

JACK:  I'm a cardiologist. (Pause.)

MAGGIE:  Please go away.

**C.** In *The Boys Next Door,* by Tom Griffin, the good-natured but mentally marginal Sheila has been "dating" the retarded Norman and has greatly admired a large ring of keys Norman wears attached to his belt. For her birthday, Norman presents her with a box covered with stuck-on bows. She opens it, and inside is her very own ring of keys. Their key lines are:

SHEILA:  Oh, Norman, keys.

NORMAN:  Try them on.

**D.** In *Feed the Hole,* by Michael Stock, Shelly and Samantha, friends since they were kids, are in a dress shop trying on outfits and talking about whether or not they are happy with their lives so far. Their key lines are:

SHELLY:  Do you like this dress, or no? It's beautiful, but—it's—

SAMANTHA:  Yeah?

SHELLY:  Definitely, try the other one. . . .

SAMANTHA:  You have to leave him.

**E.** In Donald Margulies' *July 7, 1994,* Kate is removing stitches from the palm of Ms. Pike's hand. The scene takes place in a medical clinic, and Ms. Pike, who has been abused by her husband, is five months pregnant. Their key lines are:

KATE:  *What* happened exactly?

MS. PIKE:  Hmm?

KATE:  *How'd* you hurt your hand?

MS. PIKE:  I told you, I don't know, I cut it.

**F.** In Ed Bullins' *In the Wine Time,* Lou and Cliff are a young married couple sitting on the street in front of their house on a hot summer night. They are drinking wine, and their conversation alternates between bantering and wrangling. Their key lines are:

LOU:  What should I do when I find lipstick on your shirt . . . shades I don't use? (Silence.) What should I say when I see you flirtin' with the young girls on the street and with my friends? (Silence.)

CLIFF:  (Tired.) Light me a cigarette, will ya?

**G.** In Neil Simon's *Lost in Yonkers,* Bella tries to convince her brother, Louie, that the man she wishes to marry is a good man. They hope to open a restaurant, but they need five thousand dollars to begin operations. Louie, who is prone to volatile outbursts, tries to dissuade Bella from carrying through with her intentions. Their key lines are:

BELLA: It'll only cost five thousand dollars.

LOUIE: (Laughs) Five thousand dollars? Why not five million? And who's got the five grand? Him?

**H.** In *Our Town,* by Thornton Wilder, George and Emily are on opposite sides of Main Street in Grover's Corner. George has just been elected president of the junior class, and Emily has been elected secretary and treasurer. Emily is carrying an armful of "imaginary" schoolbooks. When George crosses to Emily, their key lines are:

GEORGE: Emily, why are you mad at me?

EMILY: I'm not mad at you.

**I.** In Richard Greenberg's dark comedy, *The Dazzle,* Homer, a lawyer and the more functional of the two notorious Collyer brothers, is trying to persuade a woman named Milly to marry his brother. In this scene, Homer has persuaded his brother (by hitting him) to vacate the house in order to attend "an afternoon recital for ladies." Their key lines are:

HOMER: He responds beautifully to physical violence—he always has—he becomes an angel of docility. *(Pause.)*

MILLY: That sort of thing doesn't happen here.

HOMER: Doesn't it?

MILLY: You know, Mr.—Homer, I have been trying in these last weeks to figure you out—to sift and winnow through your behavior to me—its violent, even perverse swings—and after careful consideration, I have come to the conclusion that you are extremely hard to read.

**J.** In *The Zoo Story,* by Edward Albee, two men quarrel violently over which one has the right to occupy a particular park bench. Their key lines are:

PETER: This is my bench, and you have no right to take it away from me.

JERRY: Fight for it, then. Defend yourself; defend your bench.

## Terms and People to Know

**circles of attention**   The actor's range of concentration onstage. Stanislavski described three circles of attention: small, medium, and large.

**communion**    To give to or to receive from a person, object, or image something constituting a moment of spiritual intercourse.

**concentration**    Giving complete attention to something.

**ensemble**    The actors' internal and external reactions to one another in a mutual endeavor to project the super-objective of a play.

**public solitude**    Achieved when actors are fully focused on their immediate action without any attempt to amuse or pander to the audience.

## CHAPTER 7

# Investigating the Subconscious

*"Acting technique develops 'a conscious road to the subconscious.'"*

–Constantin Stanislavski

Everything onstage is a lie. The properties, the makeup, the costumes, the scenic environment, as well as the actor's emotions are not real. In life, we do not think about emotions such as love, hate, or anger as they are happening. Rather, these emotions occur naturally and subconsciously as a result of actual external stimuli. We think about the resulting emotions only later as we reflect on a particular event or circumstance. Onstage, however, every action, every emotion must be controlled and conscious. Characters may be insane, obsessive, uncontrollably violent, or drugged, yet actors must always remain in command of their emotional and physical being. That is one of the actor's paradoxes. Whereas emotions in life occur without thought, stage emotions result from deliberate choices and actions.

Your inner resources consist of everything you have experienced. Every personal event, every movie, every book, every photograph, every time you explore the Web, the experience goes into your memory bank and becomes an important resource from which to draw onstage. Stanislavski called his approach to the use of internal stimuli **affective memory,** which he later divided into *sense memory* and *emotion memory.* This technique was designed to produce controlled emotional reactions that actors could use to color their characters.

True emotions in life—what Stanislavski referred to as **primary emotions**—are extremely difficult to control. Our interpretation of emotions is also imprecise and vague, for we are never simply one emotion. At any given time, we may be happy, anxious, terrified, nauseous, and determined. But what is happy? What is anxious? Everyone interprets these emotions differently, and these isolated feelings meld together and change with the circumstances. They are almost impossible to define precisely, and yet audiences ultimately judge the quality of an actor's performance by his or her ability to truthfully convey these emotions.

Stanislavski referred to stage emotions as **repeated emotions,** and they differ greatly from primary emotions. If you love someone onstage, it is not real love, but it is truthful. A character's emotions are as true to the actor as the eternal verities of life, but repeated emotions have a different quality than primary emotions. Stanislavski referred to these repeated emotions as a "poetic reflection" of the actor's primary emotions. **Sonia Moore** wrote, "No actor could survive long if he had to go through a true tragic shock every time he performs. And if an actor is honest, he will admit that an authentic emotion of suffering while performing gave him true joy."[1]

Repeated emotions do not arise from actual causes; they occur because actors have experienced similar emotions in their own lives. We each have a lifetime of emotional experiences, and we all have the capacity to do anything within our physical realm. We have all experienced love, hate, jealousy, and greed, just as we have all felt incompetent, boastful, shy, and superior. We have faced every conceivable human emotion many times and under vastly different circumstances. According to scientific research, the nerves that repeatedly participate in the experience of each emotion become highly sensitive and responsive to that emotion. Therefore, through exercises, rehearsals, and performances, actors develop a conditioned reflex in which their emotions are stirred in response to the stage stimulus.

Unlike primary emotions, repeated emotions do not completely absorb us. When tragedy strikes in real life, we are completely immersed at that moment. We do not have the capacity to objectively consider our feelings. Years later, however, as we reflect upon the events and as other life encounters penetrate our memories, we have the ability to objectify our experience. This is the actor's emotional state while living through the character's emotions for the "first" time. Actors live in the present—Stanislavski's state of "I am"—but they never completely forget they are in front of an audience. Again, their repeated emotions are absolutely sincere and truthful, but they are not real. There is a distance between these emotions and the actor. You must find your own personal emotions that are analogous to those of the character you are creating. You must remember your behavior and then apply it to the character. "Then," according to Moore, "you will

Reprinted by permission of Richard Finkelstein.

**Figure 7.1**   Lynnie Godfrey in a scene from the New York State Theatre Institute's production of *Ladies of Song*. Directed by Robert Bennett Steinhauer, scenic design by Richard Finkelstein, costume design by Brent Griffin, lighting design by John McLaine. Actors strive for true emotions onstage. The powerful emotions demonstrated by the actor in this photo are not primary; instead, she substitutes analogous emotions from her own life to find truth in the circumstances.

merge with the character, and it will be difficult to know what is yours and what is the character's, because you will also be revealing yourself."[2]

Finding appropriate emotional memories is not an end in itself; they lead you to a more complete understanding of your character's desires, morals, fears, and distinct points of view regarding any person or issue in her world. Emotion memories are not complete until they are transferred to your character and made synonymous with their circumstances. Emotion memories help you believe in your given circumstances. They allow you to have faith in your relationships, and they help you to discover your character's behavior by justifying your every action.

## Recalling Sense and Emotion Memory

Fortunately, most of the time our memory serves us spontaneously, onstage as in life. Facts, figures, faces, stories, images we have known in the past—even sensory and emotional experiences—come back automatically as we need them. If you perform logical actions, believe in the given circumstances, work toward objectives and against obstacles, and establish specific relationships with onstage objects, clothing, environment, and other actors, then your past experiences will likely be subconsciously serving you without thought. Your actions and relationships, coming directly from the imaginary circumstances of the play and from connection with the other actors, should automatically tap into your inner resources and evoke the proper feeling. If, on occasion, the techniques of physical action, objectives, and relationships do not elicit the desired responses, you may need to bring a past personal experience directly to bear on the stage situation.

Although theatre history provides much evidence that actors have always made conscious use of their experiences to some degree as a specific technique, Stanislavski first extensively explored this practice in the early twentieth century. However, his early experiments in emotion memory brought actors to a state of panic that actually affected their nervous systems. Thus, he concluded that the use of emotions as a principal means to discover truth onstage was very dangerous. When Stanislavski later discovered the Method of Physical Actions and made *it* the focal point of his system, he also revolutionized the use of emotion memory. He realized that emotional recall was an indirect process. As a reliable and safe approach to tap our emotional resources, we should focus, Stanislavski decided, on recalling the sensory experiences of the situation, and, most of all, we should remember our actions. With these admonitions in mind, we shall discuss emotion memory in three steps. You ordinarily go through these steps without thinking about them, but a separate examination of each will help you when you need to make conscious use of the process.

## Retaining an Original Experience

"Time is an excellent filter for our remembered feelings," wrote Stanislavski. "Besides, it is a great artist. It not only purifies, it also transmutes even painfully realistic memories into poetry."[3] It is important for you to understand that the original experience must have occurred some time ago; some acting theorists insist that emotional memories must have occurred at least three years before their use onstage. Most of us do not have the ability to view recent events objectively. If, for example, you recently experienced the death of a parent, the rejection of a lover, or a false accusation by a close friend, you most likely will not have come to grips with your feelings as you think on these experiences. If you are overcome with emotions as you recall a particular memory, it is virtually impossible to use onstage. Over time, the memories of important events remain just as clear, but the distance allows you to view them with necessary objectivity. Childhood incidents, because they frequently remain in the mind with peculiar vividness, are often especially valuable. Regardless of which experience you use, you must have felt it deeply but accepted it emotionally.

Retaining the experience is partly a matter of natural memory and partly a matter of conscious effort. Most people are genuinely aware of what is going on around them and are likely to remember what has happened in the past. Any technique, however, that will aid you in retaining the details of an experience vividly in your mind is worth developing. Here is what we mean.

A ten-year-old boy from a small town was riding his bicycle to the corner store followed by his dog, Hilda. The boy was an only child, and Hilda was his constant companion. The pet slept with him at night, and followed the boy almost everywhere he went. As they approached an intersection of a moderately busy street, Hilda ran in front of a car and was killed. The boy released a painful cry. Unable to bear the sight of his "best friend" lying disfigured and bloody on the road, the boy jumped on his bike and rode as quickly as he could back to his house. Pedaling as fast as he could, the boy shed tears, and liquid dripped unashamedly from his nose. He cried for his mother. As he entered his yard, he jumped off his bicycle and ran through the house calling for his mother. No one was home. Not knowing what to do, the boy jumped back onto his bike and pedaled with much trepidation back to the intersection where his beloved dog was lying. As he approached the sight, he noticed a police car parked close to where the accident had occurred. The boy, with tears still streaming down his face, did not approach the officers. Instead, he simply watched as the police got a shovel from the trunk of the car and calmly lifted the carcass into a plastic bag. They then placed it in the trunk and drove away.

The boy never forgot that traumatic childhood story. As years passed, every detail remained as vivid as if it had occurred only yesterday. His bicycle, his clothing, the neighborhood, the weather, the time of day, and the sight of his dog being killed were fixed in his memory. The pain, however, eventually subsided. He overcame the shock of the moment. Time filtered his emotions, and he objectively accepted the death of what he perceived as a member of his family. But he never forgot.

# Selecting the Experience

Good actors accumulate inner resources that may serve them once they can recall the experiences objectively. In deciding what experiences to recall, actors search their past for happenings that most nearly parallel those of their characters. They may be identical, or they may be far removed.

Remember, most of our sensory and emotional experiences return automatically as we need them onstage. If you believe your character's actions, the circumstances, and "your" relationships, your real memories will subconsciously serve you without thought. Through your selected actions, you will tap into your inner resources, thus evoking true secondary emotions.

The young boy who had witnessed the death of his beloved dog grew into a fine young actor. Early in his career he was cast in the television role of a young man who witnessed the brutal murder of his father. The young actor had little problem with the majority of the scene. Through his character's verbal and physical actions, he produce truthful inner images and emotions. However, as the character described the actual murder of "his" father, the actor could not exploit the emotional depths required by this dramatic moment, especially after more than a dozen takes of the scene. The director saw the character as breaking down in uncontrollable tears in front of the jury, but the actor could not produce the effect. Fortunately for him, the young man had never experienced the death of a family member or close friend, nor witnessed a violent murder. However, he recalled the death of his dog, Hilda, in order to help him find the truth in this dramatic television scene.

More often than not you will not be able to find a close approximation to the experience of your character. Obviously, your personal experiences will not parallel those of every character you might be called on to play. Therefore, you must often resort to situations in which your feelings were similar to those of the character, although the circumstances that prompted the feelings may have been entirely different. The actor playing the young man on the witness stand had no direct parallel to the moment in the play, and he was unable to produce truthful emotions from the circumstances and his selected actions. The young man's actual memory of the death of his dog is emotionally similar to the character's experience of watching the brutal murder of his father. Although the magnitude of the death of a pet does not compare to the brutal slaughter of a parent, to a young boy of ten, there are many parallel emotions.

Another example that would most likely require you to substitute your own emotion memory into that of the character's is the potion scene (Act IV, Scene 3) from *Romeo and Juliet*. Secretly married to Romeo, Juliet has been promised by her parents to the Count Paris. To get herself out of this entanglement, she is about to take a potion to make her appear dead. She then will be placed in the family tomb, and Romeo will rescue her. Juliet is about to do something the outcome of which is uncertain and fraught with dreadful possibilities, an action that will surely call for emotions starting with fear and mounting almost to hysteria. During the moments before this horrifying act, she imagines all the things that might happen to cause her plan to fail and is distracted. What if the potion does not work at all? What if it is a poison? What if she should wake before Romeo comes and find herself alone in the tomb with the remains of all her buried ancestors? If you are to play Juliet, you must make these fears personal and believable within the given circumstances.

What experience have you had that might enable you to realize Juliet's fear? Have you been in a situation, no matter how dissimilar in its actual circumstances, that induced a feeling akin to Juliet's? Have you ever been alone, preparing to take some step the uncertain consequences of which held possibilities of danger? Unhappiness? Pain? Discomfort? Did you ever prepare to run away from home? Contemplate an elopement? Did you ever prepare to go to the hospital for an operation? To go into the army? To go away to college? To move to a new town where you might be homesick? Have you ever felt trapped while exploring a cave? Perhaps you could recall an instance of fright from your childhood. Almost everybody has experienced something like this.

For example, perhaps when you were fourteen years old you spent a weekend with an aunt who lived alone in a large house with no neighbors nearby. On the first evening, before you had become acquainted with your surroundings, your aunt was called to care for a sick friend. You boasted that you were used to staying alone, and because it was impractical to get a sitter on short notice, your aunt reluctantly left you to look after yourself for a couple of hours. You settled down in the living room, feeling grown up and independent, and looked happily at a book. Gradually you became uneasy. At home, you had activity and noise to calm you, but this place was terribly still. At home, lights all through the house made everything bright and cheerful. Here a lamp with a green shade in the living room and a lamp with a red globe in the hallway cast eerie shadows on unfamiliar surroundings.

Suddenly you were overcome with fear. A noise on the porch started you thinking of thieves and kidnappers. You had no sooner quieted those fears than a noise upstairs started you thinking of ghosts and haunted houses. It seemed impossible to stay in the house alone, but the outdoors was just as terrifying. The cell phone your parents gave you had a weak signal, and to reach the landline telephone you had to go down the hall and into the completely dark dining room.

If such an incident is your liveliest experience with fear, it will have to serve, and if you can recall it vividly, it will serve you well in preparing to play Juliet's potion scene.

## Using the Experience

Concentrate on remembering the details of the experience rather than on the emotion itself. Begin by using sensory recall. In the last example, you should attempt to remember as much as you can about the room—the lights with their bright spots and especially the dark corners; the reflection of the light on the dark, polished surfaces of the furniture; the windows, shiny black in the darkness, reflecting the quiet gloom. Remember the chair you sat on, the objects on the table beside the chair, and the pictures you looked at. Recall the odors of the room—lilacs and furniture polish. Recall the stillness and the sounds you heard (or thought you heard).

When returning to such a situation as a source for your performance of the potion scene, you will need to develop a shortcut to the heart of the memory. By breaking the memory down into its individual components, you can usually recreate the sensation of the moment by concentrating on the aspect that provides you with the most vivid connection to the situation. You should be able to get to the sensation of fear by concentrating on a specific sound, a particular odor, or the way your body temperature changed, rather than by attempting to evoke the entire experience every time you need to use it. When you can place this odor, this sound, or this body temperature within the given circumstances of the potion scene, your use of emotional memory is complete.

If you are unfamiliar with this technique, you will be surprised (after you give it an honest trial) how many details you will be able to bring back and how much the memory of the way things felt and looked and smelled will help you recapture the essence of the entire experience.

As you are working with the experience during the rehearsal period, try to remember as much detail as possible about what you did in this situation. How did you deal with the cause of your fear—the frightening shadows? The sounds on the porch? The noise upstairs? Perhaps you first pretended you were not afraid. You may have tried to renew your interest in the pictures. Did you brave your way into one of the dark corners for another book? You tried then to reassure yourself by singing as loudly as possible. Gaining a little confidence, you may have gone timidly to the window to investigate the sounds on the porch. What happened physically, when you could not bring yourself to take a good look? Remembering the childhood situation at the level of physical action should give you a range of believable choices for performing Juliet's scene. Adapting them to the given circumstances of the scene you are playing should reinforce your emotional recall.

When you attempt to remember an incident, sit quietly relaxed, free of tensions that might interfere with the flow of memory and feeling. In a sense, this technique is an application to acting of Wordsworth's famous definition of poetry: "Emotion recollected in tranquility."

Whenever incorporating the above emotion memory exercise into your rehearsal process, the final step is to make certain that anything you use from your remembered experience is believable within the given circumstances of the scene and your character. Unless you can use the feelings you have induced to help you play the actions and speak the lines of the character, you will take yourself out of the play and away from your objective. *You must especially guard against reducing moments conceived by the imagination of a master dramatist to your own personal experiences, which may be drab and smaller in scope.* One of the strongest tendencies of a student actor is to "play everything too small." Don't forget that drama, for the most part, explores the greatest—and many times the largest—moments in the lives of its characters.

Unless your director schedules time during rehearsals for such exercises, you should carry on this process during your work on the role at home or during your preparation before rehearsal and performance. The mark of a prepared and competent actor is the ready ability to access responses during rehearsals and performances on demand.

---

**Exercise 7.1**    **RECONSTRUCTING AN EXPERIENCE**    Remember a specific moment in your life when you strongly felt some emotion such as anger, hate, love, or fear. Reconstruct in your mind the detailed circumstances that caused you to experience this emotion. Perform an activity related to these circumstances until you can sense the emotion associating itself with the action.

---

It should be apparent that emotion memory is a technique better suited to study and rehearsal periods than to performance. Used correctly, it sharpens your inner resources, especially those needed to perform scenes of intense emotion. Many teachers who use this tool in the classroom spend hours with individual students, attempting to stimulate the believable recall of an emotional experience. Others think this technique offers so much potential for self-indulgence and for "playing the emotion" rather than "playing the action" that they have turned away from emotional memory altogether.

If you are serious about becoming an actor, we urge you to spend the time it will take to develop this technique, to make it yours, and to be able to use it on command. If you find that believable, true emotions do not arise just from selecting imaginative objectives and concentrating on the external elements of the physical actions you are performing, you will need a technique such as emotion memory to muster a complete mastery of the role. Another approach to emotional memory that has stood the test of time by many great actors is the use of images.

# Visualizing Inner Images

As human beings, we cannot speak without images. As you recall a place, illustrate an event, or describe a person with whom you had an encounter, images flow through your mind. Think of someone you recently met—perhaps someone you bumped into on campus. Describe her clothing. Her physique. Her age. Was she from an urban area or a small town? Was she from a wealthy or a poor family? Did her body language suggest an air of confidence or was she shy and introverted? As you think of this person, images naturally appear in your head. You cannot block them out, as they are a natural function of the human brain. These **inner images** are not literal pictures; instead, they emerge as flashes of

Used by permission of Peter Smith. Photo by Jennifer Matthews.

**Figure 7.2**   Justyna Kelley in a scene from The University of the South's production of *Dark of the Moon*. Directed by Peter Smith and Amanda Michaels, scenic design by Micah Hargrove, costume design by Jennifer Matthews, lighting design by John Womack. This actor's strong inner images onstage help to communicate truthful actions and emotions.

thought, pieces of the entire visual representation. To test this theory, try to describe an actual person, place, or event without imagery. It is impossible.

Remember, however, everything onstage is a lie. Your character's words are scripted; they belong to incomplete characters living in a fictitious world. The world of the play may closely resemble our society, or it may remind you of a nightmare. Theirs may be a world in which characters speak in verse or break into song when the moment arises. Regardless of the propinquity of their reality to our own, you have the task of merging your own life with your character's. From an unfinished character, you must create a three-dimensional human being with a distinctive personal history. Everything about your creation must be unique—the character's desires, fears, goals, morals, values. Your character must dress, behave, gesture, speak, and carry himself differently from anyone else. His entire tempo-rhythm will belong only to him. Although you are working from scripted dialogue, your character's thoughts, speech, and images must be as truthful and complete as your own.

When inferior actors speak their lines, they rush over the dialogue. They see nothing in their minds. Their words have no thoughts; their images are dead. In life, our images are spontaneous, and we sometimes take them for granted. Onstage, however, everything is conscious, including our imagery. As natural as inner images are in life, so to the beginning actor the process of communicating truthful images is extraordinarily difficult. But you must learn to clearly visualize your images so that your partners onstage see them as well. Only then will your speech and nonverbal gestures commune with the audience.

The technique of using images, then, begins with pictures of specific circumstances supplied voluntarily by the imagination. These pictures lead in turn to action, to belief, and to feeling. Again, we must recognize that feeling is the end and not the means, that the actor is concerned with *causes,* not with *effects.* The actor is like the interior decorator who wants to create a beautiful room. Decorators are concerned with color and fabric, with line and form, because they know they are the means to beauty; if properly controlled, they will produce a beautiful effect. But they also understand that trying merely to create beauty without a specific knowledge of how to use their materials would be futile.

In his introduction to *Stanislavsky on the Art of the Stage,* David Magarshack describes the process of using images as an acting technique.

> The actor needs . . . an uninterrupted series of visual images which have some connection with the given circumstances. He needs, in short, an uninterrupted line not of plain but of illustrated given circumstances. Indeed, at every moment of his presence on the stage . . . the actor must be aware of what is taking place outside him on the stage (i.e., the external given circumstances created by the producer, stage-designer, and the other artists) or of what is taking place inside him, in his own imagination, that is, those visual images which illustrate the given circumstances of the life of his part. Out of all these things there is formed, sometimes outside and sometimes inside him, an uninterrupted and endless series of inner and outer visual images, or a kind of film. While his work goes on, the film is unwinding itself endlessly, reflecting on the screen of his inner vision the illustrated given circumstances of his part, among which he lives on the stage.[4]

Most of the time, however, inner images are incomplete. Instead, as we speak our images explode in our minds and change with the speed of light. Thinking is not based on verbally organized ideas. Whereas the storytelling aspect of writing and speech metaphorically resembles the unraveling of a film, as Magarshack describes in the previous paragraph, inner images are more akin to a contemporary teen watching television or logging onto the Internet. Many teens have short attention spans, preferring to channel surf or surf the net rather than watching or reading an entire story. Rather than a logical and formalized, internal visual narrative that unfolds, the thought process, like "surfing," paints a fragmented picture of your responses to external stimuli.

**Exercise 7.2    SEEING IMAGES**

**A.** These problems are for developing the habit of seeing definite images from word stimuli. For each of the following concrete words, visualize a detailed and specific picture. See yourself in the picture, and think what you would do if you were there. Let yourself respond. Remember that you can't *make* yourself feel but that you can *let* yourself feel. You can make this exercise more valuable by writing down what you see, or, if you can draw, by making a sketch of it. Describe your picture and your actions to the members of the group, making them see the images as vividly as you do.

| | | |
|---|---|---|
| party | rally | funeral |
| beach (or forest) | snow (or thunderstorm) | camp |
| vacation | concert | antique |
| dress | fire | boyfriend (or girlfriend) |
| initiation (or ritual) | team | car |
| restaurant | pet | sister (or brother) |
| bedroom | celebrity | parent (or teacher) |
| home | date | wedding |
| graduation | sporting event | accident (or injury) |

**B.** Repeat the same process for the following abstract words. It is important that you learn to realize abstract concepts in meaningful concrete images that can stimulate responses, too.

| | | |
|---|---|---|
| serenity | love | cruelty |
| disgrace | fame | elegance |
| injustice | kindness | wealth |
| speed | happiness | indifference |
| desire | grief | jealousy |
| bigotry | glamour | mercy |
| embarrassment | poverty | beauty |
| power | infatuation | worship |

**Exercise 7.3** **IMAGE IMPROVISATIONS**   Opportunities abound in plays to use images. Present a solo improvisational scene using one of the problems described below. Illustrate the images through dialogue. The pictures should be definite, not vague and general. The images should also be from life experience, not from the theatre (that is, don't use an image of another actor in a similar circumstance). As we explained in Exercise 6.10: Key Line Improvisation, we do not expect that you will be familiar with the play. There is no score, but you will need to take a moment to consider the given circumstances. Use your imagination. Don't worry about making wrong decisions with regard to the play as a whole. In this exercise, you are only beholden to the generalized scenario. Commit yourself to sharing your images with the group.

A. In Rinne Groff's *The Ruby Sunrise,* Ruby, a teenage runaway, is something of a technological genius. The time is in the early 1930s. Ruby is staying with her aunt on a farm and is working on a project that will someday be known as television. While conducting experiments with her contraption in the barn, she determinedly tells Henry, a boarder with her aunt, about her new invention.

B. In *Our Lady of 121st Street,* by Stephen Adly Guirgis, Rooftop, a popular Los Angeles DJ, has returned to New York City for the funeral of a nun who was a much-beloved teacher at his Catholic school. The body of Sister Rose has curiously disappeared from the funeral home. Rooftop, while waiting with others for the police to solve the mystery of the missing body, decides to confess his many indiscretions to a priest at a nearby church.

C. In *The Story,* by Tracey Scott Wilson, Latisha, a young African American woman with inside knowledge of girl-gangs, recently told Yvonne, an ambitious newspaper reporter, that one of the groups was responsible for the murder of a white man in a black neighborhood. Here, Latisha reveals that it's all been a lie.

D. In *The Basic Training of Pavlo Hummel,* by David Rabe, Pavlo is a wide-eyed, totally inept soldier, born and raised in a middle-class environment. He wants to be thought of as a tough street kid, so he conjures up romantic pictures of stealing automobiles and being chased by the police.

E. In *To Gillian on Her 37th Birthday,* by Michael Brady, 16-year-old Rachel is standing outside scanning the late-summer night sky. As she traces the paths of falling stars with her finger, she slowly begins to visualize the face of her late mother, who would have been 37 that day, had she lived.

F. In *Biloxi Blues,* by Neil Simon, a young soldier named Epstein has filched the notebook in which Eugene has been writing descriptions of all his army comrades. He opens it and reads the section about himself, discovering that Eugene believes Epstein is a homosexual. (*Note:* regardless of the situation in the play, actors may improvise this scene as if they are alone as they read or as if they are reading aloud to the entire barracks. They may also assume the given circumstance that Eugene's notion is either true or false.)

**G.** In *A Delicate Balance,* by Edward Albee, Tobias recalls an instance several years in the past when a pet cat bit him, after which he took it to the veterinarian and had it killed.

**H.** In *Eleemosynary,* by Lee Blessing, Echo tells the story of her cutthroat, "take no prisoners" journey to victory in the National Spelling Bee Contest in Washington, D.C. Easily handling such words as "perspective," "glunch," and "palinode," she destroyed the confidence of her final competitor before winning with "eleemosynary."

**I.** In *Boy's Life,* by Howard Korder, Phil tells the story of a girl for whom he would have "sliced his wrists" or "eaten garbage" but who recently dumped him for being "too needy."

**J.** In *Lu Ann Hampton Laverty Oberlander,* by Preston Jones, the teenaged Lu Ann sees a picture on the classroom wall of a European castle with a tiny door at its very top. The castle stimulates her to dream about getting out of the small, stifling, Texas town in which she lives.

**K.** In Charles Busch's *Psycho Beach Party,* a satire of beach movies from the sixties, Chicklet reflects on how she got her name, her girlfriends' "kissy kissy" obsession with boys, and her all-consuming passion for surfing. (Charles Busch originated the role of Chicklet, but it may also be played by a female.)

**L.** In *A Raisin in the Sun,* by Lorraine Hansberry, Ruth, a young black woman, is preparing with her husband's family to move from crowded quarters into a large house in a white neighborhood. She anticipates the greater comfort their new home will provide as she packs bric-a-brac, accumulated over the years, into a carton. The objects provoke images from the past, and her anticipation evokes images of the future.

**M.** In *Suburbia,* by Eric Bogosian, Sooze tells the story of her brother with Down's syndrome, who died by falling into an icy stream while looking for "the doughnut lady" ten years before. As she recalls the event, she visualizes the condition of Mikey's body when they pulled him from the water later that spring.

## Planning Your Inner Monologues

In the previous exercises, you have been "surfing" your mind for visual images and describing them vividly to the group. In the process, you have unwittingly used another helpful technique called the **inner monologue.** The inner monologue is a key aspect of the interpretative art of acting, as it is essential for transforming thought into speech. Stanislavski said that actors who do not use one onstage look like "prematurely born people." Like inner images, inner monologues occur naturally in life while we are listening and thinking. Even in moments of silence, we continue to debate and influence others in our minds and with our body language.

For that reason, the word **pause** is an improper term for actors. Pause indicates a momentary suspension in the action where nothing happens. The word **silence** is more appropriate, for our stream of consciousness, our thought processes, and our attempt to infect others never stop.

In reality, inner monologues, like inner images, occur with lightning speed and lack logical organization. Consequently, modern playwrights rarely compose inner monologues. The most common examples in which the classical dramatist creates inner monologues are soliloquies and asides that supply thoughts to be spoken to the audience. Hamlet's "To be, or not to be . . ." and Macbeth's "Tomorrow, and tomorrow, and tomorrow . . ." are examples of superb inner monologues. One of the greatest modern dramatists, Eugene O'Neill, experimented with the inner monologue in *Strange Interlude,* in which he wrote "thoughts" for the actors to speak between the lines of regular dialogue. Sonia Moore tells a story in which Nemirovich-Danchenko points out how, in literature,

> good novelists frequently introduce us to the innermost thoughts of the characters—the thoughts that bring them to their decisions and actions. Mrs. Knebel mentions one of Chekhov's stories, "He Quarreled with His Wife," which consists almost entirely of the thoughts that go through a man's head after he has complained to his wife that the supper was not good. At almost the end of the story the husband speaks for the first time since his complaint. He says to his wife, "Stop crying, my little darling." This story shows what a great deal in inner monologue can lie behind one spoken sentence.[5]

Accomplished actors carefully plan their inner monologues, write them out, memorize them, and recall them at each rehearsal and performance, just as faithfully as they memorize and speak the playwright's lines. If you fail to write down your inner monologues, your thoughts will always be accidental. Thus, your work, which should be done through conscious and deliberate means, will always be unplanned and out of your control. Always keep in mind, however, that what you write down does not necessarily have to appear in complete sentences. Therefore, your inner monologues may be simple phrases and fragments of thought. During rehearsals and performances, repeat in your mind your inner monologues through every silence. Only then will *pauses* disappear.

On the other hand, you must not have an inner monologue as you speak. You know why you are speaking, why you have selected these words. You project the meaning of the words, communicate the subtext, and see the inner images. Inner monologues occur only during silences in your own lines, as others speak onstage.

In telling the group the images you had in your mind in the previous exercises, you were, in a sense, speaking a formalized inner monologue using complete sentences. You were making the inner monologue an *outer* monologue and thus receiving an initiation into this useful technique. The next exercise will allow you to make further application of it using mostly fragmented thought, as it is in life.

---

**Exercise 7.4**   **SPEAKING YOUR INNER MONOLOGUE**   Create a score of physical actions and present a solo scene centering around an activity that you do not want anyone to know about, for example: opening someone's mail or searching someone's desk. For the purpose of practice, speak your inner monologue, which may be simple phrases and fragments of thought, as you are carrying out your score. You should make use of images and justify your actions. Be sure you have a strong objective and work against an obstacle.

---

Part I has offered you a basis for developing your own method of acting. It assumes that you establish, from the very beginning, a regimen of physical exercise and vocal study that will place these two tools totally and flexibly at your command. It has concentrated on developing your inner resources so you will be able to create a believable character to communicate with your body and your voice. Your inner technique consists of three stages: (1) discovering the physical actions required to perform the role; (2) creating objectives to go with each physical action that are believable and stimulating to the imagination; and (3) learning to respond to both external and internal stimuli provided by the given circumstances of the play. Along the way, we have also helped you discover an approach to the creative state, to direct your attention to the proper focus of the moment, and to learn to see things in the special, imaginative way an actor views the world. In Part II, we shall learn how to mine the play for the raw materials of the role.

# Terms and People to Know

**affective memory**   Indicates both *sense* and *emotion memory*.

**inner monologue**   The unspoken flashes of thoughts and images that underscore the character's every action, inner monologues occur while speaking, listening, and experiencing any action.

**Moore, Sonia**   The most critically acclaimed American teacher of the *Stanislavski System*. Besides Stanislavski's own published works, hers remain the most widely read interpretation of his techniques.

**pause**  Derogatory term indicating a momentary suspension in the action where nothing happens.

**primary emotions**  True emotions in life, they are extremely difficult to control onstage.

**repeated emotions**  Stage emotions, a "poetic reflection" of your uncontrollable *primary emotions*.

**silence**  An onstage moment without dialogue, during which your stream of consciousness, your thought processes, and your attempt to infect others never stop. The more appropriate term for *pause*.

## CHAPTER 8

# Creating a Character

*"Read my plays very carefully."*

–Henrik Ibsen

Throughout Part I, we concentrated on technique training that teaches you to use your intelligence, your life experience, your imagination, and your senses as raw material for creating a character. We frequently referred to the dramatist's given circumstances but clearly placed the initial emphasis on the actor. Some of the exercises derived from published plays, but we attempted to include enough of the circumstances to provide practice in developing logical and appropriate behavior within specific parameters. However, to fully create a three-dimensional character who behaves logically within the world of the play, you must learn how to read, uncover, and use the total circumstances of a script. You must think of yourself as a detective searching for clues found on every page of the text. You must rake the script with a "fine-toothed comb" as you sift through the evidence. A would-be actor who lacks the appropriate skills (or is perhaps too lazy) to analyze the play will succeed only in creating a characterization that is both incomplete and inconsistent.

Given circumstances refer to everything the writer tells you in the script about your character and the situation she finds herself in. They are the facts, the details about which there is no discussion. They are your foundation for building a character. Actors who refuse to analyze and accept the given circumstances can literally destroy a scene—and perhaps even the entire play. Of course, it is your job to interpret the script—your physical and vocal choices, your character's rhythm and tempo, the depth of emotions, all the subjective decisions—but you cannot forgo the given circumstances. Some naive students actually believe that intense scrutiny of the script will stifle their creativity. This is nonsense. The given circumstances are your ticket to onstage freedom. Really knowing and understanding them will give you infinitely more choices as an actor, as they will provide you with a distinct point of view concerning every person, object, idea, and event that occurs around "you."

## Doing Your Homework

It is absolutely crucial for you to read the play—the whole play. Then read it again. And then read it again. At first, simply read it as an audience. Allow yourself to respond to the experience. Take notes. How does it affect you? Then, start to personalize it. Use your imagination. How can you bring this character to life? Incorporate the "magic if." What would I do *if* I were this character in these circumstances? Create a life for your character. Write down the facts—"your" personal history. Start to think in first person through the eyes of your character. Decide between the subjective comments of others and the irrefutable truth. Write down your character's images. Work on "your" simple objectives, "your" physical and psychological obstacles, "your" perspective about everything and everyone around "you."

This is your *homework*. You may not like the word, but as a future professional it is your responsibility to thoroughly study the script. Analysis is *not* just busywork—a classroom exercise that you can forget once you graduate and step into the "real" world. In fact, your homework becomes even more important in the post-graduate environment, particularly in film and television, where you may not have the luxury of months (or even weeks) of rehearsals. As a professional actor, many of your most important discoveries and decisions must be made before you ever meet the rest of the cast or set foot on the stage or set.

Once your homework is properly stored in your memory, it should become invisible. The given circumstances affect every decision you make in rehearsals and performances, but they will remain rooted in your subconscious. In the analysis phase, you are making conscious decisions about every aspect of your character. In rehearsals, however, you simply know who "you" are. This leaves you free to explore objectives, to work against obstacles, and to make tactical decisions through the eyes of your character.

Stage productions that contain living, vital characters result from a melding of the creative talents of the actor and the dramatist. Any argument over which of the two is more important is fruitless, because they are completely interdependent. The actor relies on the character created by the dramatist to provide an essential, continuing stimulus and source of inspiration. On the other hand, without the actor to bring it to life, the dramatist's character will remain dormant on the pages of the script. The final creation is the result of a true collaboration—a marriage of sorts—between actor and dramatist. For instance, the audience will see neither Strindberg's Miss Julie nor the actress's Miss Julie, but the actress *as* Strindberg's Miss Julie. Each character a playwright conceives has the potential to sustain a broad range of actions, and for a great character such as Hamlet, that number is practically unlimited. The character's final shape in a particular production will be colored both by the actions selected by the actor and by what the actor finds significant about his or her personal relationship to the part.

An actor's performance of a character consists of both an inner characterization and its outer form. To create the outer form—the way the character looks, moves, gestures, and speaks—the actor draws "from his own experience of life or that of his friends, from pictures, engravings, drawings, books, stories, novels, or from some simple incident—it makes no difference."[1] For you to perform a believable, three-dimensional characterization, you must also create the character's inner life. You accomplish this portion of your task by adopting the character's thoughts, emotions, and states of mind, drawing wherever possible on similar experiences in your own life. When you are working correctly, you make a direct connection between the character's external anatomy and your newly created inner being—the psychophysical union. That is your goal, and you must dedicate your study of the play and the role, as well as the designated period of rehearsals, to achieving it.

As we stated in Chapter 1, you can create another person only by drawing on your own experiences, actual or vicarious. No matter how you may alter your outward appearance, no matter how you may change the sound of your voice (and this outer form is necessary to complete characterization), your ability to communicate the essential truth of your role depends upon your capacity to externalize your inner resources. Even though study and observation in the preparation of a specific part may greatly expand your own natural resources, what is essentially *you* remains the same from one character to another. Remember, however, *you* are infinite. Your soul has no bottom. Your imagination and personal history grant an unlimited source for diverse portrayals.

Thus, the actor's final product is a unique creation that cannot be duplicated. No two actors will relate in the same way to the same part because they have not had identical experiences in life. "Every artistic stage character is a unique individual creation, like everything else in nature," writes Stanislavski scholar David Magarshack, continuing:

> In the process of its creation there is a "he," that is "the husband," namely the author of the play, and a "she," that is "the wife," namely the actor or actress. There is "the child"—the created part. There are in this process, besides, the moments of the first acquaintance between "him" and "her," their first friendship, their falling in love, their quarrels and differences, their reconciliations, and their union.[2]

To say that actors become creative artists in their own right in this process neither minimizes nor falsifies the creativity of the dramatist. Kenneth Branagh's Hamlet was different from Mel Gibson's Hamlet because each actor found meaning in Shakespeare's Hamlet in light of his own experience. In so doing, each was true to Shakespeare and to himself.

## Penetrating the Script

While creating a characterization that is unique and personal, you must realize and readily accept the great responsibility you owe to the dramatist. Your first step toward fulfilling that obligation is to study the play until you have gleaned all evidence that discloses the dramatist's overall purpose for the character. **Jerzy Grotowski** explained that actors must "penetrate" their roles. By definition, *penetrate* means to "enter by overcoming resistance," so Grotowski is admonishing the actors to explore and yield to the physical and psychological demands of the part as they prepare to play it. Some teachers have suggested that actors "have an affair with the script," that they read it as if it were a sensual, "juicy" story. Thus, you must open your senses to the character, reading the script over and over, each time for a different purpose.

As you read the script, two basic questions guide your study:

1. What, overall, does the character want?
2. What is he willing to do to get it?

One man, for instance, may want more than anything else to be rich and may be willing to employ any means to satisfy his desire. He may be willing to forgo all ordinary pleasures, even to sacrifice his health and the happiness of his family. He might break any law—legal or moral—that he finds to be an obstacle. Another man may also want to be rich but might not be willing to obtain his wealth by gambling with the happiness and security of his family or by taking advantage of friends and associates. One woman may want to find love and might be willing to sacrifice everything, even her pride and virtue, to gain what she wants. On the other hand, another with the same basic desire might be too proud to compromise her reputation. Still another might be too shy to let her desire be known.

If you know what "you" want and what "you" are willing to do to achieve "your" goal, you have the key to creating an honest performance. Answering these two questions provides you with the motivating force behind what your character does and says; thus, this task completely dominates your initial study of the play. Failure to understand the overall desire that motivates your character's behavior means a breakdown in understanding the dramatist's intention. This, in turn, means failure to interpret the play truthfully.

Studying a script is a process of analysis and synthesis, of taking apart and putting together. Actors analyze, or take apart, the characters, studying their behavior in relation to the other characters and to the play as a whole. Then, guided by their sensitivity and imagination, they reassemble the parts, organizing them to form an artistic creation.

## Identifying the Motivating Force

In Chapter 3, we discussed the term *simple objective,* a character's quest at any given moment expressed and pursued by use of an action verb that motivates a sequence of simple actions. The **motivating force,** on the other hand, is what your character wants overall.* Like the simple objective, you should state the motivating force in specific terms. Finding a name for this overall objective is an important step in creating a character. The name must designate a desire true to the dramatist's overall intention, and, like the simple objective, it must also stimulate the actor to action. A motivating force that does not suggest action is worthless.

Stanislavski emphasized the importance of choosing the right name, recalling his analysis of the hero in Goldoni's *The Mistress of the Inn.* "We made the mistake of using 'I wish to be a misogynist,' and we found that the play refused to yield either humour or action," he wrote. "It was only when I discovered that the hero really loved women and wished only to be accounted a misogynist that I changed to 'I wish to do my courting on the sly' and immediately the play came to life."[3]

Besides not being in accord with the dramatist's conception, "I wish to be a misogynist" was a weak choice because it was insufficiently specific. "I want to hate women" defines a general attitude but fails to suggest action. Such statements as "I want to avoid women" or "I want to take advantage of every opportunity to embarrass women" would have been better. For this character, however, they would still have been unacceptable because he did not hate women at all. And

---

*Some actors refer to the character's motivating force as the super-objective. We refer to it as motivating force simply to distinguish the character's overall desire from the super-objective of the entire play, which is explored in the next chapter.

Reprinted by permission of Richard Finkelstein.

**Figure 8.1**   Cliff Fantigrossi (*left*) and Connor Fux in a scene from
James Madison University's production of *A Flea in Her Ear*. Directed
by Roger Hall, scenic and lighting design by Richard Finkelstein,
costume design by Pam Johnson. Like the simple objective, the
motivating force must stimulate a larger sequence of actions.

what splendid possibilities for action are suggested by "I want to do my courting
on the sly."

You must state your motivating force as a *specific statement that your character can attempt to satisfy through action*. Examples of unsatisfactory statements
that cannot motivate specific action are:

+ I want to be unhappy.
+ I want to be popular.

Examples of better statements are:

+ For his indiscretions with my wife, *I want to ruin* my neighbor's reputation in
  the community.
+ *I wish to make others laugh* in order *to divert attention* away from my own illness.
+ *To exact revenge* upon my boss, *I must expose* his illegal activity.

The convention for naming the motivating force is the same as those for stating simple objectives. Begin the statement with "I want to," "I wish to," or "I must,"
and follow with an active verb expressing the overall desire of the character. Do

not follow with the verb *to be* or a verb expressing feeling, because *being* and *feeling* are conditions, not actions, and consequently cannot be acted.

Your defined motivating force must also involve activity with the other characters. As we recognized earlier, a play is a conflict. Your motivating force must demand something of the other characters and bring you in conflict with them. And it is through conflict in motivating forces that the plot unfolds and characters are revealed.

Last, the character's motivating force must mean something personal to your character. It must arouse in "you" a real desire to accomplish "your" aims. To *think* is not enough; your character must truly *want*. Stanislavski's student, **Michael Chekhov,** who later became head of the Second Moscow Art Theatre, explained that the actors must be "possessed" of their objective.[4] The motivating force is an emotional magnet that pulls "you" forward. It is not analytical; rather, it must be something for which you yearn.

## Constructing "Your" Autobiography

**Analysis,** for the most part, is a solitary task. It begins with your first reading of the script and doesn't stop until the lights fade on the final performance. You must read, evaluate, analyze, and research everything that helps illuminate your character and her world. Using the script as your primary source, you must reflect on the character's personal history, present state of being, relationships, and self-perceptions. You must consider previous and present actions and the character's future expectations. Research may include pictures, paintings, music, poetry, textures, colors, books, articles, interviews, observations, or anything that may help you in the creative process. Whether writing on your computer or scribbling in a notebook as you lie in bed, you must write down all the information revealed in your script and from your research. You must fill the pages with information and **discoveries** about your character.

From the moment you have been cast in a role, you should consider everything from your character's point of view—"I" rather than he, she, or they. Remember, "you" are unique. "You" have "your" own history, ideas, attitudes, desires, and fears. "You" have a singular attitude regarding every social and moral issue "you" face. As you begin to take notes, don't necessarily worry about spelling and grammar. Write as your character would write—taking into consideration his level of education and mental capacity. If your character is not politically correct, do not attempt to write your autobiography using this twenty-first century convention. You must be as completely subjective and biased as your character would be with regard to everything in this invented world. Also keep in mind that although you may disagree with your character about his spiritual and moral views, his choices and significant life decisions, you must never judge your character. Otherwise, you (the actor) will never be able to sustain belief in "your" (the character's) actions. Writing your analysis in first person will help you eliminate the tendency to judge your character.

Your analysis is for the most part personal and private. The majority of it should be kept from your fellow actors, and much of the time you should refrain from discussing "your" most private thoughts with your director. This does not mean to abstain from openly talking about the given circumstances and many of the issues facing your character. Anything "you" would publicly accept, defend, or share with "your" family, friends, colleagues, and the general public is perfectly acceptable for discussion with your director and colleagues. However, you should avoid sharing "your" *private* thoughts and feelings, "your" secrets. This part of your analysis is solely for your eyes. Put it under lock and key as you would a personal diary. In life, mystery surrounds the most interesting people. We never *really* know even our closest friends (and sometimes we don't understand our own actions). We may think we know our parents, our siblings, our friends, our lover, but they will always contradict themselves. They do the opposite of what we expect. They relentlessly do things that are "out of character." Sometimes they harbor thoughts and feelings that stay hidden for years. Sometimes these feelings never surface. Human beings are "walking contradictions." They are mysterious. Therefore, as in life, the most fascinating acting is surrounded by mystery. We all have secrets, and our characters are no exceptions. Sharing too much of your analysis with others will destroy "your" mystery.

During the period of analysis and study, read the play "very carefully" many times. Take note of every hint, every clue that helps you bring your creation to life. You should consider:

1. What "you" do and don't do.
2. What "you" say and don't say (keeping in mind that characters sometimes exaggerate and lie).
3. What the other characters in the play say about "you" and do to "you" (always taking into consideration the other character's perceived purpose).
4. What actions are suggested in "your" lines.
5. What comments and descriptions the playwright offers in the stage directions (remembering that not all stage directions are appropriate for your interpretation and that many times they are simply a stage manager's notes from the first production).

From there, your analysis must advance into a detailed autobiographical investigation. The dramatist provides enough information for you to understand the motivating force and the essential traits of the character, but you must almost

Photo by Zach Seat. Used by permission of Dr. Judith Midyett Pender.

**Figure 8.2**  Sara Clark in The University of Oklahoma's production of
*The Philadelphia Story*. Directed by Judith Midyett Pender, scenic design
by Alex Hutton, costume design by Aaron Turner, lighting design by
Jerry Lewis. Note the sense of mystery surrounding this character.
Hidden secrets intrigue the audience and make the performance infinitely
more interesting.

always supply an imaginary background to round out the essentials mined from
the text. Begin by writing down what you perceive as logical and true. Your initial
thoughts, however, will change—or evolve—as you go through the rehearsal
process and as you merge with your character.

To be valid, a character autobiography* should contain only details that logically extend from those provided by the dramatist. To be useful, it should contain only those particulars of specific behavior that can guide the actor's choice of objectives and relationships.

Your character's autobiography will put you on closer terms with the character you are playing, and you should prepare one as a regular part of your analysis procedure. Write down "your" images, thoughts, and inner monologues. Again, this is *not* a limitation; it is a means to openness and free expression. Full knowledge of your character that comes through analysis gives you more choices in the rehearsal process. Conversely, failure to write down your character's thoughts results in vague decisions that are difficult to repeat with consistency. Discoveries will be purely accidental, and you will stunt the growth of your character.

You may begin your character autobiography by asking "yourself" the questions listed below. Your answers to these queries will undoubtedly overlap. In answering one question, you will allude to another one. This is expected. You should not attempt to isolate one from another.

## Autobiographical Worksheet

1. **Who?**
   a. What is my personal history? (This should be a thorough investigation of your second plan, which is discussed in greater detail later in this chapter.)
   b. What is my present state of being?
   c. How do I perceive myself physically?
      i. Mentally?
      ii. Morally?
      iii. Socially?
      iv. Economically?
      v. Spiritually?
   d. What are my emotional relationships?
   e. What am I wearing?

---

*Some people refer to this as a character biography. We feel that approach will interfere with your ability to think in first person. Therefore, we refer to it as an autobiography, written in first person from your character's point of view.

### 2. **When?**

   **a.** What is the year?

   **b.** What is the date and time?

   **c.** What is the weather?

   **d.** How does "when?" affect my life?

### 3. **Where?**

   **a.** In what city am I?

   **b.** What are my immediate surroundings?

   **c.** How do the city and immediate surroundings affect my life?

   **d.** What are the social and spiritual customs and political tendencies of my family?

      **i.** Neighborhood?

     **ii.** Group?

    **iii.** Society?

### 4. **What?**

   **a.** What has just happened prior to the events in the script?

   **b.** What is happening presently?

   **c.** What is my attitude toward the unfolding events?

   **d.** How does my attitude differ from that of my family, friends, or society?

   **e.** What do I expect to happen in the future?

### 5. **Why?**

   **a.** How would I define the units of action?

   **b.** What is my simple objective for each unit?

   **c.** What noun names would I give each unit?

   **d.** What is my motivating force?

### 6. **How?**

   **a.** What stands in my way of achieving my goals?

   **b.** What is my "will" to get what I want?

Although the motivating force should be stated in a single phrase, the process of uncovering it is no simple task. Characters, like real human beings, are filled with psychological complexities. You must take pains to consider all the possibilities, finally stating the motivating force specifically and in terms that will stimulate you to action.

By now it must be apparent that discovering the motivating force is the key to getting into the part. Important as it is, actors frequently fail to understand the basic motivation clearly, to name it accurately, and to feel it fully. This failure stems from two causes:

1. Many actors don't study the play with enough care and imagination.
2. The motivating force—especially for a long and complex role—is frequently difficult to find.

You should not give up if you do not know the motivating force when you begin rehearsal; instead, keep searching throughout the creative process. During the rehearsal stage, you can play specific actions and realize the character's simple objectives from scene to scene without knowing for certain how they relate to the motivating force. In fact, you may never be convinced that you have the absolute, final answer for some characters; however, the search must not be abandoned, because the effort itself is of great value. Because of the ongoing nature of this process, your statement of the motivating force you are working with at any particular moment is always hypothetical. You must continue to explore it, test it, and be willing to change it as your understanding of the character and the play increases.

As we stated previously, analyzing your role is mostly a solitary assignment. It is your homework. Analysis does continue during rehearsal, but there are boundaries. Stanislavski, in the early years of the Moscow Art Theatre, sat around a table with his actors for weeks discussing every aspect of the play. During this time, they uncovered a wealth of information about the characters and their environment; however, Stanislavski discovered that their table work actually impeded their progress, and the characters lost some of their mystery. Simply talking about the role stood in the way of discovery through the psychophysical process. Discussion is very important, but you must learn to do it in conjunction with the rehearsal process. As you—with the guidance of your director—determine physical actions, they must connect with your psychological choices. Thus, as a serious actor, you must study the play, research "your" world, and answer many questions, but you must also understand that the analytical process is merely a means to discovering physical actions. *And the Method of Physical Actions is the only path to inspiration onstage. Analysis is not an end in itself. Therefore, you must stop talking so much in rehearsals and work on action.* Your character's autobiography is an extremely important part of the process that you work on primarily outside rehearsals and test and modify during rehearsals.

---

**Exercise 8.1**   **CONSTRUCTING A CHARACTER AUTOBIOGRAPHY**   Select a role from one of the plays listed in Appendix A at the back of this text, or choose a character from another standard full-length script. Using the above worksheet as the basis for analysis, write a complete autobiography. State your initial idea of the character's motivating force in terms that are true to the dramatist's conception and that could stimulate you to action in playing the part.

---

You are attempting to give birth to an imaginary person, a being filled with mystery and secrets, an individual who has experienced a lifetime of emotions and who is more complex than the most sophisticated computer. Without proper analysis, many actors simply do not have enough information to fully "penetrate" their characters. Thus, they play only the most primitive impressions. To fulfill his need for immediate gratification, such an actor plays the result rather than building his character one step at a time. Actors simply cannot grasp all the complexities of characterization at the beginning of the rehearsal and analytical process. Just as a fetus grows in the womb, your character takes time to gestate.

To begin the process of building your character, choose a sequence of actions in which you can most readily believe. Think of it as the foundation upon which your character will grow. Your sequence of actions need not be the first scene in which your character appears, and you shouldn't concern yourself with the level of importance of your selection. It is simply the chain of events with which you most identify with your character—one in which you can find an analogous emotion, one that stimulates your imagination, or one in which you can readily become "possessed" with the objective. From there, you begin the gestation process that leads to the development of the entire imaginary human being.

---

**Exercise 8.2    COMPLETING THE THOUGHTS**    In her Stanislavski-based book, *Free to Act*, Mira Felner developed this exercise. Using the same character as you did for Exercise 8.1, complete the following thoughts from your character's point of view. Let your responses be as spontaneous and uninhibited as possible. The more you know your character, the more revealing your answers will be.

1. I am happiest when . . .
2. I am most upset by . . .
3. If I had it my way, . . .
4. I don't understand why . . .
5. I wish . . .
6. I love to . . .
7. I hate . . .
8. I'm afraid . . .
9. Sometimes I think I . . .
10. I like to think of myself as . . .
11. Other people perceive me as . . .
12. A person's family . . .
13. If I were in charge . . .
14. The first time I met him (or any character from the play), . . .
15. I love him (or her), but . . .[5]

Did you learn anything new about your character? Were your responses consistent with "your" autobiography? This exercise is an excellent extension of your autobiographical worksheet.

## Uncovering the Units of Action

As an actor, your basic responsibility is to find, one by one, the numerous simple objectives and actions that taken together constitute your role. You carry out each action to satisfy a singular desire of your character, and each has a precise relation to your character's total behavior. Stanislavski referred to the smallest whole division of a play—one in which there is a distinct beginning, middle, and end— as a **unit of action** (or "unit" for short). Many actors refer to units as **beats.** For our purposes, however, we shall return to Stanislavski's original phrase and refer to them as units with the understanding that they are synonymous with beats. Regardless of their name, the transition between them is open to wide interpretation. Most new units are defined by a simple shift in the action—a "change of direction," so to speak. According to Charles Marowitz, it is "a section of time confined to a specific set of continuous actions, or perhaps the duration of a mood or an internal state. As soon as our actions graduate to the next unit of activity, we can be said to be in the next beat of the scene. . . . It is characterized by one overriding emotional colour."[6]

The actor and the director break down each scene into units so they can more precisely discuss the role and prepare its performance, in much the same way a conductor uses a "measure" to focus the musicians' attention on a particular part of a score. The units of action are comparable to the measures of a musical score in another way: they are primarily useful as rehearsal aids and should never be evident to the audience. "The analysis of the play's beats, the characters' actions, can and should be made before the actual staging of the play is begun," wrote **Harold Clurman.** "The actors derive a basic direction from such analysis and from *the notation of the beats in their part-books* [italics ours], a guiding line that is the foundation for their entire work in the play. Without such groundwork, we may get a display of 'general emotion' but not the meaning of the play." Your talent as an actor becomes evident in the manner in which you carry out these actions. Independent of talent, however, you must clearly present the units of action for the play to become a comprehensible and logical whole.[7]

## Scoring the Units

In Part I, you scored your exercises based primarily on improvisational technique, which is free and open to interpretation. When working with an actual script, however, you must adhere to the playwright's words. You cannot improvise the scripted language of your character. Your physical actions must:

+ reveal your character's inner life down to the smallest nuances and idiosyncrasies.

- be as imaginative and original as possible within the limits of your character. Human beings can be enormous, and they can also act irrationally and illogically given the circumstances. People are not consistent, but you must always consider the logic (or illogic) of your choices with regard to the personality of your character.

- have purpose and move you toward the attempted achievement of a simple objective.

- be absolutely truthful within the boundaries of the given circumstances.

- be dynamic and infuse energy into your acting.

- move forward the dramatic action of the play as a whole.[8]

Stanislavski stressed the necessity of seeing the role as a series of units. As soon as one simple objective that motivates a unit is satisfied, another desire arises that forms the basis for another unit. In earlier chapters, when we asked you to structure your work by clearly delineating a beginning, middle, and end to your score of physical actions, we were in effect dividing the exercise into units.

Every unit of action must be developed around a simple objective. Once an objective has been determined, it stands as the primary motivation until the character successfully achieves it or until the circumstances of the play force the character to move to a new unit and a new goal.

Once you have defined the simple objectives, you must give each unit a **noun name,** a single word that characterizes the whole section. For example, you may call a particular unit "Confrontation." The noun name will dictate certain behavior in your character and will define each unit. Only then will you *know* what the audience must understand. Defining each unit through a single word discloses its essence and propels the dramatic action forward.

Individual units must logically progress from one to another. Therefore, one noun name—the essence of that unit—will understandably lead to the next. Beginning with the noun name "Confrontation" it may follow that the second unit is entitled "Debate." This, in turn, leads to the following sequence of units: "Allies," "Battle," "Confession," "Retreat," and "Reparations." These named units form a logical progression that extends throughout the play. The movement from one unit to the next—the development of the inner life of your character—illustrates what Stanislavski referred to as the **through-line of action.** He compared the through-line of action to a traveler on a long journey. The traveler, while moving toward his destination, comes into contact with many new people and diverse situations; all the while he continues on his expedition toward his goal.

Some professional actors do their analytical work in their heads, but it is important for you to learn to write out your complete score that includes your **score of psychological actions,** which then leads you to a corresponding score of physical actions, as we have explored in Chapters 3 through 7. The example below represents an actor playing the role of Petruchio in a production of Shakespeare's *The Taming of the Shrew*. It illustrates how he scores the psychological and physical actions in two units. The actual dialogue is copied (or pasted) onto the center of an 8½″×11″ piece of paper. The dotted line within the text shows where one unit ends and a new one begins. The left-hand column represents the score of psychological actions—including the unit number, the noun name, the character's simple objective, and obstacles. It is also appropriate to place any of the character's autobiographical information and internal thoughts in this column. The column on the right is the score of physical actions, corresponding to the psychological score on the left. The actor uses **blocking notations** (e.g., X, USL, DS, etc.) as a form of shorthand. The letters in the right-hand column followed by the description of an action match up with the superscripted letters placed within the text where the impulse for that action occurs. Some actors use circled numbers instead. This is simply a matter of preference, as long as you are consistent. Note that the unit numbers for the psychological score are continuous throughout the script, while the letters (or numbers) representing the physical score are renewed at the top of each page. This simplifies your work, as your score of physical actions will be modified at every rehearsal. Finally, this example takes place on a **thrust stage** or three-quarters stage. Thus, when the actor X's (crosses) USL (upstage-left), he is still walking toward the audience.

PETRUCHIO:

I pray you do. I'll attend her here—

*Exeunt all but Petruchio.*

| | | |
|---|---|---|
| UNIT #23: Plan | And[a] woo her with some spirit when she comes! | **a)** X DR to edge of stage |
| Objective: In order to secure my financial independence, I must establish a plan to woo this wildcat by opposition. | Say that she rail, why then I'll tell her plain | |
| | She sings as sweetly as a nightingale.[b] | **b)** Kneel |
| | Say that she frown,[c] I'll say she looks as clear | **c)** Pick up rose petal that has fallen on floor |
| | As morning roses newly washed with dew. | |
| | Say she be mute and will not speak a word, | |
| | Then I'll commend her volubility[d] | **d)** Stand |
| | And say she uttereth piercing eloquence.[e] | **e)** X USL toward audience |
| Obstacles: Violent sounds emanating from other room; fear of unknown | If she do bid me pack, I'll give her thanks | |
| | As though she bid me stay by her a week.[f] | **f)** Turn DS |
| | If she deny to wed,[g] I'll crave the day | **g)** Crumple petal and drop on floor |
| | When I shall ask the banns, and when be married. | |

*Enter Katherina.*

UNIT #24: Execution

Objective: In order to execute my plan, I must counter her violent attacks with kindness.

Obstacles: Kate's temper; her disdain; her unwillingness to reciprocate; flying objects and bodily fluids

But here she comes, and now, Petruchio, speak.[h]

Good morrow, Kate, for that's your name, I hear.

KATHERINA:

Well have you heard, but something hard of hearing—

They call me Katherine that do talk of me.

PETRUCHIO:

You lie, in faith, for you are called plain Kate,

And bonny Kate,[i] and sometimes Kate the curst.

But Kate,[j] the prettiest Kate in Christendom,

Kate of Kate-Hall,[k] my super-dainty Kate—

For dainties are all Kates—and therefore, Kate,

Take this of me, Kate of my consolation:[l]

Hearing thy mildness praised in every town,[m]

Thy virtues spoke of and thy beauty sounded—

Yet not so deeply as to thee belongs—[n]

Myself am moved to woo thee for my wife.

h) Make eye contact, silence, then X R to L of table

(NOTE: As Pet moves, Kate keeps table between them.)

i) Duck to avoid being hit by flying centerpiece

j) X to US of table

k) Reacts to Kate's vulgar action

l) X DL to Kate

m) Wipe spit off face and smile

n) Grab Kate's hands

This is not the only way to score a script; it is one approach. Regardless of your eventual process, you must score your role. Remember, this is a working document. Your score lives and changes with every rehearsal. Do not "set it in stone." Therefore, you should work in pencil—keeping a big eraser close at hand.

In the end, your psychological score of actions should help disclose your character's motivating force to the audience. You should eliminate all actions not related to this purpose. The audience understands the play by following a series of logical and expressive units. You must facilitate this by communicating a believable and logical progression of actions, all of which grow from the given circumstances of your role.

Although the idea of truth remains constant, the given circumstances and the world of the play differ wildly with every production. The seeming illogic of some modern and contemporary plays—especially those identified as theatre of the absurd—is deceptive. The dramatist has written the play for a specific purpose and has given the characters some pattern of behavior. To express the absurdity they find in contemporary life, they may require from the actor a series of illogical actions. But by using speech and actions illogically, by introducing the fantastic and the ridiculous, their purpose is to express the absence of truth and meaning in modern society. As in the case of any drama, it is the actor's job to discover a motivating force that is truthful in the seemingly illogical pattern and to communicate it to the audience as clearly as possible.

Creating a character requires, more than anything else, the ability to follow a through-line of action. To do so, you must carefully perform each unit of action, always attempting to realize your objective and to relate each unit clearly to the one that follows it. A definite "terminal point" at the end of each unit and a firm "attack" at the beginning of each new unit give the play a sense of forward movement. There must also be clear cause-and-effect relationships between the units that illustrate the kind of analytical problem you will face in most plays, whether they be classic, modern, or contemporary.

---

**Exercise 8.3**   **SCORING A ROLE**   Using the example above, return to the same character for whom you completed the Autobiographical Worksheet earlier in this chapter. Study the breakdown of one scene very carefully. Then copy or cut and paste the script onto an 8½″ × 11″ sheet of paper. Divide the scene into units of action. In the left column, state your character's simple objectives and obstacles, and label and give a noun name for each unit. Notate precisely in the text where the impulses for action occur, and using corresponding notations in the right column, describe the physical actions using shorthand blocking notations where possible.

---

Characterization begins by breaking the role into small units of action, each with a clearly understood simple objective that moves the character toward accomplishing her overall goal. Discovering, enriching, and playing these units is a constant challenge throughout the rehearsals and performance. Few actors, even of the highest professional caliber (and after playing a role a great number of times), would claim they succeed in believing, with equal conviction, every unit. That, however, is the aim of all actors who seek to create art onstage, and they work to accomplish it at every rehearsal and performance. But they realize that failure to achieve complete belief at every moment does not indicate a bad actor any more than failure to return every ball indicates a bad tennis player. A good actor succeeds in believing a large proportion of what she does, just as a good tennis player succeeds in returning a high percentage of balls. The actor and the athlete both work to improve their technique to increase the ratio of their successes.

## Incorporating "Your" Second Plan

Many of the people, places, and events mentioned in a script's dialogue don't actually appear in the play. Some images are mentioned only in passing by the playwright. Regardless, it is your responsibility to discover the truth behind every

Photo by Buddy Myers. Copyright by Allied Theatre Group.

**Figure 8.3**    Steven Breese as Petruchio and Theda Reale as Katherina in Shakespeare in the Park's production of *The Taming of the Shrew* in Ft. Worth, Texas. Directed by Kenn Stilson, costume design by Rhonda Weller-Stilson, scenic design by Patrick Atkinson. A well-defined second plan helps these two actors with the first moment of intimacy between these rival characters. Also note the shared staging that places Petruchio in the power position.

action your character does and every mental picture your character imagines. **Vladimir Nemirovich-Danchenko,** co-founder of the Moscow Art Theatre with Stanislavski in 1898, believed that an actor's ability to create and communicate real inner images resulted from the completion of his *second plan.* Like Stanislavski,

Nemirovich-Danchenko believed the audience must be made aware of the whole inner life of the character, his entire destiny, while he is onstage.

When you write "your" autobiography, you are using your imagination to construct a history, a past life of the character. Although such work is necessary for creating a believable person who can live and act within the given circumstances of the play, you must concentrate your efforts on those moments in the character's life that the playwright chooses to dramatize. Besides incorporating everything in "your" autobiography, your character's **second plan** incorporates the events that occur offstage during the course of the play. These events many times are extremely important to the development of the plot. You can make use of these actions by writing a narrative version of the entire story, curtain to curtain, from the point of view of your character, and by improvising actions that happen offstage.

---

**Exercise 8.4    WRITING A SECOND PLAN**    Using the same character you selected for the three previous exercises in this chapter, write a narrative of your character's life that includes offstage events during the actual time covered by the play. Select an important offstage event in which your character is alone, score the units, and present it as a solo scene.

---

# Finding the Outer Form

Unless you have the ability to externalize your inner thoughts and feelings, you have no business onstage. Your external actions must influence the other actors and project into the audience. Most marginally talented actors have the ability to analyze and internalize a character. This, however, falls short of your goal. There must be communion with others. Otherwise, you would do just as well to stay home and "act" and "feel" for your own entertainment. If you fail to externalize your inner thoughts and feelings, you will never engage your psychophysical being. Your character will never project into the audience. The spectators will not follow the action, and your presence onstage will be illogical. Action is your only means to external expression, your sole purpose onstage.

You externalize your character through posture, manner of movement, degree of mobility, gestures, physical abnormalities, and all nonverbal modes of expression. You communicate through your character's dialect, level of articulation, choice of words, and sentence structure. You reveal your character's inner being through animation and the unique tempo-rhythms of physical and verbal actions. Clothing, makeup, and hair reveal a great deal of information about your character's self-perception. Personal objects (e.g., fans, pipes, canes, glasses, books, guns, etc.) become extensions of your imagined personality. Characters, as in life, are identified by their possessions. Everything the audience sees "you" do and hears "you" say, everything with which "you" connect, everyone with whom "you" relate projects something about your character. *Externalizing* a character is arguably your most important responsibility. The audience suspends their disbelief when they trust what they see and hear. Therefore, you must find outward forms that will help the audience believe your character.

Externals also greatly help actors sustain belief in their characters. They use their bodies as expressive instruments to project their inner being, and their external decisions reinforce their internal convictions. An especially erect posture, with chin held high and nostrils pinched, as if constantly trying to locate a slightly offensive odor, might aid an actress in characterizing the overpowering Lady Bracknell in Oscar Wilde's *The Importance of Being Earnest*. A mannerism of sucking his teeth might help an actor in demonstrating the vulgarity of Mr. Burgess in George Bernard Shaw's *Candida*. Elia Kazan's notebook for *A Streetcar Named Desire* outlines effective externals for the crude, simple, naive, sensual character of Stanley Kowalski. He sucks a cigar. He annoyingly busies himself with other things while people are talking to him.

Dramas abound with opportunities for actors to use externals as a means of deepening and extending their characterizations. For instance, the actor playing Willy Loman in Arthur Miller's *Death of a Salesman* should examine the effect of carrying heavy sample bags on the physique of an elderly man. The rounded shoulders, the body leaning forward to balance the weight of the samples, the feet hurting from too much pressure, the eyes looking at the ground to search for obstacles—all these external manifestations can help create a truthful characterization of Willy's exhaustion.

Sir Laurence Olivier often used makeup to help find his character. For example, he once told of developing the right type of nose as a key to a role. From this center, he could create a whole physical presence. However, Olivier would have been the first to emphasize that the external approach must be used in conjunction with internal motivation to develop a complete characterization.

When using externals as a means to characterization, you must observe two cautions:

1. Beware of clichés, the stereotyped mannerisms or properties that have been so frequently repeated they would occur immediately to even an unimaginative mind. For the audience, clichés no longer express individuality but only general types. They are the imitation of imitation, worn-out devices that can be executed mechanically. Consequently, they are powerless to aid in your belief in the character.

2. Be sure that the externalization either results from or leads to a specific need you can relate to your character's motivating force.

The caution we emphasized about making externals serve the motivating force may be similarly stressed for all aspects of the characterization. Everything you do, say, or wear onstage should help either create the motivating force or satisfy it. The more clearly you understand how a particular detail relates to your goal, the more significant it will be to you and your audience.

The motivating force is the unifying factor in selecting both internal and external details of characterization. All your decisions must relate to your character's motivating force; otherwise, they should be omitted. In fact, you should even avoid external character choices that are merely neutral, that is, details that perhaps do not hinder but bear no inherent relationship to your character. Neutral decisions are weak. They have no benefit and can distort the plot. Whether "you" smoke or not, whether "your" hair is long or short, whether "you" drink beer or coffee, whether "you" wear boxers or briefs, should all be determined by "your" motivating force. Every detail should make a positive contribution to the total characterization.

As an actor in production, you must focus only on your own character. That is the part you play. That is your contribution. Through individual analysis, you break down the entire script into units, complete with noun names and simple objectives. Connecting the units allows you to clearly see the through-line of action, which in turn leads to the naming of your character's motivating force. Keep in mind, however, that all this must naturally fit within the director's concept of the production, and you must have the ability to infect your partners and project your character into the audience.

You may identify your motivating force only if you have carefully completed your unit analysis along the way. Remember, however, the units are simply markers as you travel toward your destination. You cannot ignore the markers, for they lead the way. They are the fuel to be consumed on your journey. The markers also warn you of potential danger; they prevent you from wandering away from the path. However, you should not allow the markers to stand in your way. If you isolate the individual units and do not look at them as part of a connected whole, you will bog down in a multitude of shallow, unrelated details. They will merely confuse and frustrate you, as you lose sight of your destination. Analysis is your means to external freedom. It leads you to the path of discovery through the psychophysical process, as you work your way toward your character's motivating force.

# Terms and People to Know

**Adler, Stella (1901–1992)**   One of the great American acting teachers of the twentieth century. Founding member of the *Group Theatre*.

**analysis**   Your homework. Analysis includes the completion of the character autobiography, your score of physical and psychological action, and your research.

**beat**   A short silence in the dialogue (e.g., "hold the moment a beat before continuing"); also another name for *unit of action.*

**blocking**   The director's arrangement of the actors' movements with respect to one another and the stage space. Blocking helps tell the story, develop characterization, set mood, and create suspense.

**blocking notations**   The notes to yourself written beside the dialogue recording the physical movements of your score. Shorthand notations are incorporated where possible (e.g., XDR to chair = Cross downright to chair).

**character breakdown**   The description of a character for casting purposes.

**Chekhov, Michael (1891–1955)**   Russian stage and film actor, director, and teacher. Member of the Moscow Art Theatre's First Studio, Chekhov emigrated to the U.S. in 1928. His theatrical existentialism influenced and divided the Group Theatre.

**Clurman, Harold (1901–1980)**   Director, critic, author, teacher, and co-founder of the Group Theatre.

**conflict**   Two opposing forces in comedy or drama.

**cover**   Term used to define the speech or action invented by an actor to keep the audience from detecting a mistake.

**discovery**   Any new information an actor learns about the character in the rehearsal or performance process or the character learns about himself, others, or events during the course of the play.

**Grotowski, Jerzy (1933–1999)**   Director and acting theorist whose work stressed the importance of the actor; his style bordered on dance choreography. His book *Towards a Poor Theatre* and his work proved seminal in the European and American theatre.

**ground plan**   The arrangement of doors, windows, steps, levels, furniture, and so forth for a stage setting.

**motivating force**   What your character wants overall. It is sometimes referred to as the character's *super-objective* and is expressed in much the same way as the *simple objective.*

**Nemirovich-Danchenko, Vladimir (1858–1943)**   Russian co-founder—with Stanislavski—and literary manager of the Moscow Art Theatre from 1898 until his death in 1943.

**noun name**   A single word that characterizes a *unit of action* (e.g., "Confession," "Celebration," "War").

**psychological action**   A character's inner thoughts that manifest themselves through physical actions.

**score of psychological actions**   Written in your script on the opposite column from your score of physical actions, it includes the unit number, the noun name, the character's simple objective, and obstacles.

**second plan**   Incorporates the events that occur offstage during the course of the onstage action.

**through-line of action**   The chain of logical, purposeful, consecutive simple objectives that gradually disclose the motivating force.

**unit of action**   The smallest whole division of a play—one in which there is a distinct beginning, middle, and end. Also referred to as a *beat*.

## CHAPTER 9

# Expressing the Super-Objective

*"Everything should converge to carry out this super-objective."*

–Constantin Stanislavski

Richard Boleslavsky described the **super-objective** as the trunk of a great tree. The trunk is "straight, proportioned, harmonious with the rest of the tree, supporting every part of it. It is the leading strain; 'Leitmotif' in music; a director's idea of action in a play; the architect's foundation; the poet's thought in a sonnet." The actor, working with the director, interprets the trunk and then provides the branches, the elements that grow from the overall super-objective. The leaves on the tree come as a result of the union of the trunk and branches, "the brilliant presentation of the idea." The author is the sap that flows and feeds the tree.[1]

Creating a character is the actor's sole responsibility, but a single character is part of this much larger whole. Actors must relate their performance to the entire production. They must discover why the dramatist wrote the play, what she wanted it to say, and what emotional effect she wanted it to have on the audience. Ideally, the entire company will agree on the play's super-objective, and each actor will in turn build his particular role in relation to this concept.

In Chapter 8, we learned that actors must analyze their characters with considerable care to determine the motivating force behind their actions. In this chapter, we shall discover that a dramatist uses a group of characters, all motivated by different and often conflicting desires, for the purpose of expressing an overall meaning. Further, we shall be concerned with how each actor's role can help to realize the author's intention.

Several sources help actors prepare to learn about the play. They will want to know something of the playwright's life and of the circumstances under which the play was written. Knowing that *The Tempest* was probably Shakespeare's last play, and that in Prospero's farewell to his art—the practice of white magic— Shakespeare was saying farewell to his supreme artistry as a dramatist and a poet, might help an actor realize the calm, the dignity, and the finality of the overall tone of this play. An actor in Molière's plays may use the knowledge that this playwright had a young wife and that, in his several plays in which an old man is married to a young girl, his observations came from his own experience. Some of O'Neill's plays are almost completely autobiographical, and knowing about his relation with his parents and his older brother and about his life as a young man in New London, Connecticut, might well help actors select actions to illuminate O'Neill's characters and help them communicate the world of the play.

## Researching the World of the Play

Good drama always reflects, if it does not deal directly with, the social, economic, and moral values of its time. It follows that actors need to learn about the prevailing social conditions at the time a play in which they are performing was written. An actor could hardly succeed in Congreve's *The Way of the World* without learning as much as possible about the amoral behavior of upper-class society in Restoration England. On a more modern note, it might help an actor preparing to perform in one of Bertolt Brecht's intriguing dramas to know that the enigmatic German playwright was ideologically a Communist and that most of his works protest against a capitalistic society. For the corpus of dramas written about the war in Vietnam, such as David Rabe's *The Basic Training of Pavlo Hummel* or Sean Clark's *Eleven–Zulu,* the actor needs to learn about the conditions in training camps, the prevailing moral values in the combat zones, and the breach that combat experience is likely to cause between returning soldiers and their families.

One of the fascinating aspects of being an actor is the constant need to understand what makes people from all walks of life "tick." Depending on the production in which they are working at the moment, they may have to learn about conditions among the coal miners in Pennsylvania or among sharecroppers in the South, or about the treatment of American Indians. They may have to learn about proper procedure in a courtroom, in a hospital, or on a battleship.

Used by permission of the Virginia Commonwealth University. Photo by Jay Paul.

**Figure 9.1**    TJ Simmons and Jeannie Giannone in a scene from Virginia Commonwealth University's production of *Kabuki Macbeth*. Direction, scenic design, and costume design by Shozo Sato; lighting design by Laura Esch. Actors in this production undoubtedly must research Shakespearean and Japanese Kabuki theatre and possibly the historical eleventh century king of Scotland.

To understand and perform in period plays, the actor must find out about the clothes worn at the time. Actors must know not only how to wear them and move in them but also why a certain fashion prevailed. Why were stocks and farthingales worn in the Renaissance? Paniers and powdered wigs in the eighteenth century? How did Restoration gentlemen use a walking stick or Victorian ladies use a fan? Just as actors must fully understand the social, economic, and moral values of their characters' world, their understanding of fashion will make all period plays new and contemporary, clear and relevant to a contemporary audience.

Where do actors find answers to questions about the playwright's life and the historical context relating to the world of the play? First, they must be voracious readers, concentrating on both the fiction and nonfiction of the period during which the play takes place. They should study biographies of their playwright and of famous actors and other people from the period. Pictures from the period—paintings, engravings, and photos—are excellent sources for makeup and clothing, but they also indicate attitudes and atmosphere of the times. Good pictures arouse strong feelings, and good actors find ways to use the flavor of pictures in defining a believable character. For more recent periods, film and television, both fictive and documentary, provide excellent sources of behavior and social detail. To know too much about the play, the period, and the character is impossible.

The Internet is another invaluable source of information for the actor. Most young people are extremely comfortable surfing the net. We must always keep in mind, however, that the Web is unregulated, and actors should be forewarned to use only legitimate sources. John Smith's undergraduate term paper from Anywhere University that he posted on the Web last night does not constitute a legitimate source. However, Web articles found on such sites as The History Channel, Biography Channel, The Learning Channel, The Discovery Channel, A&E, MSNBC, CBS, ABC, CNN, *The New York Times* Online, or any other long-standing journal, magazine, or newspaper represent an important means to research your character and period.

Indeed, the Web is an indispensable tool, but it is not the only tool. Many young actors naively believe that doing a quick search on sites such as Google, Yahoo!, Excite, or Ask Jeeves from the comfort of their dorm rooms is all the research they will need in creating a character or exploring a particular period. To them, the Web sometimes seems immeasurable and comprehensive; the lazier the actor, the more infinite, all-powerful, and universal the Internet seems. Many of the most valuable resources can be found only in hard copy in such places as libraries and bookstores. You must supplement the legitimate work you have done on your computer. Therefore, get out of your chairs and go search "the stacks." You will be amazed.

With that said, knowledge of such matters as period and style is essential to a full understanding of the playwright's meaning. Consequently, actors find it doubly important to obtain this information; indeed, they cannot afford to ignore it. It helps them prepare to read more intelligently their chief source for interpreting the play—the script itself.

---

**Exercise 9.1**   **RESEARCHING YOUR CHARACTER'S WORLD**   Using the same character as you did for Exercises 8.1 through 8.4, research your character and the world of the play. Your work may include any and all of the resources discussed above, plus any sources suggested to you by your instructor or that you believe are appropriate. If you include critical analysis from a magazine, journal, book, or Internet source, you should highlight the portions of the text that you found useful. *From this point on, you should include research as part of your overall analysis.*

---

# Finding the Super-Objective

Although the individual character autobiographies are mostly private, all actors in the performing company must agree on what a play is about, what meaning the dramatist had in mind, before the actors can fulfill their particular functions in the cooperative effort of a dramatic production. "The main theme must be firmly fixed in the actor's mind throughout the performance. It gave birth to the writing of the play. It should also be the fountainhead of the actor's artistic creation," wrote Stanislavski. "In a play the whole stream of individual, minor objectives— all the imaginative thoughts, feelings, and actions of an actor—should converge to carry out the *super-objective* of the plot." The character's motivating force must be so closely tied to this overall idea that even the most insignificant detail, if it is not related to the super-objective, will stand out as superfluous or wrong.[2]

Harold Clurman stated emphatically that "no character of the play can be properly understood unless the play as a whole is understood." He recognized that understanding the play resolves itself into one central theme—one basic action. He considered each play from the standpoint of the characters' principal conflict, which in turn led him to the play's core. "Saroyan's *My Heart's in the Highlands*, to its New York director, was the story of people eager to give things to one another—lovers all, in a sense. For me, Odets' *Night Music* had to do with the search for a home."[3]

*Although finding the basic action is one of the director's most important tasks and sharing it with her cast is one of her most important responsibilities, the actor, if he is to be a creative artist in his own right, needs to understand the meaning of the play through his own efforts.* Only then can the actor be certain that it is *his*, that it has possessed every fiber of his imagination.

The meaning of a play cannot be determined solely from a study of its events. Story is rarely the unique feature of a dramatic work, for essentially the same story may be used to express a variety of meanings. People who are interested only in the "story" of a play are missing a good deal of its value, and a production that offers the audience nothing more than story is realizing only a part of its possibilities.

The story of *Hamlet*, as long and complex as it is, can be summarized in five sentences. Prince Hamlet has suffered the loss of his father only two months before his mother's marriage to his uncle. A ghost, whom he does not fully trust, informs the young prince that his uncle murdered his father. Unable to act until he discovers the truth, Hamlet "feigns" insanity as he furthers his investigation. Once he proves his premonition correct, the young prince exacts revenge on his father's murderer. In the end, all the principal characters die, leaving Fortinbras to "pick up the pieces." Simple, right? In fact, if this story is all the play offers, it cannot be distinguished from half the classic tragedies ever written.

Even a cursory reading of this most brilliant play will reveal the importance of a second dramatic element—character. Hamlet is an infinitely complex character, filled with frustration, wit, contradiction, and courage. Over the past four centuries, the most brilliant scholars have tried to understand his multifaceted relationships with his dead father, as well as with Gertrude, Ophelia, Claudius, and his comrades. These are complicated human beings—people, no matter their station in life, with whom we relate. We feel their joy, their pain, their desires, their frustrations, and their sense of revenge. We are engaged with their stories, but we bond with the individuals.

Story and character combine to form **plot,** and these two elements working in concert with each other allow the dramatist to make an observation on life. We have emphasized many times that revealing this super-objective is the actor's basic purpose onstage.

What observation did Shakespeare make in *Hamlet?* The play cannot be merely the story of a son's revenge. The story is not simply "a play dealing with the effect of a mother's guilt upon her son," as suggested by T. S. Eliot.[4] Such a story has little point unless it is directed toward some further end. What purpose does the action of the play serve? Of course, we become engaged by the story and empathize with the needs and emotions of the characters, but that does not relieve us from the responsibility of trying to determine the playwright's purpose, the super-objective. To be significant, any production must attempt to make clear the playwright's observations as interpreted by the artists associated with that particular performance.

Following this reasoning, the super-objective in *Hamlet,* according to Edward Gordon Craig, is the story of "man's search for the truth."[5] Sophocles' *Oedipus Rex,* on the other hand, attempts to show us an arrogant, blind, and godless "search for wisdom." Euripides' *The Bacchae* tells the story of the consequence of disobedience to the gods through the basic conflict between Pentheus and Dionysus. Thus, the super-objective may be stated as "the necessity for obedience to the gods."

Regardless of the play on which you are working, once you discover the super-objective, you must be unwavering in your commitment to this major purpose. All the events leading to the play's climax must serve this end. Your single and steadfast goal will be to clearly communicate this meaning to the spectators, for the through-line of action is complete only after the audience absorbs its significance.

The next step in interpreting the script is for the actors (and the director) to determine the basic action that grows out of its meaning, for it is this action that provides the play's dramatic conflict and through which playwrights make clear their message. Harold Clurman referred to this overarching action that embodies the meaning as the **spine.** It serves as a constant guide to the director and the actors, because it is the unifying factor for the super-objective of the entire play. To illustrate this concept, we shall examine *Romeo and Juliet,* relating the spine to the super-objective.

The play opens with a violent outbreak of the rivalry between the Montagues and the Capulets. Starting with a comic quarrel between the servants of the two houses, it next involves Benvolio and Tybalt (the younger generation), and finally the old men themselves, old Capulet calling for his sword and old Montague calling Capulet a villain. They are restrained from combat only by the jibes and pleadings of their wives. Only when the prince of Verona arrives does this unseemly brawl come to an end. It is a nasty fight, and it disgusts us with its violence and its pointlessness.

In subsequent scenes we see the Capulets and the Montagues not as enemies but as parents. We see they are not ogres but concerned parents, the Montagues with finding the cause of Romeo's depression and the Capulets with finding a suitable husband for Juliet. We wonder about this mixture of filial concern and violent hatred; that we first see Romeo and Juliet in relation to their parents is significant to understanding the play.

The conflict develops rapidly. In quick succession we see the meeting of the lovers, the balcony scene (death to Romeo if he should be discovered), the marriage, the killing of Mercutio and Tybalt, Romeo's banishment, and the death of the lovers in the tomb. We glory in the greatness of their love, but we loathe the senseless "canker'd hate" that brought about their tragedy. We are filled with wonder at their sacrifice and grateful that the ancient rivalry has ended. But how unnecessary! The parents are left with golden statues instead of living children, and they are faced with a realization of the awful price Romeo and Juliet have paid.

What is Shakespeare attempting to say with this story? What is the play's super-objective? It can probably be stated in some embodiment of the old bromide, "love conquers all." If we communicate it clearly, the audience should be sickened by the hatred between the families and rejoice for the love that overcame such bitterness. We want them to know that cankered hate brings tragedy and suffering and that it must ultimately yield to the force of love. The play's *spine*—the basic action that embodies the meaning we have just interpreted—could be stated as "to overcome all obstacles in the path of love." A production that uses this spine to guide the actors and the director throughout rehearsals and performance could provide an unforgettable experience for the audience.

To further demonstrate the concept of the spine and its relation to the super-objective, we shall look quickly at two additional classical plays. In Aristophanes' wildly popular comedy, *Lysistrata,* we may reveal the super-objective, "a feminine consciousness in a world dominated by men is the only means to solving major conflicts," by unveiling the play's spine, "sexual ritual has the power to domesticate the primitive energy found in war." In the world of *Lysistrata,* the "happy idea" is that women are on top. If mothers ran the world, Aristophanes is saying, war would not exist. The late medieval play, *Everyman,* embodies the anxieties of its age, a time when people seemed more preoccupied with death and the afterlife than with life itself. In this play, however, the author, who remains anonymous, was attempting to show a successful journey to death that parallels what a successful journey through life should be (the spine). Therefore, the super-objective is not "how to die well" but rather "how to live well." "For after death amends may no man make."

**Figure 9.2**    Evan Karlewicz, John McGuire, Joel Aroeste and David Baecker (*left to right*) in a scene from the New York State Theatre Institute's production of *Fiorello*. Directed by Pat Birch, scenic design by Richard Finkelstein, costume design by Lloyd Waiwaiole, lighting design by John McLaine. Careful analysis of your character, the world of the play, and the super-objective of the production enhances creativity.

Beginning actors sometimes have a mistaken notion that careful analysis destroys spontaneity. This attitude is difficult to defend. Acting, like any other art, is a conscious process. Spontaneity is fruitful only after careful study directs it toward the accomplishment of a purpose. The resistance to analysis may be especially strong in the case of comedy, where it is natural for the actor to assume that the purpose is simply to "be funny." Actually, a dramatist's basic intention is no different in comedy than in the so-called serious types of drama; the difference, if any, lies in the treatment. Successful actors accept without question the responsibility to know the meaning and spine of every play they undertake.

## Assuming a Dual Personality

In discharging their responsibility of communicating the play to an audience, actors assume a dual personality. Figuratively, they split themselves in two. One part is the actor in the character, and up to now this has been our primary concern. The other part remains outside the character as a **commentator,** continually pointing out the significance of each action in relation to the total meaning of what the character is doing and saying.

The actor should never "lose himself in the part." George Bernard Shaw's maxim is frequently quoted: "The one thing not forgivable in an actor is being the part instead of playing it." Shaw would have stated the case more accurately if he had said: "In addition to being the part, the actor must also play it"; then his statement would warn against losing oneself yet recognize the necessity of the divided personality.

Let us state the actor's twofold function again. He must create the character, yet to make his creation fully express the dramatist's observation, he must also find a way to tell the audience what the dramatist (and, very possibly, what he himself) thinks and feels about the character's behavior. This subtle finishing touch to developing a characterization often marks the difference between a work of art and merely playing a role. All great actors find a way to provide this *comment* without detracting in the least from the believability of their performance. *If such comment is handled well, it allows the audience to glimpse inside the mind of both the actor and the playwright.*

The actor-as-commentator must help the audience understand her character's basic impulses. The actor must guide the audience in forming an opinion of her character. By this means, actors lead the audience to an understanding of the super-objective of the entire play. The comment may say that a character is weak but essentially good, that although it may not be possible to approve of her actions, she is entitled to sympathetic understanding. It may say that another character is vain and selfish, undeserving of sympathy, and that still another is living fully and happily according to sound principles.

The comment comes from the omniscience of the actor who knows the character better than the character knows himself. In life, people rarely psychoanalyze their neuroses, their obsessions, and their fears. People who we might describe as "misfits" certainly would not see themselves in that way. Most individuals whom we deem insane consider themselves to be normal. Hamlet, perhaps more than any other character in dramatic literature, attempts to analyze himself, but does he (the character) ever understand his actions as completely as the actor portraying the role does? Do young Romeo and Juliet fully understand their emotions and actions? The actor, through analysis, must objectively recognize his character's inner and outer being and clearly communicate it to the audience by emphasizing certain details of behavior.

Actors must commit themselves to expressing the playwright's intention. To make the audience dislike a character whom the playwright intended to be received with sympathy would alter essential values. Obviously, it would be very wrong in our interpretation of *Romeo and Juliet* for the long-standing feud to seem justified and the love between the two young people to be seen as a breach of family loyalty. As a result of their comment, the actors will set the beauty and rightness of their love in contrast with the ugliness and wrongness of the obstacles against it.

And actor must be aware of her dual personality, and a part of the actor's preparation is to decide how her performance can best express the meaning of the play and whether her comment should be made obvious or subtly detectable. Remember that actors must always behave truthfully in imaginary circumstances. The idea of truth remains constant, but the world of the play drastically affects the actor's commentary and the relative size of her character and subsequent actions. The imaginary world of some plays is very similar to our own world—"the mirror up to nature." Other characters live in a nightmare, whereas still others survive in a post-apocalyptic world where nothing exists outside their immediate surroundings. In some plays, it is perfectly logical for a character to break into song and dance, whereas many other plays create a world in which characters speak in verse. Regardless, once the singular reality has been clearly defined by the playwright, the director, and the designers, it remains for the acting company to behave truthfully in that specific imaginary world.

In your analysis, you must be careful never to "pigeonhole" a play. As artists, we must not make sweeping statements regarding periods, playwrights, and genres. Is it correct to say that all classical Greek plays have the same structure? Do all the plays of Ben Jonson really resemble those of William Shakespeare? With close inspection, we may identify structural parallels; however, the differences greatly outweigh the similarities. Every extant Greek tragedy is unique, just as every Elizabethan play is distinct. In fact, the process of categorizing periods and playwrights into genres is merely an academic exercise that many artists see as ludicrous. Every play has its own reality. Each production paints an entirely new world. The theatre belongs to the theatre. There is no one style, no one method of interpretation, and no one point of view. The legendary Max Reinhardt wrote, "It would be a theory as barbaric as it is incompatible with the principles of theatrical art, to measure with the same yardstick, to press into the same mold, the wonderful wealth of the world's literature."[6] To label a playwright's approach may stifle the creative process. Every play must have its own voice. All art must have its own distinct style.

Nevertheless, actors must understand the basic structural differences between dramatic genres—academic as these labels are. Because student actors are as likely to be working with an Elizabethan tragedy as with a modern comedy, we must at least discern some of the overall and rather general demands they are likely to encounter.

The approach to the internal and external preparation of a role is essentially the same for all plays, no matter the period and no matter the genre with which it has been "lumped." Performance choices will definitely vary, depending on the extent to which the audience is allowed to be aware of the actor-as-commentator and the extent to which the actors are allowed to show their awareness of the audience. When a production labels itself as realistic or illusionistic, it is more than likely based on the tradition of the proscenium theatre, which presupposes an invisible "fourth side" through which the audience sees the actors but through which the actor must not seem to see the audience. When viewing plays produced in this tradition, audiences should have the impression that they are privileged to observe the action onstage, but that it would go on in the same way whether they were there or not. This concept of theatre is called **representational,** because the actor is attempting to represent action as it happens in life. Actors make no direct contact with their observers because to do so would destroy the illusion. Any adjustments they make to the presence of the audience (speaking in a voice loud enough to be heard, holding their lines for the laughs, and performing actions so everyone may see them) must seem "natural" or lifelike; they must be clearly motivated by the desires of the character they are playing.

It is in this kind of theatre that another one of the actor's paradoxes is most readily apparent. He must forget the audience, yet he must always keep them in mind. He must develop a technique that allows him to immerse himself in the imaginary world of the play and, at the same time, consciously adapt to the audience that is outside this invented world. The actor makes direct contact with the other actors while he makes indirect contact with the audience, and his connection—or communion—with both is reciprocal. His relationship to the spectators is always a challenge, because the real essence of theatre is what happens between the actor and the audience.

In earlier periods and in an increasing number of contemporary plays, the approach is sometimes more **presentational,** or nonillusionistic. Instead of representing events as they would happen in life, actors frankly accept the contrived circumstances under which the plays are given. Actors present the play directly to the audience without attempting to conceal the theatrical devices they are using.

The ultimate in presentationalism is the traditional Chinese theatre, in which both the performers and their audience recognize that the conditions of the theatre are not real and consequently find no necessity for creating an illusion of reality. An actor astride a pole suffices as a general on horseback. The prop person sits at the side in full view and provides hand props as the actor needs them. The magic of the Chinese theatre comes from the formal manner in which it presents truthful observations of life without attempting to represent life. Chinese actors distinguish to a much greater extent than we do the difference between *truth* and *actuality*.

In some respects the classic plays—the plays of Sophocles and Shakespeare and Sheridan and Molière—are closer to the Chinese theatre than to the more modern illusionistic stage. They are presentational, in that they do not attempt to represent life in a realistic environment. They are not as theatrical as the Chinese plays are with their visible prop people, but they permit the actor a greater frankness in recognizing the presence of the audience. Soliloquies may allow the actors to speak their characters' thoughts directly to the house, and "asides" may allow them to comment freely on the action of the play, although it is important to note that both are done *in character.* Some modern plays provide an interesting mixture of representational and presentational theatre. As an example, consider the following stage direction from Robert Patrick's play, *Kennedy's Children:*

> Wanda leans back wearily, checks the time on her travel alarm, puts her pencil down, and begins to speak. As with all the characters in the play, it is her thoughts we are hearing, and we have come in not at the beginning, but in the flow of an endless stream of revery. In no way does any character ever acknowledge the fact that another is speaking.[7]

Her actions, her attention to detail, are clearly taken directly from the realistic, representational, theatre. Speaking her thoughts is just as clearly a presentational technique.

One of the most exciting aspects of the contemporary theatre is that it has opened the door to plays and performances that establish almost every conceivable relationship, both social and physical, between the actor and the audience. One example is improvisational theatre, in which the actors create their own play, often attempting to include the audience in the improvisation. Other similar approaches are often termed environmental theatre or alternative theatre. **Augusto Boal,** an infectiously enthusiastic teacher and director from Brazil who is committed to this approach to performance, describes it as: "*theatre* in [the] most archaic application of the word. In this usage, all human beings are Actors (they act!) and Spectators (they observe!). They are Spect-Actors."[8]

Performers in this kind of theatre often advocate a social cause they strongly believe in and just as often do not create characters. Their technique is to reach the audience directly in their own persons, a method frequently called non-acting. Physical relationships are equally varied; performers often come into the aisles and walk between the rows of spectators, talking to them directly on a person-to-person basis. Other times they work in large open rooms, found spaces, in which the differentiation between the space used for performance and the space used for the audience is blurred if not totally erased. Because a major objective is to break down any barrier between actor and audience, this concept minimizes the duality of the actor.

---

**Exercise 9.2**   **RELATING THE SUPER-OBJECTIVE TO YOUR CHARACTER**   Return to the same character from Exercises 8.1 through 8.4 and 9.1, and determine the spine and super-objective of the entire play. State the meaning briefly and clearly. Then list your character's traits that are important to the total meaning, and decide to what extent you might need to comment on them to make that meaning clear. *This also should become part of your overall analysis from here out.*

---

# Terms and People to Know

**Boal, Augusto (b. 1930)**   Brazilian director, playwright, and theorist. His revolutionary models of political and cultural theatre-making—with increased interaction between the audience and actors—have gained an international reputation.

**catharsis**   A cleansing or purging of emotions.

**commenting**   A technique by which actors "distance" themselves from their roles, continually pointing out the significance of each action in relation to the total meaning of what the characters are doing and saying.

**elements of drama**   As defined in Aristotle's *Poetics,* the elements of drama in order of importance include: plot, character, thought, diction, music, and spectacle.

**inciting incident**   The precise event that serves as the catalyst for the action of the play.

**plot**   The sequence of physical and psychological actions. The combination of story and character.

**presentational theatre**   Abstract or nonrealistic theatre that seeks to imitate with a minimum amount of recognizable reference to life.

**representational theatre**   Realistic theatre that attempts to represent nature as closely as possible.

**spine**   The basic action that grows out of the play's *super-objective;* it is like a spine in the human body that holds the other parts together.

**style**   A term referring to individuality and distinctive manner of expression. Style should not be confused with genre (e.g., realism, absurdism, epic, Shakespearean, etc.).

**super-objective**   The play's central theme or intent that runs throughout the plot; what the author wanted to say. Stanislavski referred to this as *sverkhzadacha* or "super-problem."

## CHAPTER 10

# Interpreting the Lines

*"Words, words, words."*

–William Shakespeare

Interpretation of the lines begins with your first reading of the script and doesn't stop until the lights fade on the final performance. One of your prime responsibilities is to communicate the dramatist's lines to the audience. Line interpretation coincides with your exploration and discovery of your character's motivating force and the super-objective of the entire play. While you are discovering the physical actions, you must dissect each line of the play, exploring every possible meaning.

The basis for effective interpretation is a good voice. The effectiveness and range of actors largely depends on their ability to use their voices and shape their speech. Vocal training greatly improves the actor's effectiveness. We have stated before that one of our basic assumptions is that all serious actors will undertake organized voice training at the same time they are studying the principles of acting presented in this book.

The past few decades have seen a tremendous increase in the number of master voice teachers specializing in the problems of the actor. Primarily through the influence of such seminal thinkers and teachers as **Arthur Lessac, Edith**

**Skinner,** and **Kristin Linklater,** the training of the actor's voice (as well as his body) is considered a fundamental priority in good acting programs everywhere.

These teachers have shown that, assuming the absence of physiological defects, no voice is so poor that it will not respond to proper training and that no voice is so fine that it could not be better if given the advantage of proper exercise. Whatever program of voice training actors undertake, they should try to accomplish several objectives. For instance, in training their voices, they should seek to acquire:

1. *Volume,* so the actors' voices may be heard without difficulty. Onstage, even quiet, intimate scenes must be heard in the rear of the theatre. Jerzy Grotowski emphasized this objective: "Special attention should be paid to the carrying power of the voice so that the spectator not only hears the voice of the actor perfectly, but is also penetrated by it as if it were stereophonic."[1]

2. *Relaxation,* so their voices will not tire unduly during a long performance and so they will not involuntarily raise their pitch during climactic scenes. Relaxation means that the column of air carrying the sound flows freely and is not constricted by tension in the throat or the jaw. Voice tension creates undesirable empathic responses in the audience, impairs actors' expressiveness, and can cause permanent damage to their vocal mechanisms.

3. *Quality* that is pleasant to hear and capable of expressing varying emotional states. A voice that is pleasant to hear is one of the actor's most prized attributes and is to a large extent a matter of resonance.

4. *Flexibility,* so their voices are capable of a variety of volumes, qualities, and pitches. A good voice is capable of adapting to a large range of demands with maximum ease.

5. *Energy,* so the voice commands attention and makes others want to listen. It is especially important to guard against a habit (common among young actors) of "fading out"—letting the energy diminish—at the ends of sentences or phrases. In speaking, as in golf or tennis, one must learn to "follow through."

Speech training should improve:

1. *Articulation,* so the actor can be readily understood, even in passages requiring rapid speech. Although not all characters are articulate, all actors must be. Good articulation, achieved primarily through careful attention to forming the consonants, is essential to clear speech. A story is told of a very great British actress who evaluated the work of an aspiring student with the comment, "Poor dear, no consonants."

2. *Pronunciation,* so that it is free from slovenliness and provincial influences. This objective is becoming increasingly important. Television and motion

pictures that reach audiences all over the country cannot use actors whose speech identifies them with a particular region, unless regional speech is essential to the character they are playing. Absolute absence of colloquial speech is necessary for classic plays, which emphasize the universality of the characters, not their individual idiosyncrasies.

3. *Artful control of tempo and rate* to convey satisfactorily the psychological and physiological connotations of human discourse. Perhaps no other aspect of speech relates so closely to the an actor's sensitivity to the complexities of her material. Tempo also is established by proper cue pickup, so the performance moves at a pace appropriate for audience comprehension.

Most of the notable vocal training techniques we have recommended quite rightly focus on these aspects of voice and speech. Interpreting the character's lines falls more in the realm of acting technique; therefore, we shall consider that subject at this point in our overview. The art of interpretation, meaning what the actor expresses and why, is a necessary part of the study of acting, no matter what vocal training technique one uses.

In earlier chapters we noted that characters speak for the same reason that they act—to satisfy some basic desire. The question always in an actor's mind as he seeks to interpret his lines is "Why does the character say what he says at this particular moment?"

## Exploring the Subtext

"Words are pig shit," declared French poet and playwright Antonin Artaud. *You cannot act words. Words have no meaning.* When Polonius asks, "What do you read, my lord?" Hamlet responds with, "Words, words, words." **Subtext** gives meaning to your words. Stanislavski often proclaimed, "Without subtext, there is no theatre." Just as *subtext of behavior* defines the characters' actions, *subtext of words* underlies their every sound. Subtext influences everything onstage. It is the reason we go to the theatre. Subtext makes your words distinct. It colors your meaning, making it unique and unrepeatable. Every sound you utter must have a specific internal justification. Subtext allows you to transform a phrase into a verbal action by supplying this justification.

To find the subtext of words, you must discover a character's motivation beneath her lines. In seeking this motivation, you must consider (1) how a line helps your character accomplish her simple objective and (2) how a line relates to its context, especially to the preceding line. A line that does not help your character accomplish her purpose will be one of those details that Stanislavski said will stand out as "superfluous or wrong." A line that is not related to its context will baffle the audience because it will seem pointless and illogical.

**Figure 10.1** David Bunce (*sitting*) and John Romeo in a scene from the New York State Theatre Institute's production of *Man of La Mancha*. Directed by Pat Birch, scenic design by Richard Finkelstein, costume design by Robert Anton, lighting design by John McLaine. Words and actions without subtext have no meaning. The actor who is standing in this scene appears to be manipulating his partner. His text may be saying one thing, but his subtext may be quite the opposite.

The real significance of a line is rarely in the meaning of the words themselves or in the literal information they convey. Such a simple dialogue as

A: What time is it?

B: Eleven.

has no dramatic significance until the meaning beneath the lines is known. Why does one character ask the time? What is in the other character's mind when he answers?

These words can convey a number of different meanings, depending on the circumstances under which they are spoken. If Character A were on death row awaiting execution, the lines might mean

A: How much longer?

B: 'Bout an hour.

If the characters were listening to a dull and seemingly endless lecture, the lines might mean

A: Shoot me. I'm in hell.

B: It's almost over.

If the characters were making out in the back of a car, the lines might mean

A: I gotta go home.

B: It's early.

Or if the characters were preparing an important presentation, the meaning might be

A: We still okay?

B: Oh, my god. We missed our appointment.

As an actor, you must know and think your character's subtext, as it flows like an underground river just beneath the surface. Sometimes the text and subtext coincide or agree; however, you must always search for conflict between them. Conflict between what the character thinks and what he says creates drama. Stanislavski believed, "Contradiction between the text and the subtext makes the word unexpected, vivid, and significant."[2] As illustrated above, with any given line, there exists an opposite meaning, an undercurrent. Always playing the literal denotation of a word is dull. Look for alternatives. Search for **opposites.** Human beings do not always say what they think. They tell little white lies. They exaggerate. They deceive. Subtext clarifies the story for the audience, yet keeping them off guard by exploring opposites keeps them interested. It deepens their experience. Contradiction also helps engage other characters in strong transactions. Remember what we said about **mystery** and secrets in Chapter 8. It is through unpredictable subtext that you must attempt to affect the behavior of other characters in the scene and to add color and meaning to your performance.

Your success in communicating your personal interpretation of a role lies to a very considerable extent in your choice of subtext. You must speak the text that the dramatist has written, but the subtext is your own contribution. It demonstrates your insight into the role and sensitivity to the play. Subtext is grounded in the motivating force and in the simple objectives of the units, both of which have been explored in the last few chapters. In fact, subtext is the vehicle via which imagination and interpretation connect with performance.

An example of how subtext affects meaning (in this case not just of a single speech but of an entire play) is Katherina's famous "advice" at the end of *The Taming of the Shrew,* in which she describes the responsibilities of a dutiful wife. Katherina is a headstrong, willful woman who has been "tamed" by and wed to Petruchio. He wants to complete the taming by having Katherina show her obedience at the wedding banquet. With one choice of subtext, the speech makes it plain that he has brought Katherina to submission. With another choice, we know she is not tamed at all but has learned to carry on the battle of the sexes

Photo by Kenn Stilson.

**Figure 10.2**    Roseanna Whitlow (*left*) and Casee Hagan in Southeast
Missouri State University's production of *The Glass Menagerie*. Directed
by Kenn Stilson, scenic and lighting design by Dennis C. Seyer, costume
design by Sarah Moore, sound design by Philip Nacy. Connected to
opposites is the human capacity to find **humor** in every scene of every
play. Humor is the warmth of human beings in every situation—including
the most tragic. It is not about "being funny" but rather about the
interchange between people.

in a more subtle way. For this second choice, Petruchio's response—his inner
monologue while she is speaking—also has a significant effect on the total meaning. If he does not understand her subtext but takes the words for their surface
value, the tables will have been turned completely, and it will now be Katherina
who will dominate their relationship. If, on the other hand, he understands her

subtext, even though the other characters do not, he and Katherina will clearly have a lively marriage.

In *The Zoo Story*, by Edward Albee, the confrontation between Jerry and Peter over a park bench leads to Jerry's suicide. The opening moment of the play demonstrates how important a clear subtext is to a play's successful performance. As the play begins, Peter is seated on a bench reading a book. Jerry's objective in his opening line, "I've been to the zoo. I said I've been to the zoo. *MISTER, I'VE BEEN TO THE ZOO!*" is more than "to become louder until he notices me." That would distort the author's purpose and create a willful, self-centered hoodlum who might frighten Peter immediately and cause him to leave. Instead, the actor playing Jerry wants to keep Peter there, so his subtext must include the pain and desperation of a person at the end of his rope. What Jerry thinks is as important as what he says.

Stanley's subtext in the scene with Lulu from *The Birthday Party*, by Harold Pinter, prepares the audience for the visit by the mysterious Goldberg and McCann. If his reason for refusing to leave the house is not specific and substantial, the word games with Lulu and his offer to take her anywhere will lose all importance. The actor must know that Stanley is in danger and that his options of hiding in the house or running away are ways of avoiding a dreaded confrontation. The net result of the scene would be mere mental gymnastics without the underpinning of fear, which can be established only through subtext.

In *Cat on a Hot Tin Roof*, Maggie is determined to have a child by Brick. The child is an economic necessity, but a Maggie whose subtext is based only on her own survival becomes a shrew, which is not the playwright's intention. Maggie is also full of positive life force, and her desire to achieve security is reinforced by her honest caring for Brick. If the actress misses this love, the pain of Brick's rejection would be hollow and unmoving. If we are to care about Maggie, the subtext has to contain the love along with the ambition.

People go to the theatre to "hear" the subtext; they can read the text in greater comfort at home.

---

**Exercise 10.1  INVESTIGATING SUBTEXT**    A helpful exercise is to find different subtexts for the same line and to speak the subtext immediately after you have said the text. You can create your own simple lines, but here are two examples to get you started:

Don't go. (I command you to stay.)

Don't go. (If you care anything about me.)

Don't go. (It's not safe.)

Don't go. (I'm warning you.)

I love you. (But not in the way you want me to.)

I love you. (If you force me to say it, I will.)

I love you. (How can you treat me this way?)

I love you. (I don't ever want you to doubt it.)

Now, write at least two possible subtexts for each of the following lines. Speak each line, followed by your first choice of subtext. Then speak it without saying the second choice aloud, making clear its different meaning. Have a partner or the entire class check your success.

| | | |
|---|---|---|
| I hate your guts. | Baby. | Don't cry. |
| Thanks. | Get out. | Sorry. |
| You're beautiful. | Liar. | Kiss me. |
| You're late. | You shouldn't have. | You're insane. |
| Fine. | Wow. | Hi. |

The above examples should make it clear that finding the subtext of a line is not the same as paraphrasing it, or restating the words of the author in the words of the actor. Paraphrasing may be necessary when surface meaning is not immediately clear; indeed, you may find it especially worthwhile to restate in your own words the lines of a verse play. But the paraphrase will not tell you what is beneath the line and how it relates to the dramatic action and to the character's motivating force. Finding the subtext begins with understanding the character's purpose in saying the line.

## Finding the Verbal Action

The interpretation of words is *verbal action.* You must use the words, expressing your inner life and attitude through every utterance. Verbal action is stronger than physical action. It is the drive, the purpose, behind every line. It is the means by which you communicate your inner relationship with yourself, your partners, and your world. The inner images stirred by your words can make an entire audience jump with fright or howl with excitement. Verbal action is the path with which to accomplish your objectives.

In the example at the beginning of the last section, when A asks, "What time is it?" meaning "How much longer?" the verbal action is to hold back the time. When the character means "Shoot me. I'm in hell," the verbal action is to get out of a dull lecture or to make the time go faster. And when A means "I gotta go home" or "We still okay?" the inherent action is to sound an alert.

To summarize, then, the significance of a line is not on the surface but beneath it; the real meaning is found in the subtext, for it provides the justification, motivation, and interpretation behind the role. When you speak a line, you must think simultaneously of the words you are saying, their subtext, and their inherent verbal action.

Let us illustrate this crucial point with examples from Oscar Wilde's famous satire on snobbery, *The Importance of Being Earnest*. When the haughty Lady Bracknell speaks slightingly of the family background of Cecily Cardew, then Cecily's guardian, Jack Worthing, replies, "Miss Cardew is the granddaughter of the late Mr. Thomas Cardew of 149 Belgrave Square, S.W.; Gervase Park, Dorking, Surrey; and the Sporran, Fifeshire, N.B."

To give the addresses of Mr. Thomas Cardew's three residences is not Jack's purpose. Rather, the subtext is: My ward is a person of excellent family connections that may be quite as acceptable in English society as are your own, Lady Bracknell! The verbal action is to put Lady Bracknell in her place.

Earlier, Jack has been informed that Lady Bracknell hardly approves of him either. He says, "May I ask why not?" His subtext is, "I am sure I don't see why she doesn't approve of me. I am every bit as good as she is." His verbal action is to assert his equality.

The choice of the subtext determines to a considerable degree the overall effect of a line—whether it will be comic, pathetic, or melodramatic. These lines from *The Importance of Being Earnest* are, of course, comic. Their subtexts must help point up the ridiculous seriousness with which the characters take themselves.

## Relating the Lines to the Motivating Force

The subtext and the verbal action, both significant in interpreting a line, do not by themselves disclose its significance. You determine this by relating the meaning to your motivating force. By understanding how each line serves to help the character get what she wants, you will have a better chance of making the motivating force clear to the audience.

Although in any circumstances the character may be motivated in one of several ways, you must make a clear and unequivocal commitment to a motivating force before you can give a line its full value. Recall the situation in which A is on death row. The actor might decide that the condemned person feels only the primal urge to live, that he is hoping for a reprieve from the governor, or even hoping blindly for a miracle. With such a motivating force, his asking for the time will be essentially a cry for help. Instead, he might decide that the person has accepted his death as inevitable, in which case his motivating force might be "to seek redemption," and his line might be a plea for more time in which "to make atonement." Another interpretation might be that even at the point of death, the person was filled with the same bitterness that led him to commit the crime and was determined to give no one the satisfaction of seeing any sign of remorse. In this case, the line would strengthen his motivating force "to refrain from repenting." In any case, once your motivating force has been decided, you must stick to it and follow it wherever it takes you as you interpret the lines.

Confusion often arises from the use of a variety of terms to describe the actor's relationship to the role and the relationship of the role to the whole play. For clarity, let us review the definitions of those terms as we use them:

1. *Motivating force* is the character's long-range goal. It gives the character a sufficient reason to pursue the course of action demanded by the play.

2. *Super-objective* is the theme or basic line of the play and is synonymous with its *spine*. In this context it is a directional term. The motivating force of each role (sometimes referred to as the character's super-objective) must be compatible with the super-objective of the entire play.

3. The *through-line of action* is the progressive movement from one *unit* of the play to the next. It assumes a series of consistent and logical actions, a pattern of behavior that is the route an actor takes to her character's motivating force. The attempt to fulfill the objectives of the character against a series of obstacles moves the play to a conclusion, and the through-line of action is the thread that links all the character's actions.

## Relating the Lines to the Super-Objective

You also must know how your lines serve the super-objective and how they aid in communicating the play's central idea to the audience. This problem has been anticipated in such previous steps as (1) finding the character's motivating force—a process in which the lines were an important consideration, (2) relating this fundamental desire to the meaning of the play as a whole, and (3) finding the subtext and the verbal action, which, as we have seen, emerge only after the lines have been related to the motivating force.

After completing these steps, you will likely understand how the dramatist intended each line to aid in expressing its own meaning. For example, knowing that the playwright Jean-Paul Sartre believed that all people are trapped in their feelings of shame and guilt and that he used this theme in many of his works will aid in development of each character in his classic play, *No Exit*. Sonia Moore illustrates this concept:

> Like many other modern playwrights, Sartre is preoccupied with people's inability to have healthy relationships. His heroes are lonely; they need each other but are unable to approach and reach each other. Sartre's idea is that a man is always surrounded by a wall as if he were in prison. People torture themselves with constant guilt feelings and they are also tortured by the condemnation they see in the eyes of others. . . . Their

attempts to break loose from this hell are really an attempt to regain their feeling of innocence. But they cannot. Dissatisfaction with oneself makes it impossible to relate to people. The hell in the play represents the world in which a man must live whether he wants to or not. Sartre believes that a man must create for himself the values to live by. It is what a man does that defines him. By creating his own values, he creates himself, or as Sartre says, finds an exit. Sartre believes that man chooses his values and makes himself.[3]

Before you can begin creating your individual role in Sartre's play, you must understand the character's feelings of isolation, feelings of guilt, his burning desire to escape, and his frustration when he discovers the futility of his actions. You will fully understand your character only if you understand the author's meaning of the entire script.

Every unit of action must be carefully examined in the context of the super-objective interpreted by each particular production. No element of the production is excused from this basic demand. The actor's task is to hold to this interpretation with an unyielding grip and to make everything she says or does flow from some variation on the theme. Actors must turn the interpretation into action, and subtext is one of their major tools for doing so.

Once again, Oscar Wilde's *The Importance of Being Earnest* can serve as a contrasting example of the problem of relating the lines to the super-objective. This play is a satire on the snobbish upper classes at the close of the nineteenth century, who sought to relieve their boredom by concentrating on inconsequentials. Wilde saw the comic possibilities in the affectations of such people, and he ridiculed them good-naturedly in this farce. The plot has to do with two young ladies whose virtually sole requirement for a husband is that his name be Ernest, a requirement that compels both Jack and Algernon to arrange to be rechristened. The actors in this play must see that their lines serve Wilde's purpose of having fun at the expense of these people.

The following dialogue drips with Jack's boredom and underscores the eagerness with which Algernon engages in trivial pursuits.

ALGERNON: . . . may I dine with you tonight at Willis's?

JACK: I suppose so, if you want to.

ALGERNON: Yes, but you must be serious about it. I hate people who are not serious about meals. It is so shallow of them.

And later:

ALGERNON: . . . Now, my dear boy, if we want to get a good table at Willis's, we really must go and dress. Do you know it is nearly seven?

JACK: Oh! It always is nearly seven.

ALGERNON: Well, I'm hungry.

JACK: I never knew you when you weren't. . . .

ALGERNON: What shall we do after dinner? Go to a theatre?

JACK: Oh no! I loathe listening.

ALGERNON: Well, let us go to the Club?

JACK: Oh, no! I hate talking.

ALGERNON: Well, we might trot round to the Empire at ten?

JACK: Oh, no! I can't bear looking at things. It is so silly.

ALGERNON: Well, what shall we do?

JACK: Nothing!

ALGERNON: It is awfully hard work doing nothing. However, I don't mind
hard work where there is no definite object of any kind.

Clearly, Algernon's verbal action stands in opposition with Jack's. Algernon's
objective is "to relieve his boredom," while Jack's objective is "to remain inert."
Just as actors must search for contradictions and opposites with their own lines,
they must also explore contrasts with other characters. Contrast leads to conflict,
and conflict is the heart of drama.

Playwrights make their basic intention clearer and stronger by using contrasting elements. In such cases, the relationship of certain characters' lines to the total
meaning is one of contrast with the central theme. The meaning is thus painted
more sharply, just as colors appear brighter when contrasted with other colors.

Several examples of the use of contrasting elements appear in *Romeo and
Juliet*. Remember that we found its theme to be the triumph of young love over
"canker'd hate." Although Romeo and Juliet both meet a tragic death, their love
is triumphant. Because of it, the Montagues and the Capulets end their ancient
feud, and civil brawls no longer disturb the quiet of Verona's streets.

Triumphant love is expressed throughout the play in Juliet's lines:

My bounty is as boundless as the sea,
My love is as deep—the more I give to thee
The more I have, for both are infinite.

and Romeo's:

O my love! my wife!
Death that has suck'd the honey of thy breath
Hath had no power yet upon thy beauty.
Thou art not conquer'd—Beauty's ensign yet
Is crimson in thy lips and in thy cheeks,
And Death's pale flag is not advanced there.

The final beauty of their love is moving and memorable because it stands
out in relief against the hatred of old Montague and old Capulet, the Nurse's
vulgarity, Mercutio's mockery, Tybalt's malice, and Lady Capulet's coldness. The

lines of these characters are related to the total meaning through contrast, and it is important that the actors understand this relationship. For instance, Romeo's romantic love seems stronger because it rises above the jibes and cynicism of Mercutio's mocking lines. Tybalt's malicious lines put Romeo's newfound love to a test and bring about the duel that causes Romeo's banishment. Throughout the play, Juliet's warmth and generosity stand out against her mother's unyielding practicality. Lady Capulet rejects Juliet with:

> Talk not to me, for I'll not speak a word,
> Do as thou wilt, for I have done with thee.

These particular lines underscore the desperation of Juliet's predicament and propel her toward her final course of action.

Although the Nurse's character is vastly different from that of Lady Capulet, she serves a similar purpose in providing dramatic contrast—her bawdiness against Juliet's sweetness and purity. Her advice to marry the Count Paris for practical reasons, when Juliet is already secretly married to the banished Romeo, is revolting to a person of Juliet's innocence:

> I think it best you marry'd with the County.
> O, he's a lovely gentleman!
> Romeo's a dishclout to him. An eagle, madam,
> Hath not so green, so quick, so fair an eye
> As Paris hath. Beshrew my very heart,
> I think you're happy in this second match,
> For it excels your first, or if 't did not
> Your first is dead—or 'twere as good he were,
> As living here and you no use of him.

In such instances, relating the lines to the super-objective means making them provide dramatic contrasts. Knowing when this is so and how various relationships unfold demands a complete understanding of the play as a whole. No individual line can be interpreted without a complete command of the play's global meaning. Even difficult lines will yield to honest interpretation once this meaning has been mastered.

---

**Exercise 10.2  INTERPRETING EACH LINE**   Return to the same character you studied in Chapters 8 and 9, and select a sequence of lines from one unit of action. Study it carefully. For each of your character's lines, determine its:

- ✦ subtext
- ✦ relationship to "your" motivating force
- ✦ verbal action
- ✦ relationship to the super-objective

Write out this information, as it will complete your score of physical actions. *From here out, this too should be included in your overall analysis.*

---

# Believing Your Character's Manner of Speaking

The lines are composed of two elements, both of which are vital:

**1.** The content: what the lines say, including both text and subtext.

**2.** The form: the manner in which the content is expressed, including vocabulary, grammar, pronunciation, and articulation.

We have explored how the actor detects the content of the lines, so we shall now consider the problem of believing the manner in which the character speaks. Different speakers may express the same meaning in a variety of ways:

**1.** I hope it ain't gointa rain an' spoil the picnic we was plannin' fer so long.

**2.** I trust inclement weather will not mar the outing we have been anticipating for such a time.

These two lines are alike in content, and their surface meanings are identical. The subtext could be the same, and both lines could bear the same relation to the speaker's motivating force. But neither is expressed in a manner that the average actor would find "natural." The actor's problem is to understand the background of the character's speech so she can believe the manner of speaking in the same way she believes in the character's actions.

For the most part, the dramatist imposes the characters' manner of speech by choosing the vocabulary and the grammar, both of which should be accepted as given circumstances by the actor. Occasionally, as a part of the externalization of their characters, actors may introduce variations in pronunciation and articulation. For instance, they might play characters with a dialect, a stammer, or "baby talk." Like all good externalizations, such characteristics should support inner traits and help both the actor and the audience believe them. Baby talk, for example, might be helpful in characterizing a woman who had been pampered by her parents and whose motivating force is to get the same attention from her husband. Such decisions about the speech of the character are subject to the same intense scrutiny as are other character externals and are justified only if they enable the actor to realize the dramatist's intentions.

Actors study their characters' speech habits in the same way they study other traits provided by the dramatist: They try to find justification for them in the play. They also may need to supply, as they did when justifying actions, imaginary circumstances true to the playwright's conception that help explain why the characters speak the way they do (discussed further in Chapter 11).

If the character's manner of speaking is similar to the actor's or if he has frequently heard others speak in a similar way, he will have little difficulty. The speech background of Trisha, Meredith, and Frances in *Five Women Wearing the*

© 2003 Utah Shakespearean Festival. Photo by Karl Hugh.

**Figure 10.3**   Henry Woronicz as Richard in *Richard III*, 2003. Actors performing in Shakespearean plays must believe the verse and poetic prose language of their characters.

*Same Dress,* by Alan Ball, is so immediately comprehensible that it presents no problem to most young American actors. The entire play takes place in Meredith's bedroom, while her sister's wedding reception is in full swing outside. The following dialogue is typical.

TRISHA: (*Looking at her reflection in the vanity mirror.*) God, would you look at me? I look terrible.

MEREDITH: You look like a million bucks, as usual.

TRISHA: I had to put about a gallon of white-out underneath my eyes this morning. (*She pulls a cosmetics bag from her purse and begins to skillfully retouch her make-up. . . .*) So Frances, did you enjoy the wedding?

FRANCES: Yes, it was so beautiful.

MEREDITH: It was ridiculous.

FRANCES: Tracy's dress sure was something.

MEREDITH: Yeah, it was a float.

TRISHA: You've got to hand it to her, though, she carried it off. I could never wear anything like that with a straight face.

MEREDITH: She didn't wear it. It wore *her.* If she has any sense at all, she'll put it on a mannequin and just roll around the reception and leave herself free to mingle.

TRISHA: I shudder to think how much that thing cost.

MEREDITH: Six.

TRISHA: (*Turns to her.*) That's obscene.

FRANCES: Six hundred dollars?

MEREDITH: Six *thousand.*

TRISHA: She talked me into designing her invitations for *free,* and then she made me go through *eight* revisions, and she spent six thousand dollars on her *dress?* That is totally obscene.[4]

On the other hand, the speech in Eugene O'Neill's *Desire Under the Elms* presents a problem. Simeon and Peter, both in their thirties, are square-shouldered, homely, bovine men of the earth who live on a New England farm in 1850.

SIMEON (*grudgingly*): Purty.

PETER: Ay-eh.

SIMEON (*suddenly*): Eighteen year ago.

PETER: What?

SIMEON: Jenn. My woman. She died.

PETER: I'd fergot.

SIMEON: I rec'lect—now an' agin. Makes it lonesome. She'd hair long's a
hoss' tail—an' yeller like gold!

PETER: Waal—she's gone.[5]

The average actor will find it difficult to believe this manner of speaking in terms of his own experience. The actor may have no doubt that the speech is right for the character. He may understand the regional factors that have produced this unique, musical language. Still, he is aware that his own speech is quite different, and such a disparity is not always easy to reconcile.

Regional dialect is learned over a lifetime of improper reinforcement from family and friends. It is a difficult habit to break. Many actors struggle with hearing subtle differences of articulation, vowel placement, and speech rhythms that differ from their own. Their early efforts are often mechanical and imitative. Actors must record and listen to themselves as they try to form the sounds in accordance with the dialogue on the printed page. Some playwrights are remarkably skillful in their use of phonetic spellings to indicate speech variations. Eugene O'Neill was a master of writing dialogue phonetically; George Bernard Shaw also represented Cockney English in this way. Actors also may listen to recordings or imitate actual models if they are fortunate enough to know someone whose speech is similar.

If this external approach is to serve its purpose, however, it must lead the actor to believe her character's speech. And believing the speech should, in turn, increase her belief in the characters. In other words, as the actor becomes convinced she has developed a true manner of speaking, she will have a greater conviction in her total characterization. Diction—the way of expressing oneself—is one of the actor's principal resources in creating a character.

Trisha, Meredith, and Frances are average, upper-middle-class, young women who speak in a contemporary vernacular. Simeon and Peter, on the other hand, are modest folk who express their thoughts and feelings as best they can, as colorful as their speech often is. As you probably recall, we meet people in *The Importance of Being Earnest* with quite a different background. Algernon Moncrieff is, by his own admission, "immensely overeducated." He speaks not only to express his ideas but also to impress his hearers with his cleverness and his aptness of phrasing. We have known for some time that speech is an action; now we see that the manner of speaking can carry with it its own dramatic intention.

All the characters in *The Importance of Being Earnest* exhibit a kind of "speech embroidery" indicative of their elegance and earnest artificiality. The following lines of Gwendolen Fairfax are an example. She is talking to Cecily

Cardew, whom she has learned is Jack Worthing's ward. Gwendolen and Jack have recently become engaged.

> GWENDOLEN: Oh! It is strange he never mentioned to me that he had a ward. How secretive of him! He grows more interesting hourly. I am not sure, however, that the news inspires me with feelings of unmixed delight. (*Rising and going to her.*) I am very fond of you, Cecily; I have liked you ever since I met you! But I am bound to state that now that I know that you are Mr. Worthing's ward, I cannot help expressing a wish you were—well, just a little older than you seem to be—and not quite so very alluring in appearance. In fact, if I may speak candidly—

> CECILY: Pray do! I think that whenever one has anything unpleasant to say, one should always be quite candid.

> GWENDOLEN: Well, to speak with perfect candour, Cecily, I wish that you were fully forty-two, and more than usually plain for your age. Ernest has a strong upright nature. He is the very soul of truth and honor. Disloyalty would be as impossible to him as deception. But even men of the noblest possible moral character are extremely susceptible to the influence of the physical charms of others. Modern, no less than Ancient History, supplies us with many most painful examples of what I refer to. If it were not so, indeed, History would be quite unreadable.

Taking command of these lines will provide quite a test for young American actors. Just learning to "say" them will not be enough. They must understand the ostentation and snobbery that produced such a vocabulary and structure. Only then can they begin to believe the speech and actions of the characters, and they must believe them before they can make an adequate comment on their ridiculousness.

Believing the characters' manner of speaking is a matter of understanding the influences in their background that have determined their way of speech, of justifying the characters' speech in terms of their background. The actor is constantly faced with such questions as

1. Why does one character have such an extensive vocabulary, whereas another speaks almost entirely in words of one syllable?

2. Why does one character speak in long, involved sentences, whereas another speaks in halting fragments?

3. Why does one character speak with faultlessly correct grammar, whereas another says "he don't," "we was," and "I seen"?

4. Why does one character say "you gentlemen," whereas another says "you guys"?

Why does one character say "yeah," whereas another says "ay-eh," and yet another says "yes"?

---

**Exercise 10.3  STUDYING SPEECH PATTERNS**   Choose a character whose manner of speaking varies from your own. Study the speech, and practice the lines until you believe you are truthfully reproducing the character's manner of speaking. If possible, use actual models, sound recordings, or phonetic transcriptions.

---

# Motivating the Longer Speech

So far in this discussion of interpreting the lines, we have concentrated on the importance of motivation, of relating the lines to the characters' basic desires and understanding how each line helps the characters get what they want. For the most part, we have been thinking of lines no longer than a sentence or two. Long speeches frequently pose exceptionally difficult problems of interpretation. Usually, the best way to approach them is to break such speeches into small parts, find the subtext of each segment, and relate it to the character's motivating force. In other words, long, complicated speeches should be treated as if they were a series of shorter, more manageable lines. You should avoid the temptation to motivate all speeches as a single idea. Some long, complex speeches may contain several units.

When discovering and arranging the units of a longer speech for performance, remember that each section should have a clearly stated verbal action. In many long speeches, you can easily detect the familiar, classical, three-part structure—the beginning, the middle, and the end. Other speeches may have only two parts, and still others may have five, or seven. You should never divide a speech into so many units that you cannot keep its overall pattern in mind; otherwise, it will seem to the audience to lack structure or form. Sometimes, of course, speeches are broken off, either by the speaker or by another character, before they reach a structural ending.

A speech from *Golden Boy,* by Clifford Odets, will serve as an illustration. Joe Bonaparte, on the eve of his twenty-first birthday, is telling his father he wants to break away from the restraints of home so he may have "wonderful things from life." He thinks he can find what he wants by becoming a prize fighter. But Mr. Bonaparte, a humane and kindly man, wants Joe to find happiness as a violinist and has paid a lot of money for a fine violin that he plans to give Joe for his birthday. Others present in the scene are Frank, Joe's older brother who travels about a good deal, and Mr. Carp, a neighbor who owns an *Encyclopaedia Britannica.*

Mr. Bonaparte: Sit down, Joe—resta you'self.

Joe:  Don't want to sit. Every birthday I ever had I sat around. Now'sa time for standing. Poppa, I have to tell you—I don't like myself, past, present, and future. Do you know there are men who have wonderful things from life? Do you think they're better than me? Do you think I like this feeling of no possessions? Of learning about the world from Carp's encyclopedia? Frank don't know what it means—he travels around, sees the world! (*Turning to Frank*) You don't know what it means to sit around here and watch the months go ticking by! Do you think that's a life for a boy my age? Tomorrow's my birthday! I change my life![6]

Joe's purpose in this speech is to make his father see that he is going to change his way of life and that the change will mean a difference in their relationship. His verbal action is to break away from his home and his father. He is excited and resentful, but the speech does not come easily and he cannot say it all at once. Once said, he also feels it necessary to defend his decision. Through all this, his relationship with his father creates a psychological obstacle to every verbal action in every unit. The speech may be divided into three structural parts:

1. Verbal action: *to assert his independence from his father.*

   Don't want to sit. Every birthday I ever had I sat around. Now'sa time for standing.

2. Verbal action: *to defend his decision to break away from his father.* This is the middle part, the development leading to the climax. Joe gives several reasons for his decision, and he plays each reason with increasing intensity:

   Poppa, I have to tell you—I don't like myself, past, present, and future. Do you know there are men who have wonderful things from life? Do you think they're better than me? Do you think I like this feeling of no possessions? Of learning about the world from Carp's encyclopedia? Frank don't know what it means—he travels around, sees the world! (*Turning to Frank*) You don't know what it means to sit around here and watch the months go ticking by! Do you think that's a life for a boy my age?

3. Verbal action: *to defy his family.* This is the climax of the speech.

   Tomorrow's my birthday! I change my life!

---

**Exercise 10.4  PRACTICE MATERIAL FOR LONGER SPEECHES**   The following speeches provide material for practice in interpreting lines. Read the play each speech has been selected from, because the significance of any speech lies in its relationship to the play. Determine the motivating force of the character. Break the speech into units. Find the verbal actions. Make a score of physical actions. Memorize the speech. As you rehearse it, look for the separate motivation for each unit, and relate its meaning to the objective of the speech as a whole. If the language is different from your own, study the speech background of the character.

**A.** Masha in *The Three Sisters*, by Anton Chekhov, adapted by David Mamet[7]

> MASHA: My sisters? My Clown Soul. My Jolly Soul is heavy, do you want to know? It is. Hear my confession. For I am in torment and my Guilty Knowledge sears my Heart. My sinful Mystery. My secret which screams to be told. I am in love and I love someone. I love a man. You have just seen him. The man that I love. Vershinin. [. . .] What am I to do? You tell me. He was *strange* to me. At first. I *thought* about him. Often. I felt sorry for him. I . . . I "grew to love him." I did. I grew to love him. His *voice* . . . his *ways* . . . his *misfortunes* . . . his two little *girls* . . .
>
> You won't hear it? Olga? You won't hear it? Why? I love him. He loves me. It's my Fate, do you see? This love. It's as simple as that. Yes. Yes, it's frightening. Yes. But it's *mine*. It's what I *am*. Yes. My darling. Yes. It's *life* s'what it is. We *live* it, and look what it does to us. We read a novel, and it's clear. It's so *spelled out*. This *isn't* clear. *Nothing* is clear. And *no* one has a final *true* idea of anything. It's "life." We have to *decide*. Each of us. We. Have. To DECIDE: what *is*, what it *means*, what we *want*. My darling sisters. (*Pause.*) That's what the thing is. And now I've confessed. And I'll be silent. (*Pause.*) As the grave. (*Pause.*) Silence.

**B.** Young Roy in *No Mercy*, by Constance Congdon[8]

> YOUNG ROY: I'm not afraid of tarantulas. I'm really not afraid of anything out here. Two months ago, if I thought I'd be here in New Mexico, well, I would've laughed. I got my orders home in Berlin, and they told us we'd get a month off then go back to, you know, clean up. But when I reported for duty, they put us on this train and the next thing I know, we're heading west. A whole train of soldiers heading west for no reason. Seemed like then. And we stopped in Nebraska—*Nebraska*—for three days and played baseball to kill time. And still we have no idea where we were going or why. And then, and then, back on the train and further west, and the ground starts to change. My buddy wakes me up and presses my face to the window. Lord! There's a herd of antelope galloping alongside the train and I look up and got my breath took away again! Mountains! Blue-green, almost black the pine is so thick. They are so still and big, they look painted on. Well, that's when I knew I was going somewhere important. Something about the speed of that train—I swear once we got close to here, we went faster and faster—I think those guys could've lost control like that. (*Snaps fingers.*) I mean, that prairie blurred into the desert and the day *went by*. And then, bang, we were stopped. Cause we were here. Stopped. Dead. And it was so quiet. The sky was full of stars. And I could feel that train moving inside me for the whole

next day. [. . .] This is just about the most exciting thing that has ever happened, sir. I mean, I missed the invention of the motor car, I missed Christopher Columbus, I missed the time when Lord Jesus was walking around the earth, I missed the invention, no, *discovery* of electricity. I was beginning to think that absolutely nothing was ever gonna happen to me. You know? When I think that the smartest men, why, in the whole world are here. And all the knowledge that's went into this, from way back there. When the first guy got an idea, like a little light bulb going on over his head, and wham, he invents that light bulb. And then another guys makes it better. And another guy says, "We got a light bulb, we need a socket." And then, wham, we got a socket. And then a lamp. And then, the next thing you know, the whole world is lit up. Lamps everywhere! No more darkness.

**C.** Arlene in *Getting Out*, by Marsha Norman[9]

ARLENE:  This chaplain said I had . . . said Arlie was my hateful self and she was hurtin' me and God would find some way to take her away . . . and it was God's will so I could be the meek . . . the meek, them that's quiet and good and git whatever they want . . . I forgit that word . . . they git the earth. [. . .] And that's why I done it. [. . .] They tol' me . . . after I's out an it was all over . . . they said it was three whole nights at first, me screamin' to God to come git Arlie and kill her. They give me this medicine an thought I's better . . . then that night it happened, the officer was in the dorm doin' count . . . an they didn't hear nuthin' but they come back out where I was an I'm standin' there tellin' 'em to come see, real quiet I'm tellin' 'em, but there's all this blood all over my shirt an I got this fork I'm holdin' real tight in my hand . . . (*Clenches one hand now, the other hand fumbling with the front of her dress as if she's going to show Ruby*) this fork, they said Doris stole it from the kitchen an give it to me so I'd kill myself and shut up botherin' her . . . an there's all these holes all over me where I been stabbin' myself an I'm sayin' Arlie is dead for what she done to me, Arlie is dead and it's God's will . . . I didn't scream it, I was jus' sayin' it over and over . . . Arlie is dead, Arlie is dead . . . they couldn't git that fork outta my hand till . . . I woke up in the infirmary an they said I almost died. They said they's glad I didn't. (*Smiling*) They said did I feel better now an they was real nice, bringing me chocolate puddin'. [. . .] An then pretty soon, I's well, an officers was sayin' they's seein' such a change in me an givin' me yarn to knit sweaters an how'd I like to have a new skirt to wear an sometimes lettin' me chew gum. They said things ain't never been as clean as when I's doin' the housekeepin' at the dorm. (*So proud*) An then I got in the honor cottage an nobody was foolin' with me no more or nuthin'. An I didn't git mad like before or nuthin'. I jus' done my work an knit . . . an I don't think about it, what happened, 'cept . . . (*Now losing control*) people here keep callin' me Arlie and . . . (*Has trouble saying "Arlie"*) I didn't mean to do it, what I done. . . .

**D.** Dave in *The Dreaded Word*, by Galanty Miller[10]

DAVE:  Sometimes I think having a family would be nice. But sometimes I don't. Sometimes I think having a steady job for the rest of my life and making a lot of money would be nice. But sometimes I don't. Like you said, I don't know where the finish line is. I wish God would just come down and tell me what to do. I wish he would say, "Get married. That's what success is. Have two kids, not one and not three but two." Whether I like the results or not, I just wish I knew what I was supposed to do, what the ending was. You would think God would do that when you're like eighteen or something. He'd invite you up for a beer and tell you what your purpose is. "Okay, Dave, here's what I want you to do. I want you to get your Master's degree, but don't go any further in school. Then I want you to keep your first job after school for about a year. Then I want you to keep your second job for the rest of your life." Life would be so much easier if God was more social. (*Pause*) Do you believe in God?

**E.** Scarlet in *Coyote Ugly*, by Lynn Siefert[11]

SCARLET:  I blame my whole life on that Hide-a-Bed. I was produced on it after one night of hot sex. Who knows. Ma tried to get rid of me but I was too serious about living. She took ice showers and sat out late waiting for the chill. She beat me with her fist while I was still inside her and that's why she can't lay a hand on me now. There was this creep had pink hair and one eye name of Danny Dog used to drive Red around before he worked for a living. This one eye of his was glass. Just some old marble he'd stuck in. He didn't have no brakes so he'd pick Red up by punching it from the road, coasting to the house, sliding into a three-sixty, swinging Red into the rear, then gunning it fast back to the road. One day he gunned it so hard his marble eye popped out and he drove up onto the porch. Ma come running out screaming and hollering all pooched out with me inside her. HEY YOU WHAT ARE YOU UP TO YOU GO ON HOME NOW, Ma said. Danny Dog pointed to the eye in the palm of his hand. Ma give the pickup a shove. Danny Dog beat it to the road without a look back. Right then. When she was least expecting me, I popped out like Danny Dog's eyeball. Ma fell down kicking and cussing with me still hooked up to her. I hated her already so I bit her. I bit her and I bit her. She started running. She ran dragging me behind her all the way to Phoenix. You want to know what happened to my neck? She ran and I flew out behind. She felt like nothing by then but she was driven driven driven. She ran up the front steps of a man's house. Man's name was Keeper. Sign on the porch said SCISSORS SHARPENED. Ma rang the bell. I bit her feet. She pulled on the front door. She pulled so hard the whole house came off in her hand. That's all I remember.

**F.** Kent in *La Turista*, by Sam Shepard[12]

KENT: Yes, sir! Nothing like a little amoebic dysentery to build up a man's immunity to his environment. That's the trouble with the States you know. Everything's so clean and pure and immaculate up there that a man doesn't even have a chance to build up his own immunity. They're breeding a bunch of lily livered weaklings up there simply by not having a little dirty water around to toughen people up. Before you know it them people ain't going to be able to travel nowhere outside their own country on account of their low resistance. An isolated land of purification. That's what I'd call it. Now they got some minds, I'll grant you that. But the mind ain't nothing without the old body tagging along behind to follow things through. And the old body ain't nothing without a little amoeba. [. . .] Yes sir! That's always been true as long as man's been around on this earth and it ain't going to stop just on account of a few high falootin' ideas about comfort and leisure. No sirree! Why it'll get so bad up there that even foreigners won't be able to come in on account of they won't be able to take the cleanliness. Their systems will act the same way in reverse. Nobody can come in and nobody can get out. An isolated land. That's what I call it. [. . .] Then the next step is in-breeding in a culture like that where there's no one coming in and no one getting out. Incest! Yes sirree! The land will fall apart. Just take your Indians for example. Look what's happened to them through incest. Smaller and smaller! Shorter life span! Rotten teeth! Low resistance! The population shrinks. The people die away. Extinction! Destruction! Rot and ruin! I see it all now clearly before me! The Greatest Society on its way down hill.

**G.** Rosacoke in *Early Dark*, by Reynolds Price[13]

ROSACOKE: You had punished me for laughing that morning in church, and I wanted to die—which was nothing unusual—but guessed I could live if I breathed a little air, so I picked up a bucket and walked to the woods to hunt some nuts and win you back. It was getting on late. I was hoping you were worried. I was past Mr. Isaac's in the really deep woods. The leaves were all gone, but I hadn't found a nut. Still I knew of one tree Mildred Sutton had showed me—I was headed for that—and I found it finally. It was loaded— pecans the size of sparrows—and in the top fork a boy, a stranger to me. I was not even scared. He seemed to live there, twenty yards off the ground, staring out dead-level. I said "Are you strong enough to shake your tree?"—"If I wanted to," he said. I said "Well, want to please; I'm standing here hungry." He thought and then braced his long legs and arms and rocked four times— pecans nearly killed me. I rummaged round and filled my bucket, my pockets. He had still not faced me; so I said "Don't you want to share some of my pecans?" Then he looked down and smiled and said "I heard they were God's." I said "No, really they belong to Mr. Isaac Alston. He can't see this far."—"I can see him," he said. "You may can see Philadelphia," I said—he was looking back north—and he nodded to that but didn't look down. "How old are you?" I said. He said "Fifteen" and shut up again. "I'm thirteen," I said. He said "You'll live" and smiled once more toward Philadelphia and I came on home. I wanted him then and every day since.

**H.** Michael in *Two Rooms,* by Lee Blessing[14]

(*Blindfolded and sitting alone on a mat, Michael, who has been taken hostage by a militant group somewhere in Beirut, talks to his wife, Lainie, in his mind.*)

MICHAEL: (*A beat.*) War isn't a tear in the fabric of things, it is the fabric. If earth is our mother, our father is war. The chief priority we have on earth is to vie with each other for a place to stand. Does any of this make sense, Lainie? I'm trying to explain why this has happened to us. Americans fight all the time— lots of wars. But always far away. We haven't had to fight for the soil we stand on in a century. We've forgotten that level of sacrifice. These people haven't. Everyone in this country—Christian, Sunni Moslem, Shi'ite, Palestinian, Israeli—everyone is fighting for the ground. The ground itself. They stand here or nowhere. So it's easy for them to give up their lives. Small sacrifice. It's easy for them to kill, too. Small sacrifice. You know how being here, being swallowed up by it, makes me feel? Like I'm finally part of the real world. For the first time. Lainie, something in me never felt . . . affected . . . until this happened. You know what it makes me think of? Shiloh. Vicksburg. The Wilderness. What those places must have been like: suffocating, endless, bleeding disaster. Stacking of bodies ten deep for a few feet of *our ground*. Don't you see? We're not different from these people, we've just forgotten. We think this urge doesn't exist anymore. We abstract everything, we objectify. We talk about global politics, how all this affects the balance of power. Do you know what a twenty-year-old Shi'ite thinks of the balance of power?

**I.** Marie-Antoinette in *The Queen's Knight,* by Frank Cossa[15]

(*In October 1793, from her cell in Paris, the former Queen of France faces death.*)

QUEEN: I have been a prisoner of these people for four years. I watched them march to the gates of the palace and slaughter six hundred Swiss guards. I watched as all my friends were murdered or driven into exile. I watched them execute my husband who was their King. I watched them drag my children screaming from my arms so that after a year I don't know if they're alive or dead. I have lived in this room for seventy-six days. They allow me two dresses, no undergarments, no cloak, no blanket against the dampness that runs down the walls. There is never any firewood. There is always a guard outside my cell who must keep his eyes on me at all times. At all times. Some days ago the Princess de Lamballe, my last loyal friend, returned from a safe exile to be near me in my difficult time. She came here to visit me. The mob saw her and I watched them tear her to pieces. Her head was impaled on a stake and raised up to my window there. (*She points.*) One man made himself moustaches out of her private hair while the others, laughing and cheering, threw parts of her . . . her body up at me. You see, monsieur, for four years one horror has followed another. They have allowed me no comfort, no rest. They have spared me no cruelty, no shock, no terror. And you wish me to ask these people for . . . (*She turns, slowly again, to look at him.*) a favor?

**J.**  Chrissy in *In the Boom Boom Room*, by David Rabe[16]

CHRISSY:  Shut up! I think I said for you to shut up! Did I not say I am not in the mood? I am not in the mood! I got stuff to do I want it to be alone I do it. I gotta be makin' some resolutions about my stupid life. I can't not bite my fingernails. I can't not do it. I can't keep 'em long and red, because I'm a person and I'm a nervous person, and I diet and diet I might as well eat a barrel a marshmallows. My voice is not sexy or appealing. I try to raise it. I try to lower it. I got a list a good things to say to a man in bed, I say stupid stuff made up outa my head. My hands are too big. My stockings bag all the time. Nothin' keeps me a man I want anyway. I mean, how'm I gonna look like that? (*Seizing a glamour magazine, she thrusts the cover, the face of a beautiful woman, at him.*) I can't do it. Not ever. [. . .] And then maybe I finally get it right and my nails are long and red, I got on a new pretty dress, and I go out—I got earrings and perfume, new shiny shoes and rings all aglittery on my fingers, and they bring me back here and strip me down and a hunk of meat is all I am. Goddamn that rotten stinking Al and let him run off the end a the earth with that weird Ralphie! (*Running across the room, she collapses onto the bed.*)

---

# Terms and People to Know

**ad lib**   Coming from the Latin *ad libitum* ("at pleasure"), the term applies to lines supplied by the actor wherever they may be required to fill in for an otherwise undesirable pause.

**aside**   An onstage line shared with the audience but supposedly unheard by the other actors on stage. Although they are a regular convention in plays of the seventeenth, eighteenth, and nineteenth centuries, modern dramatists rarely use asides.

**humor**   Found in every scene of every play, humor is the warmth of human beings in every situation—including the most tragic. It is not about "being funny" but rather about the interchange between people.

**Lessac, Arthur (b. 1909)**   One of the greatest twentieth century teachers of voice, speech, singing, and movement in the world.

**Linklater, Kristin (b. 1935)**   Originally from Scotland and trained at the London Academy of Music and Dramatic Art, Linklater is one of the foremost voice teachers in the world today. Her book and approach, *Freeing the Natural Voice*, has influenced a generation of actors.

**mystery**   Found in the most fascinating portrayals, all great acting contains an element of mystery, an inexplicable quality that intrigues an audience by leaving unanswered questions about a person's behavior or motives.

**opposite**   A contradiction between the text and the *subtext*, which makes the word or action unexpected, vivid, and significant.

**secret**   Found in all great acting, a person's private history that makes them infinitely more interesting by enhancing an audience's insatiable curiosity about the inner lives of others.

**Skinner, Edith (1904–1981)**   One of the leading teachers of good speech in North America, Skinner's book, *Speaking with Distinction*, helped train some of today's finest actors.

**subtext**   The actor's continuous flashes of thoughts that give meaning to the dialogue and the stage directions. Referred to by Stanislavski as "illustrated subtext," an actor must have specific images for everyone and everything that is spoken, heard, or experienced on stage.

# Communicating the Subtext

*"The value of words is not in the words themselves but in the subtext they contain."*

–Constantin Stanislavski

Many actors assume that if they understand the general meaning of a line and have an idea of its overall purpose, they will read the line correctly without further conscious effort. However faulty this assumption may be, it is reasonably understandable that many actors make this mistake when speaking straightforward prose dialogue. But many plays (all classics and a considerable number of contemporary works) are not written in simple prose. They nearly always use a range of rhetorical and poetic devices, and their vocabulary is frequently baffling. In these plays, actors must pay attention to both content and form if they are to communicate the full value of the dialogue to an audience.

To engage in a comprehensive study of the uses of rhetorical and poetic devices demands much more space and time than we can give it here. We must, however, explore the more common means playwrights use to make their dialogue effective. Understanding these strategies will stimulate you to examine the dramatist's lines more closely. Only by such careful scrutiny can you detect all subtlety of meaning and aptness of form. Because communication is the actor's primary responsibility and because language is a major means of communication,

**Figure 11.1**   Clyde Ruffin as Prospero in *The Tempest* at Shakespeare in the Park in Ft. Worth, Texas. Directed by Kenn Stilson, scenic design by Nelson Robinson, costume design by Dawn DeWitt, lighting design by Jeffrey Childs. Shakespearean actors must have the ability to think antithetically and to clearly communicate mental images through verse and poetic prose.

it goes without saying that successful actors constantly deepen their sensitivity to words and sharpen their ability to communicate their meaning.

## Understanding Words

Actors must know the meanings of their words! This advice is so obvious you may resent having it said. Yet it is not uncommon for actors to go into rehearsals not only ignorant of what their lines mean but also ignorant of their ignorance. As an actor, you should own a good standard dictionary—or have immediate access to a computer dictionary—and use it frequently, even looking up words when you think you know the meaning. You also need access to special sources: dictionaries of slang and colloquial speech are two prominent examples. For almost all period plays, you will also need a glossary and a well-annotated edition of the text.

You need to study such sources conscientiously in order to discover the meaning of the play's words. Let us return to *Romeo and Juliet* for an illustration. Juliet's first line in the balcony scene (Act II, Scene 2), spoken to herself after she has just met Romeo at the Capulet ball and fallen in love with him, is:

O Romeo, Romeo! wherefore art thou Romeo?

Without having a complete understanding of the words, actresses will inevitably misread the line by emphasizing *art* and thus making it mean "Where are you, Romeo?" with some such subtext as "I yearn to know where you are, what you are doing, whether you are longing for me as I am longing for you." But a simple check of the dictionary will disclose that *wherefore* does not mean "where"; it means "why." *Wherefore* then becomes the emphatic word, and the correct subtext is "Why do you, whom I have come to love, have to be called Romeo, the son of our great enemy?" This reading leads logically to the next line:

Deny thy father, and refuse thy name;
Or, if thou wilt not, be but sworn my love,
And I'll no longer be a Capulet.

In analyzing the meaning of Juliet's first line, note also the absence of a comma between *thou* and *Romeo*—Romeo is not being addressed. Attention to punctuation helps greatly in finding the meaning of a speech. Incidentally, Juliet uses *wherefore* in the same sense in expressing her alarm when Romeo reveals his presence in the Capulet orchard:

How cams't thou hither, tell me, and *wherefore?*

She means how did you manage to get in here and why did you come?

Several other usages in the same scene further illustrate the necessity of paying close attention to the meanings of the words. After Juliet has said her famous "that which we call a rose / By any other name would smell as sweet," she continues:

So Romeo would, were he not Romeo call'd,
Retain that dear perfection which he *owes*
Without that title.

A few lines later, fearing Romeo will think she is too forward in declaring her love, she says: In truth, fair Montague, I am too *fond.*

If your edition of the script has a good glossary, you will discover that *owes* in Shakespeare usually means *owns* and that *fond* usually means *foolish.* Juliet is not saying, "I love you too much," she is saying, "I am foolish to declare my love to someone I have known only an hour and whose family is an enemy to my family." This feeling is expressed more fully later in the lines:

I have no joy in this contract tonight:
It is too rash, too unadvis'd, too sudden;

Words that look familiar but that the dramatist uses with an unfamiliar meaning can be particularly deceiving.

Let us move to a related problem of interpretation. After Juliet has warned Romeo that he will be killed if any of her kinsmen find him in their orchard, he says:

> My life were better ended by their hate,
> Than death *prorogued,* wanting of thy love.

The word *prorogued* is not likely to be in the average student's vocabulary. It means "postponed" or "delayed." Romeo is saying, "It is better to be killed at once by your kinsmen than to endure a living death without your love." To make this meaning clear, six words in the line must have some degree of emphasis:

> My *life* were better *ended* by their *hate,*
> Than *death prorogued,* wanting of thy *love.*

Selecting the word or words to emphasize is important when interpreting the lines. The selection is determined by the meaning of the words and by the context in which they are used. We will call these the **operative words.** In this sense, *operative* means "exerting the force necessary to produce an appropriate effect," and we choose this term because it suggests the active influence that certain words have in communicating a meaning. Think of the simple sentence "I gave him the revolver." If we exclude the article, any one of the four words might be operative, depending on the meaning intended. Operative words are not, of course, chosen arbitrarily. Although different actors will make different choices, the choices the actors make should reveal their understanding of the playwright's text and their sensitivity to the uses of language.

Of course, vocabulary needs attention in all plays, not just verse plays from other periods. Actors from one ethnicity, social class, or geographical region may not be immediately familiar with the slang and syntax used by characters from another ethnicity, social class, or region. And most American actors will need help with the meaning of this Cockney dialogue in Edward Bond's *Early Morning:*

> LEN:  We'd bin stood there 'ours, and me guts starts t' rumble. 'Owever, I
>   don't let on. But then she 'as t' say "I ain arf pecky."
>
> JOYCE:  Thass yer sense a consideration, ain it! I'd 'eard your gut.
>
> LEN:  I 'ad an empty gut many times, girl. That don't mean I'm on the
>   danger list. But when you starts rabbitin' about bein' pecky I. . . .
>   You're a rabbitin' ol' git! 'Ear that?[1]

In fact, practically every play demands close examination of its particular idiom. Michael Weller's *Moonchildren* depends heavily on the audience's familiarity with college slang of the 1960s; *Short Eyes,* by Miguel Piñero, makes heavy use of ethnic and prison slang (the term *short eyes* itself is prison slang for a child molester); and one would have to know a whole range of urban or "street" slang to extract nuances of meaning from many of the lines in plays representing that social class.

## Handling Sentences

An actor who is ignorant of the basic rules of grammar cannot possibly interpret and communicate a playwright's lines. No matter what the role or the play, you must have the ability to recognize subjects and predicates, modifying words, phrases, and clauses, and you must understand the principles of subordination and pronoun reference. Jerzy Grotowski wrote:

> The ability to handle sentences is important and necessary in acting. The sentence is an integral unit, emotional and logical, that can be sustained by a single expiratory and melodic wave. It is a whirlwind concentrated on an epicentrum [focal center] formed by the logical accent or accents. The vowels at this epicentrum should not be shortened but rather prolonged slightly in order to give them a special value, taking good care not to break up the unity of the sentence with unjustified pauses. . . .
>
> In poetry too, the sentence must be considered as a logical and emotional entity to be pronounced in one single respiratory wave. Several lines (one and a half, two, or more) often constitute the sentence.[2]

Understanding the sentence as a structural unit, recognizing the relationship and relative importance of its different parts, determining the operative words (or logical accents as Grotowski called them), and keeping the sentence moving toward its epicentrum is one of your principal areas of concern in dealing with the language of a play. Grotowski's warning against unjustified pauses should be heeded, because unnecessary pauses, whether for an intake of breath or for any other reason, obscure the relationship of the parts of the sentence, which blurs the meaning, and destroy the rhythmic flow that is essential to the form. Good actors handle sentences so the words are constantly moving forward toward a focal point. The problem can be more complex than Grotowski suggests. In *The Tempest,* Prospero's "Farewell to His Art" (Act V, Scene 1) has a sentence that is seventeen-and-a-half lines long, and Juliet's potion speech (Act IV, Scene 3) has a sentence of eighteen lines. Let's look at some sentences, less complex than those just mentioned, that illustrate this problem.

In *Major Barbara,* by George Bernard Shaw, Lady Britomart answers the protest that she treats her grown-up offspring like children.

> I have always made you my companions and friends, and allowed you perfect freedom to do and say whatever you liked, so long as you liked what I could *approve* of.[3]

Here is a sentence of thirty-one words that can be handled as a "single melodic wave," culminating in the operative word *approve*. To select *approve* as the operative word does not mean that other words in the sentence do not have a degree of importance and should not receive some manner of emphasis. But *approve* is a logical choice, because in Lady Britomart's mind her approval is more important than the freedom she claims to allow. It helps reveal her dominating character, and it highlights the comic contradiction of the line by suggesting that she is blameworthy of the very charge she is denying.

The following line from Arthur Kopit's *Indians* presents a similar, but more difficult, problem. John Grass, a young Indian, testifies before a group of senators sent by the President of the United States, the Great Father, to investigate charges of mistreatment. He talks about the futile and bungling attempts of a missionary bishop to help the situation:

> But when we told him we did not wish to be Christians but wished to be like our fathers, and dance the sundance, and fight bravely against the Shawnee and the Crow! And pray to the Great Spirits who made the four winds, and the earth, and made man from the dust of this earth, Bishop Marty *hit* us![4]

This is a group of fifty-nine words, punctuated as two sentences but constituting a single logical and emotional entity, always moving toward the operative word *hit*. Grammatically, "Bishop Marty hit us" is the principal clause, and *hit* is the main verb of the entire unit. Logically, it is John Grass's purpose to impress on the senators the mistreatment the Indians have received, in spite of what (to them, at least) has been a reasonable attitude. Emotionally, he feels very deeply about the physical abuse they have suffered. Kopit's choice of the word *hit* is peculiarly expressive of John Grass's uncomplicated earnestness and naiveté.

In *Blues for Mister Charlie,* by James Baldwin, a mature white man tells about his love for a young African American woman:

> I used to look at her, the way she moved, so beautiful and free, and I'd wonder if at night, when she might be on her way home from someplace, any of those boys at school had said *ugly things* to her.[5]

The speaker realized that at the school they attended, an African American girl's permitting any kind of relationship with a Caucasian boy subjected her to a good deal of cruel comment. In expressing this concern, the whole sentence must move forward to *ugly things*. This speech also affords the actor a chance to observe the principles of subordination, to pick out the main structure, the "skeleton," and to relate the less important parts to it. Here is the skeleton of this sentence:

> I used to look at her . . . and I'd wonder if . . . any of those boys . . . had said ugly things to her.

The other parts must be made subordinate.

**Exercise 11.1  FINDING OPERATIVE WORDS**   Select a speech of at least twelve lines spoken by a character in a play on which you are working. Look up all the words (with the exception, perhaps, of articles and conjunctions) to make certain you understand the possible range of meanings of the passage. If necessary, do a prosaic, line-by-line paraphrase—especially if the speech is from a verse play. Find the operative words.

Remember, each sentence may have more than one operative word, but each sentence should be unified into a single structure with its parts related to the whole through the proper use of subordination. Memorize this speech, and rehearse it until you have control of both its meaning and its form.

# Building a Progression

In the previous section, we stressed the importance of finding the operative words and of directing the rest of the sentence toward them—if not like a whirlwind, as Grotowski suggested, at least in some form of progression. We must feel when actors are speaking that their lines are "going somewhere," and following this **progression** keeps the audience listening. Even moments of silence (not to be confused with unnecessary pauses) must drive the dramatic action forward. Actors, like travelers, must keep moving toward some predetermined destination, and they must structure their dialogue with this direction in mind.

Besides the examples already cited, dramatists have other ways of giving direction and forward movement to their lines. The simplest is a series of two or more parts, in which each part receives increasing emphasis as the series progresses. One of the best-known lines in dramatic literature, the beginning of Antony's funeral oration for Julius Caesar (Act III, Scene 2), is such a series:

Friends, Romans, countrymen, lend me your ears

In Act I, Scene 1 of *Romeo and Juliet,* Shakespeare uses a similar construction when the Prince of Verona breaks up the street brawl between the Montagues and the Capulets:

Rebellious subjects, enemies to peace,
Profaners of this neighbour-stained steel—
Will they not hear? What ho! you men, you beasts. . . .

In *The Lady's Not for Burning,* by Christopher Fry, Jennet has told how her father, an alchemist, once accidentally turned base metal into gold and how he died trying to rediscover the formula. The cynical Thomas Mendip answers that if he had been successful:

. . . you
Would be eulogized, lionized, probably
Canonized for your divine mishap.[6]

Effective handling of progressions requires looking to the end of the series and building it to a climax.

Playwrights may also use a **ladder device,** in which the idea is "stepped up," like ascending the rungs of a ladder, by a careful progression of words. Starting at the bottom, one must look to the top rung. In Act V, Scene 2 of *Hamlet,* Claudius makes the following toast to Hamlet before the duel he has plotted between Hamlet and Laertes:

> And let the *kettle* to the *trumpet* speak,
> The *trumpet* to the *cannoneer* without,
> The *cannons* to the *heavens,* the *heavens* to the *earth:*
> "Now the king drinks to Hamlet!"

Hamlet's mother (Act III, Scene 4) is overcome with grief when he makes her aware of her guilty behavior:

> Be thou assur'd, if words be made of *breath,*
> And *breath* of *life,* I have no *life* to *breathe*
> What thou hast said to me.

A delightfully complex example of this device occurs in Act V, Scene 2 of *As You Like It* when Rosalind tells Orlando how Celia and Oliver fell in love:

> . . . For your brother and my sister no sooner *met,* but they *look'd;* no sooner *look'd,* but they *lov'd;* no sooner *lov'd,* but they *sigh'd;* no sooner *sigh'd,* but they ask'd one another the *reason;* no sooner knew the *reason,* but they sought the *remedy.* And in these degrees have they made a pair of stairs to marriage, which they will *climb incontinent,* or else *be* incontinent before marriage.

Another way dramatists "progress" the lines is by piling, one on top of another, details that accumulate to create a total effect. This is called a **periodic structure.** Here, the term *periodic* means "consisting of a series of repeated stages," which well describes this method. The repeated stages build to a climax, with no trailing subordinate elements afterward to minimize their effectiveness. Again, this structure is easily recognized when read silently but requires careful handling when spoken. From the very beginning, the actor must look forward to the end and keep moving toward it. Shakespeare often used periodic structure; a classic example is John of Gaunt's soaring description of England in Act II, Scene 1 of *Richard II:*

> This royal throne of kings, this scept'red isle,
> This earth of majesty, this seat of Mars,
> This other Eden, demiparadise,
> This fortress built by Nature for herself
> Against infection and the hand of war,

This happy breed of men, this little world,
This precious stone set in a silver sea,
Which serves it in the office of a wall
Or as a moat defensive to a house
Against the envy of less happier lands;
This blessed plot, this earth, this realm, this
England. . . .

This great speech actually contains several more "stages" before the final climax. Speaking it well is a strong challenge for even the finest actor, but practicing it will prepare you to deliver simpler instances of this structure with ease.

And prepare you must, for all good playwrights use periodic structure, although not always so formally as the ringing example from *Richard II*. Sean O'Casey uses it in *Juno and the Paycock*, when Mrs. Madigan describes how "her man" used to court her:

"That'll scratch your lovely, little white neck," says he, ketchin' hould of a danglin' bramble branch, holdin' clusters of the loveliest flowers you ever seen, an' breakin' it off, so that his arm fell, accidental like, roun' me waist, an' as I felt it tightenin', an tightenin', an tightenin', I thought me buzzom was every minute goin' to burst out into a roystherin' song about "The little green leaves that were shakin' on the threes, The gallivantin' buttherflies, an' buzzin' o' the bees!"[7]

Arthur Kopit uses this same type of periodic structure for building a progression in *Indians* when Wild Bill Hickok is standing over the beautiful Teskanjavila:

Hickok, fastest shooter in the West, 'cept for Billy the Kid, who ain't as accurate; Hickok, deadliest shooter in the West, 'cept for Doc Holliday, who wields a sawed-off shotgun, which ain't fair; Hickok, shootinest shooter in the West, 'cept for Jesse James, who's absolutely indiscriminate; this Hickok, strong as an eagle, tall as a mountain, swift as the wind, fierce as a rattle-snake—a legend in his own time, or any other— this Hickok stands now above an Indian maiden. . . .[8]

It is interesting to note how, for comic effect, Kopit has Teskanjavila ruin the climax of Hickok's splendid speech, forcing him to weaken the periodic structure by adding subordinate elements:

TESKANJAVILA: I'm not an Indian and I'm not a maiden!

HICKOK: Who's not an Indian and not a maiden, but looks pretty good anyhow. . . .

# Thinking Antithetically

"Suit the action to the word, the word to the action." Particularly with the plays of William Shakespeare, you must look for **antitheses.** As Shakespeare also wrote in *Richard II*, ". . . set the word itself against the word. . . ." "We can easily overlook it because we don't use antithesis very much today, particularly in our everyday speech," said John Barton, Associate Director of the Royal Shakespeare Company. "Yet Shakespeare was deeply imbued with the sense of it. He *thought* antithetically. It was the way his sentences over and over found their shape and their meaning. . . . 'Antithesis' is in a way a bad word for something very practical. It sounds obscure and learned."[9]

Perhaps it would simply be better to use Shakespeare's description and set one word or phrase against another. This is yet another of the actor's paradoxes. Although you must constantly build your progressions toward culminating points, you must also refer to what has already been said. Every word must either *qualify* what has preceded it or change the direction of the action. "If we don't set up one word," added Barton, "we won't prepare for another to qualify it. And if the next word doesn't build on the first and move the sentence on, both the audience and the actor may lose their way."[10] In this manner, we think antithetically. Actors frequently do not understand antithetical construction and consequently choose to "operate" on a word or phrase that has already been emphasized, rather than to find the antithesis that will advance the idea. Hamlet's "To be, or not to be" (Act III, Scene 1) is a simple antithetical phrase. However, the operative words found in the next sentence are less clear.

> Whether 'tis nobler in the mind to suffer
> The slings and arrows of outrageous fortune,
> Or to take arms against a sea of troubles,
> And by opposing end them?

*Sea of troubles* refers back to and, in this case, is synonymous with *outrageous fortune*. The operative words that carry the idea forward thus are *take arms*.

Portia's famous mercy speech in *The Merchant of Venice* (Act IV, Scene 1) begins with an antithetical phrase. After all legal recourses to save Antonio's life have been fruitless, she declares that Shylock must be merciful. But he retorts with:

> On what compulsion must I? tell me that.

And Portia answers

> The quality of mercy is not strained,
> It droppeth as the gentle rain from heaven
> Upon the place beneath. . . .

*Strained* means *forced* or *compelled* and is used antithetically against Shylock's *compulsion.* If an actor does not use the antithetical phrasing to clarify subtext, the audience will not follow the progression. The use of antithesis looks backward; however, it is a primary means of driving the dramatic action forward.

Contrasting two words or phrases or emphasizing the possibility of two or more alternatives is another means of speaking antithetically. When you recognize this device in a line, it is almost impossible to read it without correctly emphasizing each of the different terms or alternatives. This mode of expression is apparent in such well-known sayings as "It is more blessed to *give* than to *receive*" or by the double-contrast in "To *err* is *human;* to *forgive, divine.*" A few examples, from both contemporary and classic plays, will further clarify this usage:

> Respect what *other people see* and touch even if it's the opposite of what *you see* and touch![11]

> An investigation of *my* affairs would lead to an investigation of *his* affairs. . . .[12]

> ALICE: Kurt, we're *leaving.*

> EDGAR: You're *staying.*[13]

> I pray you, father, *being* weak, *seem* so.[14]

> I have *hope* to *live,* and am *prepar'd* to *die.*[15]

> And let my *liver* rather *heat* with *wine*

> Than my *heart cool* with mortifying *groans.*[16]

> Let that fool *kill hisse'f.* Ain't no call for *you to he'p him.*[17]

> OL' CAP'N: Who's been putting these integrationary ideas in my boy's head? Was it you—I'm asking you a question, dammit! Was it *you?*

> IDELLA: Why don't you ask *him?*[18]

## Sharing Imagery

In Chapter 7 we discussed the technique of relating to images or pictures that actors supply from their imagination. Playwrights also make extensive use of images in their dialogue, and communicating these images to the audience through the dramatist's words is one of the actor's major tasks in handling language. Peter Brook explained:

> The exchange of impressions through images is our basic language: at the moment when one man expresses an image at that same instant the other man meets him in belief. The shared association is the language— if the association evokes nothing in the second person, if there is no instance of shared illusion, there is no exchange. . . . The vividness and

Photo by Mark Garvin.

**Figure 11.2**   Elizabeth Van Dyke and Marcus Naylor in *No Niggers, No Jews, No Dogs,* by John Henry Redwood, produced by Philadelphia Theatre Company—World Premiere Winter 2001. The eyes are the mirror of the soul, and truthful imagery shows itself most vividly through the eyes of the actor.

the fullness of this momentary illusion depends on his [the speaker's] conviction and skill.[19]

Laurence Perrine defined imagery as "the representation through language of sense experience." And, of course, sensory experience is one of the pleasures derived from going to the theatre. Perrine's definition continues:

> The word *image* perhaps most often suggests a mental picture, some-thing seen in the mind's eye—and visual imagery is the most frequently occurring kind. . . . But an image may also represent a sound; a smell; a taste; a tactile experience, such as hardness, wetness, or cold; an internal sensation, such as hunger, thirst, or nausea; or movement or tension in the muscles or joints.[20]

Images are either *literal* or *figurative,* although they both serve the same purpose of providing a vivid sensory experience. A figurative image expresses something in terms ordinarily used for expressing something else; thus, some comparison is either stated or implied. A literal image is a direct description couched in terms intended to stimulate a sensory response. "The russet dawn colors the eastern sky" and "She talks about her secret as she sleeps upon her pillow" are literal images. But in *Hamlet* and *Macbeth,* Shakespeare says in figurative language:

> But look, the morn in russet mantle clad,
> Walks o'er the dew of yon high eastward hill,

and

> Infected minds
> To their deaf pillows will discharge their secrets.

The terminology relating to imagery can be very complex; indeed, more than two hundred kinds of figurative speech have been identified. It is neither necessary nor desirable for you to become entangled in such subtlety. It is essential, however, that for both literal and figurative images you appreciate the sensory experience the playwright is expressing. For figurative language, you must also understand the aptness of the comparison. Most important of all, you must respond to imagery with all your senses before you can communicate it to an audience. Sam Shepard's description in *Red Cross* of swimming in the rain provides a rich example:

> JIM: . . . Your body stays warm inside. It's just the outside that gets wet. It's really neat. I mean you can dive under water and hold your breath. You stay under for about five minutes. You stay down there and there's nothing but water all around you. Nothing but marine life. You stay down as long as you can until your lungs start to ache. They feel like they're going to burst open. Then just at the point where you can't stand it any more you force yourself to the top. You explode out of the water gasping for air, and all this rain hits you in the face. You ought to try it.[21]

Shakespeare created exquisite images. Consider this example from *Macbeth:*

Now does he feel
His secret murders sticking on his hands.

and from *King Lear:*

Thou art a bile,
A plague-sore, an embossed carbuncle,
In my corrupted blood.

Imagery has particular power to affect the emotions of both the actor and his audience. Consider Constance's moving lament for her lost son in *The Life and Death of King John:*

Grief fills the room up of my absent child,
Lies in his bed, walks up and down with me,
Puts on his pretty looks, repeats his words,
Remembers me of all his gracious parts,
Stuffs out his vacant garments with his form.

Imagery can be beautiful, as in Romeo's rhapsody when he first sees Juliet:

O, she doth teach the torches to burn bright.
It seems she hangs upon the cheek of night
As a rich jewel in an Ethiop's ear.

It can be folksy, as in O'Casey's *The Shadow of a Gunman*:

Mrs. Henderson: I'm afraid he'll never make a fortune out of what he's
sellin'. . . . Every time he comes to our place I buy a package o'
hairpins from him to give him a little encouragement. I 'clare to God I
have as many pins now as ud make a wire mattress for a double bed.[22]

It can be earthy, as in Davis's *Purlie Victorious:*

Ol' Cap'n: You don't know, boy, what a strong stomach it takes to stomach
you. Just look at you sitting there—all slopped over like something the
horses dropped; steam, stink and all![23]

---

**Exercise 11.2   PRACTICE MATERIAL FOR COMMUNICATING SUBTEXT**   Work on several of the following speeches, exploring the language and using it fully to communicate the words, images, and overall meaning.

**A.** Taw in *August Snow*, by Reynolds Price[24]

Taw: Since I was an orphan so early in life, I taught myself to avoid dreams—
dreams at night, good or bad. They seemed one strain I could spare myself;

Used by permission of the Virginia Commonwealth University. Photo by Jay Paul.

**Figure 11.3**    James Manno, Robert Miller, and Megan Carboni in a scene from Virginia Commonwealth University's production of *Metamorphoses*. Directed by Ron Nakahara, scenic design by Ron Keller, costume design by Karl Green. The strong visual images in this scene have a powerful effect upon both the actor and the audience.

and I honestly think, in all these years, I've never had two dozen dreams—not to speak of. Neal dreams like a dog by the stove when he's here, the rare nights I get to guard his sleep. Last night though when I finally dozed, sad as I was, I lived through a dream as real as day. I'd finished my teacher's diploma and was ready to save the world around me, all children. What thrilled me was *that*—they were all young and not too hard yet to help. I'd show them the main thing an orphan knows—how to tuck your jaw and brave hails of pain and come out strong as a good drayhorse or a rock-ribbed house on a cliff by water. But once I entered my class the first day and trimmed my pencil and faced the desks, I saw they'd given me twenty grown men—all with straight sets of teeth. I prayed I was wrong, that I'd got the wrong room. Still I said my name, and the oldest man at the back of the room stood tall at last in a black serge suit and said, "Don't wait another minute to start. We've paid our way." I had a quick chill of fright that I'd fail; but then I thought of the week they died—my mother and father, of Spanish flu—and I knew I did have a big truth to tell, the main one to know. I opened my mouth and taught those grown men every last fact an orphan needs and learns from the day she's left—courage and trust and a craving for time.

**B.** Jonathan in *Sight Unseen*, by Donald Margulies[25]

JONATHAN:  I went to pack up his house the other day? My parents' house? All his clothes, my old room, my mother's sewing machine, all those rooms of furniture. Strange being in a place where no one lives anymore. [. . .] (*A beat*) Anyway, what I found was, he'd taken all the family pictures, everything that was in albums, shoved in drawers—hundreds of them—and covered an entire wall with them, floor to ceiling, side to side. I first saw it years ago, when he'd started. It was his Sistine Chapel; it took him years. He took my hand (I'll never forget this) he took my hand—he was beaming: "*You're* an artist," he said to me, "*you'll* appreciate this." He was so proud of himself I thought I was gonna cry. Proud and also in a strange way competitive? [. . .]

So, there was this wall. The Waxman family through the ages. Black-and-white, sepia, Kodachrome. My great-grandparents in the shtetl, my brother's baby pictures on top of my parents' courtship, me at my bar mitzvah. Well, it was kind of breathtaking. I mean, the sweep of it, it really was kind of beautiful. I came closer to examine it—I wanted to see how he'd gotten them all up there—and then I saw the staples. [. . .]

Staples! Tearing through the faces and the bodies. "Look what you've done," I wanted to say. "How could you be so thoughtless? You've ruined everything!" But of course I didn't say that. How could I? He was like a little boy. Beaming. Instead I said, "Dad! What a wonder job!" (*A beat*) So, there I was alone in his house, pulling staples out of our family photos. These documents that showed where I came from. Did they *mean* anything to him at all? I mean as artifacts, as proof of a former civilization, when my mother was vibrant and he was young and strong and we were a family? (*A beat*) That's all gone now, Patty. It's all gone.

**C.** Marion in *Abingdon Square*, by Maria Irene Fornes[26]

MARION:  It was he. There was no doubt in my mind. I say him and I knew it was he. [. . .] I took a book and buried my head in it. I was afraid. I thought if he saw me he would know and I would die. He didn't. I saw him leave. For a moment I was relieved he hadn't seen me and I stayed behind the stacks. But then I was afraid I'd lose him. I went to the front and I watched him walk away through the glass windows. Then, I followed him . . . a while . . . but then I lost him because I didn't want to get too near him. I went back there each day. To the bookstore and to the place where I had lost him. A few days later I saw him again and I followed him. Each time I saw him I followed him. I stood in corners and in doorways until I saw him pass. Then I followed him. I was cautious but he became aware of me. One day he turned a corner and I hurried behind him. He was there, around the corner, waiting for me.

I screamed and he laughed. He grabbed me by the arm. And I ran. I ran desperately. I saw an open entranceway to a basement and I ran in. I hid there till it was dark. Not till then did I dare come out. When I saw that he wasn't there I came home. I haven't been outside since then. I'll never go out again, not even to the corner. I don't want to see him. I don't want him to see me. I'm ashamed of myself. I'm a worthless person. I don't know how I could have done what I did. I have to do penance.

**D.** Eddie in *Fool for Love,* by Sam Shepard[27]

(*After pushing his half-sister's boyfriend, Martin, against the wall and pulling him to the ground, Eddie tells the story of their father's mysterious walks and the beginning of his love affair with his half-sister.*)

EDDIE:  But one night I asked him if I could go with him. And he took me. We walked straight out across the fields together. In the dark. And I remember it was just plowed and our feet sank down in the powder and the dirt came up over the tops of my shoes and weighed me down. I wanted to stop and empty my shoes out but he wouldn't stop. He kept walking straight ahead and I was afraid of losing him in the dark so I just kept up as best I could. And we were completely silent the whole time. Never said a word to each other. We could barely see a foot in front of us, it was so dark. And these white owls kept swooping down out of nowhere, hunting for jackrabbits. Diving right past our heads, then disappearing. And we just kept walking silent like that for miles until we got to town. I could see the drive-in movie way off in the distance. That was the first thing I saw. Just square patches of color shifting. Then vague faces began to appear. And, as we got closer, I could recognize one of the faces. It was Spencer Tracy. Spencer Tracy moving his mouth. Speaking without words. Speaking to a woman in a red dress. Then we stopped at a liquor store and he made me wait outside in the parking lot while he bought a bottle. And there were all these Mexican migrant workers standing around a pick-up truck with red mud all over the tires. They were drinking beer and laughing and I remember being jealous of them and I didn't know why. And I remember seeing the old man through the glass door of the liquor store as he paid for the bottle. And I remember feeling sorry for him and I didn't know why. Then he came outside with the bottle wrapped in a brown paper sack and as soon as he came out, all the Mexican men stopped laughing. They just stared at us as we walked away. And we walked right through town. Past the donut shop, past the miniature golf course, past the Chevron station. And he opened the bottle up and offered it to me. Before he even took a drink, he offered it to me first. And I took it and drank it and handed it back to him. And we just kept passing it back and forth like that as we walked until we drank the whole thing dry. And we never said a word the whole time.

**E.** Mags in *Painting Churches*, by Tina Howe[28]

MAGS:  It was wintertime, because I noticed I'd left some crayons on top of my
radiator and they'd melted down into these beautiful shimmering globs, like
spilled jello, trembling and pulsing. [. . .] Naturally, I wanted to try it myself,
so I grabbed a red one and pressed it down against the hissing lid. It oozed
and bubbled like raspberry jam! [. . .] I mean, that radiator was really hot! It
took incredible will power not to let go, but I held on, whispering, "Mags, if
you let go of this crayon, you'll be run over by a truck on Newberry Street,
so help you God!" . . . So I pressed down harder, my fingers steaming and
blistering. [. . .] Once I'd melted one, I was hooked! I finished off my entire
supply in one night, mixing color over color until my head swam! . . . The
heat, the smell, the brilliance that sank and rose . . . I'd never felt such
exhilaration! . . . Every week I spent my allowance on crayons. I must have
cleared out every box of Crayolas in the city! [. . .] AFTER THREE MONTHS
THAT RADIATOR WAS . . . SPECTACULAR! I MEAN, IT LOOKED LIKE
SOME COLOSSAL FRUITCAKE, FIVE FEET TALL . . .! [. . .] It was a knockout;
shimmering with pinks and blues, lavenders and maroons, turquoise and
golds, oranges and creams. . . . For every color, I imagined a taste . . .
YELLOW: lemon curls dipped in sugar . . . RED: glazed cherries laced with
rum . . . GREEN: tiny peppermint leaves veined with chocolate . . .
PURPLE:—[. . .] And then the frosting . . . ahhh, the frosting! A satiny mix of
white and silver . . . I kept it hidden under blankets during the day. . . . My
huge . . . (*She starts laughing*) looming . . . teetering sweet—[. . .] I was so . . .
*hungry* . . . losing weight every week. I looked like a scarecrow what with
the bags under my eyes and bits of crayon wrapper leaking out of my clothes.
It's a wonder you didn't notice. But finally you came to my rescue . . . if you
could call what happened a rescue. It was more like a rout! The winter
was almost over. . . . It was very late at night. . . . I must have been having
a nightmare because suddenly you and Daddy were at my bed, shaking
me. . . . I quickly glanced towards the radiator to see if it was covered. . . .
*It wasn't!* It glittered and towered in the moonlight like some . . . gigantic
Viennese pastry!

**F.** Leo Hart in *Coastal Disturbances*, by Tina Howe[29]

LEO:  . . . All the guys in school were in love with her. We used to fantasize: if she
has extra fingers, what *else* does she have tucked out of view . . . ? [. . .] We
couldn't figure out what she was doing in Essex. She must have been
studying with some famous organist in the area. She didn't stay long. Only a
year, but what a year . . . ! I used to climb the elm tree next to the First
Congregational Church where she practiced in the evening and watch her. I
lived in that fucking tree! On a clear night, there were as many as forty guys
up there with binoculars. But no one was as loyal as me. . . . It's funny, I

don't remember the music at all, and she was really good. I mean, when she cut loose with those preludes and fugues, she practically shook the stained glass right off the walls—those lambs and apostles jitterbugged like nothing you ever saw. . . . No, it was all her—the way she hunched over the keys, how her hair fell across her face, and of course all those flying fingers. Sometimes I counted as many as eight on a hand. . . . Finally, I couldn't take it anymore, I had to do something. I'll never forget it. . . . One night I was up in my tree as usual, when all of a sudden I found myself marching right up into the organ loft and bam—there I was, face to face with her. She was so flushed and beautiful, I could hardly keep my balance. . . . I reached out to steady myself and set off this blizzard of sheet music. She lets out this piercing scream as if she's just met up with Jack the Ripper, I mean we are talking disaster city here . . . and then I notice some of her fingers kind of . . . disappearing down into her palm . . . and she's wriggling around on the bench as if she's trying to hide something. [. . .] It was awful. [. . .] I threw myself at her feet. [. . .] I began telling her that I loved her, that I'd always love her, that I wanted to marry her and be with her forever. But she didn't seem to understand so I grabbed her. [. . .] I wanted to protect her. By this time, she was screaming in every foreign language you've ever heard. The louder she screamed, the tighter I held on to her. It was a nightmare. [. . .] It was shortly after that, that her family moved away. I thought I'd never recover. I mooned around for almost two years. I'll tell you one thing—she could have given one hell of a backrub.

**G.** Pooty in *Reckless*, by Craig Lucas[30]

POOTY:  When I lost the use of my legs a friend drove me up here to Springfield to take a look at this place where they worked with the handicapped. I watched the physical therapists working with the patients and there was one: I remember he was working with a quadriplegic. I thought he was the most beautiful man I'd ever seen. A light shining out through his skin. And I thought if I couldn't be with him I'd die. But I knew I would just be one more crippled dame as far as he was concerned, so my friend helped to get me registered as deaf and disabled. I used to teach sign language to the hearing impaired. I thought if I were somehow needier than the rest I would get special attention. I realized soon enough: everyone gets special attention where Lloyd is concerned. But by then it was too late. He was in love with me, with my honesty. He learned to sign; he told me how he'd run away from a bad marriage and changed his name so he wouldn't have to pay child support. He got me a job at Hands Across the Sea and I couldn't bring myself to tell him that I had another name and another life, that I'd run away too, because I owed the government so much money and wasn't able to pay after the accident. I believe in honesty. I believe in total honesty. And I need him and he needs me to be the person he thinks I am and I am that person, I really am that person. I'm a crippled deaf girl, short and stout. Here is my wheelchair, here is my mouth. [. . .] When he goes out I babble. I recite poetry I remember from grade school. I talk back to the television. I even call people on the phone and say it's a wrong number just to have a conversation. I'm afraid I'm going to open my mouth to scream one day and . . . (*She does; no sound*)

**H.** Alen in *The Reeves Tale,* by Don Nigro[31]

(*Alen is plotting a rendezvous with Sim and Abby's daughter, Molkin.*)

ALEN: I got it all planned, like a military operation, just like the Bay of Pigs or something. Okay, bad example. Look, we got three beds here, right? Just like the three bears. Now, before Sim hired us, they slept Sim and Abby in the one over on the end, right? [. . .] They're disoriented, John, because to make room for us, we got Molkin's old bed on the other end, which you and me share, and she's in the near bed with Abby, and Sim's in the middle with Pap. So once Sim gets to snoring good, and Molkin goes to sleep, what does Abby do? She goes out in the kitchen and smokes a cigarette. Every night. Just like clockwork. So when she goes out for her smoke, you follow her out there and keep her busy for half an hour or so, talk to her or something. Hell, screw her on the table if she'll let you. That asshole Sim is driving her nuts. She could probably use a little something to take her mind off her life. You know, you two being so sensitive and all. [. . .] John, that girl ain't been a flower since she was fourteen. She knows what she's doing, believe me. And Abby don't care. What does she care? Come on, take a chance. You might get lucky. This is America, here. This is like the spirit of free enterprise at work, John. You know what I mean? John? Please?

**I.** Li'l Bit in *How I Learned to Drive,* by Paula Vogel[32]

(*Li'l Bit is describing a night she remembers from her childhood in the context of a driving lesson.*)

LI'L BIT: In a parking lot overlooking the Beltsville Agricultural Farms in suburban Maryland. Less than a mile away, the crumbling concrete of U.S. One wends its way past one-room revival churches, the porno drive-in, the boarded up motels with For Sale signs tumbling down. . . . it's a warm summer evening. Here on the land the Department of Agriculture owns, the smell of the leather dashboard. You can still imagine how Maryland used to be, before the malls took over. This countryside was once dotted with farmhouses—from their porches you could have witnessed the Civil War raging in the front fields. Oh yes. There's a moon over Maryland tonight, that spills into the car where I sit beside a man old enough to be—did I mention how still the night is? Damp soil and tranquil air. It's the kind of night that makes a middle-aged man with a mortgage feel like a country boy again.

**J.** Sebastian in *Raised in Captivity,* by Nicky Silver[33]

SEBASTIAN:   It was hot, August, and the temperature must've reached a hundred and ten in that front yard. There were about two dozen children there, none of whom I particularly liked, and none of whom was having a particularly good time. We just sat there, sad, withered children on a patch of brown, burned-up grass. My mother had, as always, planned every moment of the day with military precision. Two o'clock: three-legged races. Two fifteen: passing oranges under our chins. At three o'clock, the entertainment arrived. A clown: Mr. Giggles. Mr. Giggles was *extremely* old. It's true that all adults seem old to small children, but Mr. Giggles would have seemed *very-old* to very old people! He was old. . . . In any event, Mr. Giggles made flowers spring from umbrellas and foam balls appear from behind our ears. He was maniacally cheerful, despite the fact that none of us joined in or laughed or moved. Mr. Giggles thought some singing might rouse us from our collective coma. He sang "A Hundred Bottles of Beer on the Wall." Only we were ten, so he sang "A Hundred Bottles of *Milk* on the Wall." . . . He sang loudly and with what should have been infectious joy: "A hundred bottles of milk on the wall, a hundred bottles of milk!" And we tried! We did. At first. . . . Mr. Giggles ran around in a desperate frenzy, wild for us to perform—but it was so hot! . . . I just stopped. I lay down, put my head on the earth and shut my eyes. Well, Mr. Giggles ran over and knelt down and sang *right* at me, loud, shouting more than singing really. Screaming right at me: "EIGHTY-TWO BOTTLES OF MILK ON THE WALL! EIGHTY-TWO BOTTLES OF MILK!" I refused to stir. I just opened my eyes and stared at this *fascist* clown. Then another little boy stopped. . . . Giggles leapt upon him and shrieked with rage, "EIGHTY-ONE BOTTLES OF MILK ON THE WALL! EIGHTY-ONE BOTTLES OF MILK!" Then very quickly, other children followed suit. . . . By now Mr. Giggles was in the throes of a demented fit! Running crazily from child to child, screaming, spit flying out of him, sweat spraying off of him.—But he would not give up! By now, no one was singing, . . . I watched as Giggles flapped his arms like spastic birds and lost the count completely: "FORTY-TWO BOTTLES OF MILK ON THE WALL! FORTY-EIGHT BOTTLES OF MILK!" And then he fell over in a sad, wet, broken-pencil heap. . . . "He's dead," I whispered. Bernadette shrieked and ran in horror from the yard and into the street, where a bread truck swerved to avoid her and ran headlong into a mammoth oak tree, shaking from its perch our cat, which fell to an ugly, bloody death, impaled by the truck's antenna and splattered on the windshield.

# Terms and People to Know

**antithesis**   Setting one word or phrase against another word or phrase. Shakespeare's line, "Suit the action to the word, the word to the action," is an example of an antithetical phrase.

**build**   To increase the intensity of a line or physical action to reach a climax.

**ladder device**   Playwright's device in which an idea is "stepped up," like ascending the rungs of a ladder, by a careful *progression* of words.

**operative word**   A key word or logical accent within the structure of each phrase of dialogue.

**pacing**   The rate of speed at which the actors speak their lines, pick up their cues, act upon their impulses, telescope the dialogue, and hold the moments of silence.

**periodic structure**   Playwriting device in which details are piled one on top of another to increase dramatic effect.

**"pick up cues"**   A direction for the actor to begin a counteraction immediately on the impulse to do so—whether it be internally within another person's verbal or physical action (see *telescoping*) or at the end of a fellow actor's action.

**pointing**   Giving special emphasis to a word, phrase, or action.

**progression**   The forward movement of lines and dramatic action toward a predetermined destination.

**tag line**   The last line of a scene or an act. It usually needs to be *pointed*.

**telescoping**   Overlapping speeches so one actor speaks before another has finished. It is a realistic technique for providing the illusion of accelerated *pace* and building a climax.

**top**   To "build" or intensify a line or physical action higher than the one that preceded it.

# Getting the Job

> "... for every actor who gets hired for a part,
> fifty or a hundred or two hundred do not. An
> actor is forever trying to get a part; an actor is
> forever getting rejected, never knowing why,
> simply not wanted."[1]
>
> –Michael Shurtleff

**A**udition. The word itself sends a shock wave through every actor's body. The audition is entirely artificial; in many ways, it contradicts the technique training taught in legitimate acting classes. True, auditioning is a *form* of acting; however, it is not the same as performing in a play or film or on television, where you are engulfed into an imaginary world and "working off" your fellow actors. In the audition, there are no props, no set, no costumes. If you are lucky, the audition will take place in a theatre, but more times than not they will occur in an empty studio, hotel room, or conference hall. Indeed, auditioning is a necessary evil, and it will continue to plague actors until someone discovers a better way to cast a production.

No matter how great your talent, how extensive your training, how vast your experience—unless you are one of a few exceptions—you must audition to land a role. The actor's first encounter with the director is usually at this nerve-racking experience. Michael Shurtleff, whose book on auditioning has become the bible on the subject, warns, "In order to act, it is necessary to audition. . . . All the training in the world can go for naught if the actor in the reading situation can't convince the auditors he can perform the role."[2] Many good actors simply are not cast because they lack appropriate auditioning skills. It is naive to think that directors and producers should simply have faith in your abilities and trust your résumé in lieu of auditioning. With hundreds of actors vying for the same role, it is a buyer's market. Directors will hire someone they *know* they can trust, and this trust will begin with the audition.

Your ability to audition with professional competence defines your life and career as an actor. It is your one opportunity to make a first impression. Directors will not hire someone who lacks self-confidence or is intimidated by the audition process. You must present yourself as a working professional. You must be tenacious, removing the concept of rejection from your vocabulary. You must believe in your own talent and experience, and you must seize the moment as it arises.

How do you set yourself apart from others who are equally talented and just as right for the role? How do you present yourself in a positive manner without sounding conceited? Obnoxious? Loud? You begin by knowing and liking yourself. You must know your strengths and weaknesses—both internal and external. You must be comfortable with your body. Whether you like it or not, you are "selling" your talent and body. And you must find creative ways to do so.

From the director's point of view, the audition is a simple, time-saving way to become familiar with numerous actors and to attempt to identify those who most closely resemble their concept of the characters in the play being cast. The director uses the audition to find an actor who has the talent and the technique to play a certain role, who is physically right for the part, and who will blend well with the other cast members. Of course, if the audition is for a repertory company or a stock company, the directors are also looking for versatility. They are not against you. In fact, they are on your side. They simply want to mount a successful production of the play, and to do so they need the right actors. They hope you will be "the one" for which they are searching; they are pulling for you.

In most auditions, whether for stage, television, or film, an actor presents a **cold reading** from the script. Often actors receive the scene when they arrive for the audition and have only a short time to look it over. At other times, they simply may be interviewed by the director or asked to do a prepared monologue or scene for the occasion.

It has become customary at many auditions attended by representatives from various companies that actors be allotted a total of three minutes, during which they present one dramatic and one comedic piece prepared before their arrival.

At the Southeastern Theatre Conference Auditions, for example, the actor is allowed only ninety seconds to present a monologue and a song—and this includes the introduction, transition, and ending. After hearing the prepared auditions, companies conduct individual **callbacks** for further readings and interviews.

Usually, however, actors will audition for a particular production of a particular play. Most directors have their own system for holding auditions, and an actor should not be alarmed at one who uses unusual methods to determine a performer's suitability for a role. In *A Chorus Line,* a musical about dancers auditioning for a Broadway musical, the "director" asks the dancers to talk about themselves as well as to dance. Some of the dancers rise to the occasion; others do not.

Before launching directly into the preparation and presentation of the audition, let us take a moment to discuss the business.

## Understanding the Business of Acting

Actors are artists. Many of them do not like to think of theatre as a business. The truth is, without business skills—particularly in the area of marketing—no one will ever see your talent. You may be an artist, but *you* are also a business. You are the CEO, the CFO, and the sole shareholder of "You, Inc." The studio system is dead. An agent or personal manager will only get you so far. You have only yourself to rely on. You must take charge of your own affairs. In doing so, you must have a plan—including both short-term and long-term goals. You must know where you hope to be in one year. Five years. Ten years. And you must have a well-formed strategy of how you intend to accomplish your goals. You do not have to live in New York, Chicago, or Los Angeles to begin working on your plan. Rather, you must make things happen for "You, Inc.," one step at a time, beginning right now from wherever you are currently living.

As the CEO of your company, you must maintain your appearance. This does not mean that you have to present yourself as a Rush Limbaugh–style conservative, but most working actors present themselves as working professionals. Think of top actors such as Denzel Washington, Tom Hanks, Julia Roberts, and Mel Gibson. They do not have conspicuous body piercing, tattoos, or alternative hairstyles. As beautiful as they are, they present themselves as someone to whom we can all relate. They are individuals, but each one of them could be our neighbor, our friend.

Top actors also maintain their physiques. You must get in shape and stay in shape. This is particularly true in television and film, where you are either physically fit and considered for **straight parts** or a **character actor** who plays unusual or eccentric individuals. Our profession is not politically correct. Directors *are* looking at your body and how well you communicate with it. They *are* looking at your sexuality. They *are* judging your face, your hair, and your clothing.

Therefore, if you wish to "make it" in this business, you must maintain your physical appearance.

As a working professional, you should also consider your office supplies and equipment. Agents and casting directors must have immediate access to you twenty-four hours a day, seven days a week. You must have:

+ An answering service or machine with remote access.

+ A cell phone that you carry with you at all times.

+ Access to a fax machine.

+ Access to a computer and the Internet.

+ An e-mail address that you check several times each day.

+ Paper and pens by all telephones.

+ Maps of the city in which you are working and the ability to navigate from them.

+ A record book and filing system for all items pertaining to your career.

+ (Keep your receipts, for as a working actor, you are allowed tax breaks on your mileage, industry-related magazine and book purchases, research, educational expenses, etc.)

+ A current subscription to various trade magazines and newsletters such as: *Backstage, Black Talent News, Variety, Ross Reports, Latino Heat, Hollywood Reporter, Chicago Connection, American Theatre,* etc.

In other industries you have a business card, dossier, cover letter, letter of introduction and a résumé. As an actor you have your **headshot** and **résumé** to certify your professional background. They will not get you the job, but they might get you the audition. A good picture and résumé must create an interest in the eye and mind of the reviewer. The casting director must want to see the person behind the image in the photo and described on the résumé. If these marketing tools do not serve you well, you have done worse than waste your money; you have actually spent hard-earned cash to sabotage your own career. *Your headshot and résumé are your most important marketing tools.* Many times they are your *only* means by which to open the door to an audition that could lead to a job. If either one of these tools is not working for you, it is working against you. If your headshot fails to project your individuality, then you have paid someone a lot of money to obstruct your career. Remember, your picture and résumé are the only items you leave behind after the audition.

With regard to headshots, there are no "rules," but here are some general guidelines:

+ Avoid the temptation to save money by using a friend who dabbles in photography: Hire a professional photographer with experience in shooting headshots.

+ Look at portfolios showing examples of the photographer's work. Ask for references.

+ The most basic or classic look is a **black and white** of the head and shoulders, with the focus on the face. Trends change, but this is always acceptable. In this market, actors do not use color pictures.

+ Your picture, whether smiling or serious, needs to have direct eye contact with the camera—and there needs to be something "going on" in your eyes.

+ The phrase, "make love to the camera" may sound cliché, but that is exactly what you must do. A commercial look is usually a smiling or upbeat one, while a film look can be more serious. Many actors have two, even three different shots.

+ Have a natural look, and avoid using too much makeup. If you are uncomfortable doing your own, often the photographer can recommend a makeup artist.

+ Keep it simple. Avoid black-and-white clothing and busy patterns. Bring several tops with different collars and necklines to the photo shoot.

+ If shooting outside, rather than in a studio, avoid distracting backgrounds.

+ The classic size is 8″×10″. These come with various border choices, so check with your agent or colleagues to verify the best choice for your market.

+ Have your name embossed on the front of all reproductions.

In short, a casting director wants to see a photograph that really looks like you, not someone on the cover of *Vogue* or *GQ*. Your individuality is what separates you from the crowd, and that individuality should be used and expressed in a professionally produced headshot showing you at your best.

Your résumé should contain the history of your theatrical life. At the most basic level, it should contain personal, descriptive information. It must tell the producer or director about your training and your experience and about the people with whom you've worked, the kinds of theatres and productions in your background, and your union affiliations (**SAG, AFTRA, Equity**), if any. The résumé serves as the chief source of information about you. It should be accurate and arranged in a manner that is easy to comprehend. Here are general guidelines with regard to résumés:

+ Put your résumé on your computer so that it can be updated regularly.

+ Keep it to a single page, cut to fit your 8″×10″ headshot. Staple it to the backside of your photograph.

+ Specify your union affiliation (SAG, AFTRA, or AEA), if appropriate, directly under your name at the top of the page. If you are a member of the Equity Membership Candidacy (**EMC**) Program, you may list this.

+ Do not list your actual age or the age range you think you play. Why limit the director's vision or creativity?

**Figure 12.1**    Lauren Zapko

+ Give the name, address, and telephone number of your agent and/or manager if you have one. If you do not yet have an agent, use a post office box and an answering service.

+ You may wish to list your e-mail address. *Do not list your actual landline telephone number or physical home address!* You do not know the people for whom you are auditioning, and you are putting yourself in danger by including this information.

+ List your most important credits, beginning with your strongest. Once you have gained experience, you will begin with your most recent credits.

+ When starting out, do not be afraid to list small roles and *bit parts* (even background or "atmosphere" in film or TV, but be sure to specify it as *extra* work). You can list collegiate and other non-professional credits as long as you specify where the work was done.

+ Credits should include the title of the piece, the role, and the director and/or producing organization.

+ If you do not have any credits, list your classes and workshops. It shows you are committed to the business.

+ Be honest. The theatre is a small, close-knit community in which everybody seems to know everyone else. Lying will only get you in trouble. Remember, everybody started once. There is no shame in being a beginner.

+ List any special abilities you have: athletic skills, dancing, acrobatics, singing, dialects, foreign languages, musical instruments, magic, etc. Appraise yourself realistically and do not put down something you have only done once or twice.

+ You may be expected to deliver on your special skills.

+ Describe your professional training, educational background, etc. This is the best place to list your workshops, but keep it selective.

+ List your height, weight, and hair and eye color.

Your résumé, like your picture, must give as truthful a view of you as possible. Padded lists of roles you have performed in acting class simply do not fool auditors. Do not be ashamed of who you are. Present yourself with pride.

The sample résumé on page 243 was prepared by a recent graduate to use in conjunction with auditions for summer jobs at professional or semiprofessional theatres. Certain terms are boldfaced just to let you know they can be found in the "Terms and People to Know" section. Although the needs of producing organizations vary, you should present your training and experience in the best possible light without overstating the case. Names and phone numbers of people who can vouch for your abilities are also useful.

If you are participating in a large audition site where many different casting directors will be present, do your homework before the audition. Secure the

# LAUREN ZAPKO

P. O. Box 1000                                    (724) 555-1212 — cell
Pittsburgh, PA 15105                          laurenzapko@yahoo.com

## EXPERIENCE

| | | |
|---|---|---|
| *Beauty and the Beast* | Silly Girl | North Carolina Theatre |
| *Jekyll & Hyde (w/ Sebastian Bach)* | Red Rat Girl | North Carolina Theatre |
| *Ragtime* | Mrs. Whitstein | North Carolina Theatre |
| *My Fair Lady* | Ensemble | North Carolina Theatre |
| *Anything Goes* | Assistant Choreographer | Elon University |
| *A Grand Night for Singing* | Singer | Elon University |
| *CLO MiniStar* | Singer/Dance | Pittsburgh CLO Academy |
| *Casper: The Musical* | Teen **Chorus** | Pittsburgh CLO Mainstage |
| *Bye, Bye Birdie* | Teen Chorus | Pittsburgh CLO Mainstage |
| *Joseph and the Amazing . . .* | Teen Chorus | Pittsburgh CLO Mainstage |
| *La Cenerentola* | Supernumerary | Pittsburgh Opera |
| *Don Giovanni* | Supernumerary | Pittsburgh Opera |
| *A Chorus Line* | Cassie (**understudy**) | Pittsburgh Musical Theatre |
| *Oklahoma!* | Ellen/Postcard Girl | Pittsburgh Musical Theatre |
| *A Funny Thing Happened . . .* | Vibrata | Center Theatre Players |
| *The Pirates of Penzance* | Daughter | Center Theatre Players |
| *Funky Fairytales* | Cinderella | RWS & Associates, NYC |
| *Clear Channel Worldwide* | Lead Performer | RWS & Associates, NYC |
| *International Children's Games* | Dancer | The Wizard of Ahs |
| *Rockettes California Intensive* | Teaching Assistant / Counselor | Radio City Music Hall |

## TRAINING

| | |
|---|---|
| BFA in Musical Theatre candidate, Elon University | (expected graduation, 2007) |
| Broadway Theatre Project | Ann Reinking |
| Carnegie Mellon University | Voice w/ Stephen Totter |
| Pittsburgh CLO Academy of Musical Theatre | |
|    Pre-Professional Program | Jazz, Tap, Ballet, Conditioning |
| Pennsylvania Governor's School for the Arts | Jazz, Modern, Ballet |
| Paula Scriva's Dance Studio | Ballet, Pointe, Tap, Jazz |
| Richard E. Raugh Conservatory | Young Performers Institute |
| Master Classes | Ben Vereen, Terrance Mann, Frank Wildhorn, |
| | John Kander, Michael Rupert, Dave Clemmons |

## MISCELLANEOUS

Henry Mancini Award – Outstanding Supporting Actress/Leading Actress (two-time recipient); National Association of Teachers of Singing Competitor (Regional Finalist); Outstanding Young Woman Finalist, Southeastern Theatre Conference

## SPECIAL SKILLS

Baton Twirling, Sword Fighting, Runway Model, PA Drivers License (automatic/manual), Valid Passport

Photo by Kenn Stilson.

**Figure 12.2**    A group of nervous actors in the waiting area prior to auditioning at the 2005 Southeastern Theatre Conference auditions in Greensboro, North Carolina.

names and addresses of the theatres in which you have interest. Send ahead of time your résumé, headshot, and a simple cover letter explaining your background and interest in their company along with your audition number. The following represents a good example of a letter sent to the director before a production of Shakespeare in the Park's *The Tempest,* in Ft. Worth, Texas.

Dear Mr. Smith,

   I am a second year MFA degree candidate at Columbia University. Training with Andrei Serban, Priscilla Smith, and Anne Bogart has given me the opportunity to study and perform Classic Greek, Spanish Golden Age, Chekhov, and Shakespearean plays. I have heard wonderful things about your company and understand you are producing Shakespeare's The Tempest. I would love the opportunity to be called back and to meet with you in person at the Strawhat Auditions next week. I am #103. Enclosed please find my headshot and résumé.

Respectfully,

Nicholas Cutelli

Similarly, you should always send a thank you note after the audition. You obviously cannot write to every company at a large audition site, but you should send a note to everyone who called you back—particularly if they *do not* cast you. Your note should be handwritten. E-mails are not acceptable. The following are good examples of simple and yet effective thank you notes from that same production.

Dear Mr. Smith,

Thank you so very much for calling me back and interviewing me in Miami last weekend. Your comments proved invaluable, and your production of *The Tempest* sounds exciting. I truly hope to be a part of your company.

Best regards,
Meagan Edmonds

Dear Mr. Smith,

Thank you for auditioning me at SETC. Although you have not cast me, I certainly hope you will keep me in mind for next year. I will be performing this summer at the Barn Theatre in August, Michigan.

Sincerely,
Emily Wilson

This is a professional business practice that will pay off.

# Preparing Your Audition

Whether you are participating in one of the large **cattle-call** auditions or reading for a single role in a play, you will want to be ready to present one or more prepared monologues. Selecting this material is simultaneously the most difficult and the most important task you will face. Guidelines and cheap advice about what works and what does not work are plentiful, but because directors vary so greatly in their tastes and their needs, no definitive scheme exists. A few suggestions may help:

+ Your material represents ninety percent of your time onstage; therefore, select something you like. You will be living with the piece for a considerable period of hard work. Do not add to the drudgery of it by starting with something you hate or about which you feel indifferent.

+ Use material well within your grasp and understanding. Although "type casting" has developed a bad connotation, all actors should realize the range of roles for which they are best suited. Those roles constitute your "type." It is unwise to select an audition piece from material outside this range. A director may eventually cast you for a part that demands a considerable stretch in age and temperament, but you will show yourself best in roles that are close to what you believe to be your best aptitudes.

+ Unless the director specifically requests them, avoid dialects, as they will needlessly complicate your presentation.

+ Try to select material that will not be performed twenty times by other actors at the same audition. You cannot be clairvoyant, but new and alternative material will give you a distinct advantage. When several actors perform the same piece, the director not only tires of hearing it but also has an opportunity that would not otherwise be feasible to make a direct comparison between you and the other actors. Any selection taken directly from a monologue book is overused. Monologue books are good sources to find characters; however, we suggest you locate the full script and select another monologue by the same person.

+ Sexually explicit or extremely offensive material can work against you, particularly if it is not based on humor. While eccentric selections may be attention-getters, remember that your material is a reflection of your taste. Auditors are not necessarily prudish, but in view of the brief time you have to present yourself, it is always best to leave a positive impression.

+ Avoid climactic material that requires great depth or intensity of emotion. There simply is not enough time to achieve these emotional peaks effectively and honestly.

+ Avoid dull and passive pieces that dwell on character or plot exposition. Sometimes referred to as "remember when" monologues, it is extremely difficult to engage your audience in such a short amount of time with these narrative pieces. Always look for speeches written in first person that deal with an immediate psychological or emotional problem rather than the telling of a story in past tense with no clearly defined objective.

+ Your monologue should be from a well-written piece of literature and involve a character who is pursuing an immediate simple objective while working against an obstacle.

+ Nearly anything you select as audition material will need to be "cut" to fit the playing time you are likely to be allotted at the audition. If you are given sixty seconds, your monologue should be no longer than forty-five seconds. If you are given two minutes, prepare ninety seconds. There is no such thing as a monologue that is too short. And actors who exceed an established time limit appear to be undisciplined and unlikely to follow direction.

+ Edit for clarity. Selections should be self-explanatory with a distinct beginning, middle, and ending.

If you are choosing a song, all the above guidelines apply, but remember these additional points:

+ Although good vocal quality is important, character always comes first. Character colors the voice and humanizes the song. Your song should "show off" your voice, but it also should reveal your acting skills.

+ Choose a song that is stylistically similar to the show for which you are auditioning. Obviously, if you are auditioning for *Grease,* you will want to look at rock-and-roll songs, up-tempo songs, or ballads. If you are auditioning for *Big River,* perhaps a country-and-western or folk song would be more appropriate.

+ Unless the director specifically requests it, do not audition with a song from the show being cast. However, you should *know* every song from that particular show for the callback.

+ Avoid big production numbers and dance numbers. That is a separate audition.

+ Avoid narration or story songs (i.e., Robert Preston songs). This will simply project any discomfort you may have with singing.

+ No signature songs! Some songs are simply off limits because they have been eternally associated with the original performer. Therefore, unless you wish to be compared with Ethel Merman, do not audition with "There's No Business Like Show Business."

+ Always be prepared to do more than one piece. Particularly in a callback situation, casting directors will inevitably ask to see additional pieces.

All actors should have an **audition portfolio** consisting of a variety of prepared monologues and songs. Your portfolio should consist of:

| 9 Monologues | 9 Songs |
|---|---|
| 1:30 contemporary comedic | 16-bar up-tempo |
| 1:30 Shakespeare comedic | 16-bar ballad |
| 1:30 contemporary dramatic | up-tempo standard |
| 1:30 Shakespeare dramatic | ballad standard |
| :45 contemporary comedic | rock and roll |
| :45 Shakespeare comedic | 50s (triplet feel) |
| :45 contemporary dramatic | patter song |
| :45 Shakespeare dramatic | classical aria |
| Shakespeare sonnet | country and western |

**Figure 12.3** Physical warm-ups prior to dance auditions at the 2005 Southeastern Theatre Conference auditions in Greensboro.

Over half your Shakespeare should be in verse. You may choose other verse plays, but you should be careful to find good contemporary translations.

Even after you have a full complement of monologues and songs in your portfolio, early preparation is an absolute necessity for every audition. You should begin rehearsing your pieces weeks before the actual audition. Do not wait until the last minute! You should consider the following when rehearsing your prepared pieces:

+ Study the entire script and analyze the actions and objectives of the character exactly as you would if you were preparing to perform the role in a production. Think of your audition as a "ninety-second, one-act play, starring you."

+ For the most part, you should not expect to use furniture in your staging. Audition sites will sometimes allow you to use a straight-backed chair, but you should be careful not to use it as a "crutch" or as a device to hide behind during your presentation. It can weaken your audition. You should also know that casting directors sitting beyond the second or third row in a large hall would not be able to see you in a seated position.

+ Your movement should clarify your simple objective, utilizing a minimum of space—preferably staying within a radius of five to ten feet.

+ Focus your attention into the house, not in the wings.

+ Avoid all gimmicks!

+ No props should be used unless the item is something you might normally wear or carry (i.e., glasses, handkerchief, wristwatch, scarf, or jacket).

+ Consider your audience. This is one of the most common responses given by adjudicators on critique sheets. Keep in mind that there are really very few actual monologues in modern drama; rather, they are duologues. Therefore, you must ask yourself, "To whom am 'I' speaking?" Are you speaking to the audience as a friend? Are you speaking to one person? A small group?

+ Take dynamic risks. Human beings are big. They make big decisions. How many times have you heard someone say, "If you put that onstage, nobody would believe it." This is nonsense. However, do not confuse risk taking with indicating—false, unmotivated speech and movement. Risk taking is synonymous with decision making. Risk taking can be very subtle indeed, just as it can be extremely overt. As long as you stay within the bounds of truth in imaginary circumstances, you *can* believe your actions.

+ Explore the distinct tempo-rhythm of each character in your portfolio. In an audition situation, you are trying to show your range. The greatest actors are "chameleons." Each character a great actor portrays has a distinct tempo-rhythm that manifests itself through her speech, posture, walk, and gestures.

+ Get a coach. Many audition sites such as SETC, CETA, NETC, UPTA, Strawhat, Midwest, and U/RTA feel so strongly about this issue that the name of the coach appears next to the actor's name on the audition form to ensure that the actor has had every benefit of proper preparation.*

## Auditioning

After agreeing to an audition, your presence is expected. If you are unable to attend, you must give them sufficient notice, and you must have a good reason for your absence. Your audition begins the moment you walk out your front door. There are many horror stories of actors who have had confrontations with people on their way to the audition, and that person turned out to be the casting director. Because you probably will not recognize the director, you must be nice to everyone (and we mean *everyone*). This is particularly true once you arrive at the audition check-in, where many times directors will wander through the lobby inspecting the talent. You must also arrive at least fifteen minutes early to fill

---

*See Appendix C for audition site listings and contact information.

out forms and adjust to your space. Nothing looks more unprofessional than tardiness.

Once you have checked in with the stage manager and filled out the appropriate paperwork, do not leave the audition site without permission. You must also be prepared to stay longer than expected. If you are scheduled to audition at three o'clock, do not schedule to be at work by four. If they request that you stay and you cannot, they will probably excuse you, but it will most likely cost you the job.

As a professional in pursuit of a job, your dress should reflect your professionalism. Consider the following with regard to dress:

+ Your clothing should flatter your figure—whatever your body size and type—and expose your personality. Actresses may want to consider wearing a dress, being that most female characters will be in dresses in most plays written before the 1960s or set before that era.

+ No jeans or sloppy clothing. Tyrone Guthrie was fond of saying that people who dress like slobs very nearly always turn out to be slobs.

+ Some actors like to dress in a manner suggestive of the role for which they are auditioning. If you choose to do so, make your selection subtle so your "costume" will not overpower your performance.

+ Avoid printed words and busy patterns on clothing, and avoid large, noisy jewelry. These can be major distractions, and they draw focus away from you.

+ Wear appropriate footwear. Casting directors *do* look at your feet. No sneakers, flip-flops, sandals, or Birkenstocks. Fred Silver tells the story of a wealthy actor who "thought shoes were so important that he left his fortune to Actors' Equity Association, to set up a fund to provide shoes for actors so they could make rounds without ever having to look 'down at the heels.'"[3]

+ If you wear a hat, they will assume you are bald. Hats will also create a shadow over the top portion of your face under lights.

+ Be careful with glasses, as they sometimes cause a glare.

+ If you are auditioning at a large cattle-call audition, always wear the same clothing that you wore at the initial audition to every callback.

Once you have signed in, use your techniques for relaxation to control your nervousness. Remember that relaxation involves both mind and body. You must be able to remove at will any condition that blocks your intellectual thought process or your ability to command your voice and body to perform at their full range of flexibility. Actors use a variety of methods to achieve total relaxation. For some, yoga or transcendental meditation provides the answer. Others prefer a vigorous routine of physical exercise. Find a method that works for you, and keep in mind that many audition sites provide a warm-up space with a piano.

Photo by Kenn Stilson.

**Figure 12.4**    An actor auditioning in a conference ballroom for over 115 individual summer companies at the 2005 Southeastern Theatre Conference in Greensboro.

If at all possible, you should preview the performance space before your audition. This will give you a decided advantage over those walking into the space for the first time. If you are allowed to watch the preceding auditions, you can learn from others' mistakes, and it will allow you to become more comfortable in the space.

Be careful not to fall into the trap of being "psyched-out" by the other actors. Actors talk while waiting to audition. They love to talk about themselves. Many young actors are intimidated by the "competition." They find it unbelievable that all these other actors—who are their own ages—have such composure and are thoroughly experienced professionals. People exaggerate to impress others. Do not accept everything you are told as the truth. Their credits are probably no more impressive than yours, and sometimes their credentials are simply fabricated. Trust yourself and your abilities. Do not denigrate your own past. You are not in competition with any one single person at the audition. The role is between you and the director. Remember this definition of success: "When preparation meets opportunity." This is your opportunity; take advantage of it.

If you are singing, carefully and specifically go over your music with the accompanist as you wait in the wings or off to the side. Your music should be clearly marked, and it is your job to establish the tempo. You may tap it out for the pianist ahead of time. Also remember that the pianist will follow your lead during the audition, not the other way around. Your music must be in the correct key. You cannot expect an accompanist to transpose for you on sight. Finally, make sure to "back" or matt your music so it will stand by itself.

Upon entering the acting arena, smile and relax. Directors read a lot into the way an actor enters the stage. Try to control your nerves, and maintain a confident, pleasant, and positive persona. Before your introduction, make physical contact with the space. Place the chair in the appropriate place, even if this means moving it only a few inches. If you do not need the chair, move it out of your way. Find the light. Casting directors cannot understand actors who refuse to act in the light. Also, find your offstage focal points to help you sustain belief in the fourth side. Remember, these focal points should be located in the auditorium (e.g., exit sign, column, door, or any clearly visible inanimate and stationary object).

As you begin to address the casting personnel, rid yourself of all pretenses. Be yourself. Do not apologize. We are not referring to literally saying, "I'm sorry," but rather apologizing with your gait, your gestures, your eyes, and your vocal inflection. Relax. You are the reason they are there. One of the biggest fallacies is that actors feel that those watching are the competition and want them to fail. Everyone involved in the casting process wants you to succeed. In fact, they will jump for joy if they perceive you to be the next Gwyneth Paltrow or Al Pacino.

Stand during your introduction. Actors who walk into the space, sit down, and introduce themselves come across as being intimidated by the situation. If a stage manager announces your arrival and mispronounces your name, do not correct her or show irritation. Casting directors will not hire actors who seem to be "prima donnas" or "divas." Clearly and professionally state your name and number (if necessary). This is perhaps the most important part of your audition. Take a moment, and then launch into your first monologue or song.

Your transition and exit are also extremely important parts of the audition process. Take your time between pieces. This is a common problem, usually caused by nerves or inadequate preparation, and it breaks the dramatic illusion. After you have completed your prepared material, you may wish to repeat your name (and number if you have one). This could be the last thing they hear you say as you exit the room. If time is called, do not keep going, even if it is the last sentence or last musical phrase. Simply say, "Thank you," and exit. Do not show frustration with the timekeeper (or the accompanist). You cannot blame him for your lack of preparation. Also, the auditors will sense your frustration, which may cost you a callback. Maintain your composure as you exit. Many casting directors look at the exit as the most important part of auditioning.

Cold readings require a different kind of effort. Most directors would certainly prefer that you not memorize the text, but you certainly may, and should, study the script if it is available before attending the auditions. The director will

Photo by Kenn Stilson.

**Figure 12.5**   Actor Casee Hagan checks to see the number of callbacks she received shortly after her audition at the 2005 Southeastern Theatre Conference auditions in Greensboro.

not expect a fully developed characterization in a cold reading. She will, however, expect you to make decisions about your character—even if they are wrong—and establish a relationship with your reading partner. She will also expect you to perform well under pressure and to show that you can quickly focus on an objective and perform it well enough to bring your words to life.

If you are allowed to hear others read, be wary of the tendency either to copy an effective decision or to try too hard to be different. Another warning: Do not attempt to guess what the director wants. Center your energies on understanding the script well enough to give an intelligent reading that shows you can make defensible choices. Believing is a part of auditioning, too. You must be able to believe in your abilities and in the words you are speaking.

Use your script in a cold reading, but do not be overly dependent on it. It is a map for your reading and interpretation. Hold it in one hand away from your body to free your ability to gesture. You should also make eye contact with your reading partner—*infect* him. Sometimes you will read with a casting assistant as you speak. Generally, they are not actors and will just "read." Do not fall into the trap of reading as they do. Trust your own instincts and deliver a full performance reading to the best of your ability.

Do not allow yourself to lose control of the reading. Listen to your partner and react realistically to the situation. In other words, do not "ham it up." Less is usually better, depending on the material. Even in broad comedy, go only as far as the action and dialogue take you. Do not try to be funny. Simply play your objective, and rely on your technique.

Take your time. Never rush through your reading, unless the script states that the character is talking very fast. Take your moments. If you feel a rising nervous sensation, take a deep breath—never dropping character—and continue. Of course, you will make mistakes. All actors do throughout their careers. No matter what happens, stay focused. If you get a really bad start on a reading, it is perfectly permissible and entirely professional to say "I'd like to start over, please." Take a moment and begin again. You will be respected for this kind of command of your reading. After all, this is your time and maybe your only time for this person or production group. If you make multiple mistakes and cannot continue, simply say "Thank you. It was very nice meeting you" and leave. Never apologize! The casting director may not have even noticed your mistake. Often actors are cast in roles when they themselves felt they gave an awful reading.

Be proud of your work, and do not apologize for your presence!

---

### Exercise 12.1  CONSTRUCTING YOUR PORTFOLIO

1. Using the above list, begin working on your portfolio. Find monologues and songs you believe would serve you well as audition pieces.

2. Prepare and perform in class a three-minute audition (non-singing) containing two pieces: one comic and one serious; choose one from a classic and one from a modern play.

3. Prepare your résumé on your computer, and update it regularly as you achieve additional training and experience.

4. Research the professional photographers in your area who specialize in theatre, film, and television headshots. Peruse their portfolios and compare prices. As soon as you have the money, schedule an appointment.

5. Investigate your local audition scene. Find publications and hotlines that will inform you of upcoming events.

6. Research and make an appointment with a reputable talent agent for commercial work.

7. Investigate the combined audition sites listed in Appendix B. Plan to attend one or more of these auditions.

## Terms and People to Know

**Actors' Equity Association (AEA)**   Also known simply as Equity, this is the union representing stage actors and stage managers.

**American Federation of Television and Radio Artists (AFTRA)**   The union representing television and radio actors.

**audition**   A tryout for a film, TV, or stage role. Usually auditions involve a presentation of prepared material and reading from a script, but they can also require improvisation. Also called a tryout.

**audition portfolio**   Prepared audition material, consisting of a variety of monologues and songs, that can be used at any given tryout.

**bio**   Short for actor biography. A *résumé* in narrative form, usually for a printed program or press release.

**black and white**   Synonymous with *headshot.*

**callback**   Any follow-up interview or *audition.*

**casting director**   The person responsible for choosing the initial performers for later consideration by the producer or director.

**cattle call**   An open *audition* where anyone can attend.

**character part**   Contrasted to *straight part,* a role usually depicting an elderly, unusual, or eccentric individual.

**chorus**   An unnamed role usually with few individual lines. Also referred to as an *extra, bit part,* supernumerary, or walk-on.

**cold reading**   Unrehearsed reading of a scene, usually at an *audition.*

**cold submission**   Sending an unsolicited *headshot* and *résumé* to an industry professional.

**company**   A group of actors who perform together either in an individual play or for a season.

**contact sheet**   Numerous small images of potential *headshots* printed on 8″×10″ paper. Also known as proofs.

**director**   Has the ultimate responsibility for the artistic interpretation of the script through her control of the actors and supporting production team.

**double**   To play more than one role in a single play.

**Equity Membership Candidacy (EMC)**   A program devised by *AEA* to help you gain membership into the union. You may join the EMC program once you have been hired—with a non-Equity contract—as an actor or stage manager with a participating Equity company. After completing fifty weeks (or points), you have up to five years to join the union; your accumulation of points does not have to be consecutive or from the same company. You pay a $100 fee when joining this program and the balance of the $1,000 AEA initiation fee with your first union contract. Note: The EMC program can be bypassed either partially or entirely if you are offered a role at an Equity theatre under an Equity contract and pay the $1,000 fee.

**headshot**   A general term for an actor's picture used for *auditioning* and marketing purposes. These black and white photos are also referred to as 8″×10″s— the picture's dimensions—and glossies.

**monologue**   A character's continuous dialogue without interruption by another character; also a speech delivered while alone on stage.

**parent union**   An actor's first professional union that may provide eligibility into other acting unions.

**pension and health payment**   An additional amount of money paid by the employer to cover employee benefits under union contract.

**postcard**   A 4″×6″ picture of an actor with name and other information, intended to remind industry professionals of an actor's recent credits and other news.

**résumé**   List of credits, training, and special skills, usually attached to an 8″×10″ *headshot*.

**Screen Actors Guild (SAG)**   The union representing film actors.

**showcase**   A stage show designed to promote actors by allowing them to perform in short venues with industry attendance.

**Showcase Code**   In 99-seat (or fewer) theatres that are otherwise professional, an agreement under which Equity waives contract provisions under certain circumstances. Previously known as "Equity Waiver," a term still used informally.

**standard union contract**   The standard format contract approved by the unions and offered to most union performers before the job.

**straight part**   A role without marked eccentricities, normally a young man or young woman.

**talent agent**   The liaison between the actor and casting director. Union-affiliated talent agents can only accept a ten percent commission from their clients.

**talent manager**   Another form of representation for the actor, managers do not have a set commission base nor do they have any union affiliations, but they usually work more closely with individual actors.

**trades**   Short for "trade papers," the newspapers and periodicals such as the *Hollywood Reporter* and *Variety* that specifically feature information on the entertainment industry.

**understudy**   A performer hired to do a role if the lead player is unable to perform.

**waiver**   Union-approved permission for deviation from the terms of a standard contract.

**workshop**   A class where actors can learn from industry professionals, often for a limited number of sessions.

# Transforming into Character

*"Success is transient, evanescent. The real
passion lies in the poignant acquisition of
knowledge about all the shading and
subtleties of the creative secrets."*

–Constantin Stanislavski

Ultimately, you are working toward the complete incarnation of a character, a
piece of art you have created using the text and given circumstances, along with
your personal history and imagination. To reach your onstage goal, you must
fully experience every aspect of your imaginary person. You must believe in the
power of "if." You must have complete faith in the world of the play (or film), as
you must accept your character's every action as true. From the beginning of the
rehearsal process, you must "transform" yourself into the life of another human
being, a gradual progression Stanislavski referred to as **reincarnation.**

Just as real life evolves over an extended period of time, the mystery of inspiration behind a secondary onstage life does not occur in a single burst. The
psychology of the human soul is too deep and too complex to comprehend in a
solitary moment. *One of the primary purposes of this book has been to help you develop a logical rehearsal and performance method that helps you move away from
yourself and into the physical body and mental consciousness of your character.*

Used by permission of the Virginia Commonwealth University.

**Figure 13.1**   Bev Appleton in a scene from Virginia Commonwealth University's production of *Sueño*. Directed by William Roudebush, scenic design by Ron Keller, costume design by Elizabeth Weiss Hopper, lighting design by Lou Szari. Reincarnation, the **transformation** from self into that of the character, takes time to develop.

The average academic rehearsal period for a **straight play** is approximately six weeks; it's eight to ten weeks for a musical or classical play written in verse. Since the complete transformation from self into your character usually takes the entire rehearsal period, you should not concern yourself with reincarnation. Once you have done your script analysis, it is incumbent upon you as an actor to remain in the present while onstage. To do this, you must focus on "your" immediate circumstances—"your" relationships, moment before, simple objectives, tactical decisions, and adjustments to obstacles. Only by concentrating on the moment-by-moment existence of your character can you become one with him or her—subordinating yourself to "your" thoughts, feelings, and behavior. Only then can the reincarnation from self into that of your character take place.[1]

Your transformation into character begins in earnest the moment you see your name on the **cast list.** You have a specific role. The homework process began prior to auditions, but now it intensifies. It is your responsibility to fully engage in a thorough analysis of the script while researching your character. However, it is also time for you to begin rehearsals. Only now do you have the advantage of working under the guidance of a director. A good director, who has also thoroughly analyzed the script and who has fashioned a strong artistic vision, helps you shape your analysis and character transformation so it will make the greatest possible contribution to the overall production. The director will help you create a character that is true to the dramatist's intention and according to his or her interpretation for that particular production.

The director's interpretation becomes the foundation for the master plan—a map often intricately complicated in its detail—for coordinating all aspects of the production into an artistic whole. Your specific transformation into character is a vital part of that plan, and much rehearsal time is spent on its development and its relationship to the other characters in the play. You must also learn how to use all the elements of modern theatre to reinforce your character, including lights, scenery, costumes, sound, and many more. You must learn to maintain your composure in a demanding and often pressure-packed group enterprise. Producing a play is a fine example of cooperative effort—a process described by Harold Clurman as "the relating of a number of talents to a single meaning."[2]

There are many specific types of rehearsals—i.e., **reading, blocking, working, run-through, cue-to-cue, technical, technical run-through,** and **dress**—but for the actor there are always five principal overlapping phases that make up the overall rehearsal process.

1. Finding the meaning

2. Developing your character

3. Creating and refining the form

4. Making technical adjustments

5. Polishing for performance

# Finding the Meaning

If a production is to realize its possibilities, if it is to be the "relating of a number of talents to a single meaning," everyone working on the production must understand what that single meaning is. And everyone must understand how each particular part, small or large as it may be, contributes to the expression of it. Indeed, the final success or failure of the production will rest in all likelihood on that part of the rehearsal period devoted to finding the meaning of the play.

Production teams depend on the director initially to possess a more thorough knowledge of the play than anyone else and to share her vision with them at the first meeting. The various production personnel take the director's interpretation and superimpose their own ideas before taking them back to the director, who usually incorporates all or parts of each artist's contribution into the artistic whole. Usually, the schedule will call for a number of reading rehearsals, in which actors sit in a circle reading aloud their individual parts and discussing the play with the director and with each other. Other members of the production team will often be invited to these sessions. Remember, however, that you must always guard against sharing too much personal information about your character with the entire group. Again, recall our comments in Chapter 8 about mystery and secrets.

The important thing is that everyone clearly understands what the play means. Until this common understanding has been reached, the group is likely to be working at cross purposes, and the rehearsals cannot proceed effectively.

Once the interpretation is set, you begin to search for your character's motivating force and its relationship to the super-objective. Here again agreement between you and the director is necessary, and the reading rehearsals usually produce this understanding. At the same time, you begin to consider the problem of line interpretation—of relating the lines to the character's motivating force and to the meaning of the play as a whole.

There are two schools of thought with regard to the amount of table work. Some contemporary directors sit around a table with their cast and read and discuss the play for as much as a third of the entire rehearsal period, a practice Stanislavski used at the beginning of the twentieth century at the Moscow Art Theatre. He eventually realized—and most contemporary directors agree—that too much table work actually impedes the psychophysical process. Actors must learn "to act," not just discuss. Through actions, you are forced to consider the psychological motivation, thus finding a harmony between substance and shape. So, as we previously suggested, you must learn to analyze the script in juxtaposition with the physical exploration that occurs in rehearsals. The process of physical and psychological exploration is never finished, as new and deeper meanings are certain to reveal themselves during all kinds of rehearsals and, indeed, during performances.

Reprinted by permission of Richard Finkelstein.

**Figure 13.2** Elise Marie Boyd in a scene from James Madison University's production of Medea. Directed by Tom King; scenic and lighting design by Richard Finkelstein; costume design by Jenner Brunk. Style is the director's unique overall interpretation of the dramatist's script. Every aspect of production—including the acting—must be unified and define the style.

Although the director and actors are teammates, sharing the goal of excellence, they have different responsibilities. The director is the team captain, who ultimately decides which particular actions move the play toward the desired effect. The director also interacts with other team members—set designer, lighting designer, costume designer, property master—and, most of all, with the playwright, either directly or through the play. A play is not just an imitation of an action but is also a work of art requiring unity, structure, and focus, all of which a director must create. The director guides you in much the same way an acting teacher guides an acting class—supervising the production: inspiring your own analysis, growth, and development, and serving as a formal friend.

College actors sometimes expect directors to give them too much direction. You are a creator. In addition to transforming into your role, showing up at rehearsals, and adapting to different directorial methods and to your fellow actors, you should be self-reliant. Self-observation is an important part of artistic growth. Actors who refuse to look objectively at their own work are destined to a life in community theatre. When asked to review their performance, they either say such things as "Fabulous," or "Great" or else blame their lackluster work on the audience. Actors who cannot—or will not—articulate "what worked" and "what didn't work" will never grow. Actors who will not take responsibility for their own work will forever remain amateurs. As Uta Hagen said, "the actors will cease to improve in their parts unless they themselves have learned to recognize their flaws and how to correct them."[3] As a young professional actor, you must understand that the director is there to guide you through the process, but you must have the ability to explore, make decisions, and evaluate your own work.

# Developing Your Character

With the meaning of the play in mind, you are ready to concentrate on characterization. At this time most actors find their greatest satisfaction as creative artists, and, as we have seen, the temptation is great to rush to this phase before the proper groundwork has been established. In this series of rehearsals, you explore your inner resources to discover how you can use your experiences to understand the problems of the character. You use your imagination to supply additional circumstances to round out the character's background and to aid yourself in believing the action. You observe people and objects to find helpful details. You continue to read, study paintings, and listen to music if you need to enlarge your experience to understand any aspect of the play.

By this time, you have completed the task of breaking your role down into units of action. You know the simple objective of each unit and can relate it to the character's motivating force. You devise a score of physical actions through which you can realize your objectives, and you explore various "tactics" for working against obstacles in each unit, both at home by yourself and at rehearsals with the other actors.

At the same time, you are determining the motivation behind each line, discovering its subtext and verbal action, and relating it to the character's motivating force. If the character's speech differs from your own, you have the added task of learning to reproduce it believably by listening to speakers with a similar background or to recordings.

Chances are that you will be called on during these rehearsals to have completed the memorization of your lines and cues. As with the amount of table work, there are two schools of thought with regard to memorization of lines. Some directors warn against memorizing the lines before you know your subtext and have your inner monologues and inner images. They feel that if you memorize the lines too early, your intonations may be entirely wrong. They believe that once you have done the necessary preparation, the lines will easily follow. Other directors, however, demand that you memorize the lines from the beginning. Stanislavski and Nemirovich-Danchenko debated this issue. Today, Russian directors agree with Nemirovich-Danchenko. "Before an actor can understand and make a dramatist's language, style and unique diction his own, the lines must first be memorized," wrote Sonia Moore about Stanislavski's point of view. "Even if an actor understands a character's actions and motivations, without the text he will not be able to understand fully the subtext or its relationship to the text."[4] Both arguments are valid, and chances are you will develop a technique that falls somewhere in the middle. Regardless, you must take this responsibility seriously and complete it by the time you are asked to be "off book," a moment that varies from director to director.

Accurate memorization is your responsibility. You owe it to the dramatist, who is dependent on you for the truthful representation of the work, and you owe it to your fellow players, whose own lines must be motivated by what has gone before.

# Creating and Refining the Form

Yevgeny Vakhtangov, director of the Moscow Art Theatre's First Studio, used to say that "Art is search, not finished form." In the early stages of blocking rehearsals, you are exploring the character, inventing the **business,** creating the form. However, throughout the investigative process—a process that doesn't fully conclude until the lights fade on the final performance—you are refining the form. The period of first discovery is undoubtedly the most exciting part of the creative process, and at some point you will be asked to **freeze** your major movements. However, you must *never* allow your investigation of form to end. As long as you can improve, make new discoveries, enhance the second plan, and uncover better actions and tactics, the artistic development of your character will continue. You are not bound by your early discoveries. Theatrical form is never "set in stone." Through self-observation, you continue the *process of exploration,* for that is the entire purpose of rehearsals—no matter how close to opening night.

By using the techniques discussed in this book, your work will never grow stale. However, once your verbal and physical actions become nothing more than mechanical repetition, your performance is dead. And it will grow worse with every subsequent presentation. The moment you stop working, the truthfulness of your actions and subsequent emotions will become mere accidents. Art will only exist as long as there is exploration of outer form. Stanislavski referred to it as the state of **"I am."** He said, "Right here. Right now. Today." At every rehearsal, you must, as your character, relive the moments of action as if they were happening for the first time. You must continually ask yourself, "What would I do *if*

I were this character in this circumstance?" What are "my" actions? What is "my" objective? What are "my" expectations? What am "I" willing to do to get what "I" want? What adaptations am "I" willing to explore?

You must play your objectives and work against your obstacles each time you put on your character's clothing. This is your path to uncovering the "mystery of inspiration." With the proper inner work at every rehearsal and performance, your work will remain fresh. Your character will continue to grow. Inspiration comes as a result of hard work! And repeated inspiration comes as a result of even harder work! That is the way it is—no matter how great your talent.

In the early working rehearsals, the initial creation of form is a rewarding, and sometimes agonizing, process. Again, transformation—the process of reincarnation—does not spring full-blown from the director's or your imagination; rather, it grows slowly. It comes in bits and pieces and cannot be forced. Although parts of it may need to be "grafted on from the outside," as Stanislavski said in his supplement to *Creating a Role,* it cannot be wholly imposed in this fashion. It comes from the combined imaginations of you and the director, stimulated initially by the playwright and later by the responses of the actors to one another and to the products of other artists—props, settings, costumes, and lights, for example. It must develop organically as the character develops. Form grows out of character and character out of form, so, enigmatic as it sounds, what a character is determines what she does, and what she does determines what she is.

Most of the time, the ground plan determines the actor's large movements (entrances and exits, crosses from one area to another). The director and designers determine these before rehearsals begin, aware that the most important consideration in making the ground plan is the movement it will impose on the actors. The large movements become apparent as soon as the ground plan is explained, and the actors accept these new conditions and motivate them. In fact, the blocking, the ground plan, the director's concept, the scenic design, the costume design, the prop design, and the lighting design all join the playwright's words as part of the actor's given circumstances.

Some movements and other physical activities are inherent in the lines. Examples are crossing to answer the doorbell or telephone, serving tea, or less obvious indications such as Petruchio's threat to Katherina (*The Taming of the Shrew*): "I swear I'll cuff you, if you strike again" or Juliet's plea to Romeo: "Wilt thou be gone? It is not yet near day." Most acting editions of plays also describe physicalization in their stage directions, but you must examine this material carefully.

In all likelihood the printed instructions will relate to a ground plan and set of circumstances entirely different from those of the current production, and the director often may tell you to ignore them entirely. Even including all these sources, it is necessary to invent additional movement and physical activity, relying on your impulses. Remember that physical objectives help you believe in your character and express his or her desires in ways the audience can see and understand. During working rehearsals, you and the director use your imaginations to devise movement and business that will give outer form to inner characterization.

You also use these rehearsals as a testing ground for what externals of manner, dress, action, and so forth you can use to reinforce the characterization. These externals are vital because, as we recall from earlier chapters, doing is believing. You are likely to believe the character to the extent you can translate the character's desires into action. Such small things as using a handkerchief, eating a sandwich, turning on a light, or writing down an address provide physical motivations on which you can concentrate your attention.

Determining the amount and nature of the physical activity is a matter to be settled between you and the director. Good directors frequently make suggestions, but you have both the opportunity and the responsibility to originate small actions that will help create form. Nowhere is the quality of your imagination more evident than in this phase of your work. Of course, to claim the stage, all business must be justified in terms of the total meaning of the play and the production.

Costumes and properties are vastly important in creating the form of both the role and the production. If you establish a proper relationship to them, they become in themselves excellent "actors," and they are essential to the creation of physical image. "A costume or an object appropriate to a stage figure ceases to be a simple material thing, it acquires a kind of sanctity for an actor," wrote Stanislavski. "You can tell a true artist by his attitudes towards his costume and properties."[5]

## Making Technical Adjustments

As you enter the run-through rehearsals, you will begin to work in the setting, with the properties that will be used in performance, in costume, and under the lights. At this time, adjustments are always necessary. The furniture may take up more space than the small chairs and tables with which you have been working. Opening and closing actual doors may require more time than you have been allowing. The position of a piano may have to be changed to improve the sight lines for the audience. Manipulating the clothing may require more care than anticipated. A climactic scene may have to be played farther downstage so that it may be lighted effectively. Such adjustments are an inevitable part of rehearsal. Experienced actors recognize the need for these changes and immediately find ways (sometimes by inventing additional "circumstances") to motivate them in terms of their characters' desires.

During technical rehearsals certain actions may have to be repeated over and over to allow the lighting and sound crews to coordinate their timing with that of the actors. You are responsible for handling these painstaking rehearsals calmly and pleasantly. Although it may seem that the development of the production has come to a standstill or actually regressed, you must remember that you have now had many weeks of rehearsals and that the technical production crews are attempting to catch up in one or two nights. You must recognize that the technical crew will catch up quickly. Also be aware that only through these rehearsals can the entire company become the smooth-working team it will take to make the production a success.

# Polishing for Performance

The final technical run-through rehearsals, including the dress rehearsals, are devoted to polishing for performance. At this time, your blocking is set—although your work continues—and feelings of tentativeness must disappear. During the earlier rehearsals, you have made many discoveries. You have experimented with details of business, movement, and line reading. Throughout the entire period, you have explored details that will allow you to believe in your character. These rehearsals are, in fact, a continual process of selection and rejection. By the time the play is ready for polishing, however, your major choices must be relatively firm. During the final rehearsals, you need to have confidence in your characterization and in the technical support for the production, as only then can you be comfortable and assured in your performance.

Much attention in run-through rehearsals turns to timing and **projection,** although both will have been anticipated earlier. Timing is a matter of pace and rhythm, pertaining to the tempo at which lines are spoken and business and movement are executed and to the rapidity at which cues are picked up. As long as you feel uncertain about the details of your performance, you cannot establish and maintain a tempo.

A sense of timing is one of the subtlest elements of stage technique. For its development, you must have experience before an audience. Too slow a tempo will not hold interest, but too fast a tempo will obscure the meaning. Too consistent a tempo will become monotonous; too varied a tempo will seem jerky and illogical. If you are slow to pick up cues, the play's tempo will falter between speeches. If you are too fast in speaking your lines, their meaning will be blurred. To the expert ear, this blurring clearly indicates that you are not using your lines to accomplish a verbal action. Maintaining too constant a tempo indicates you are not hearing and feeling different tempo-rhythms for varying structural units.

An important consideration in timing is the use of *silences.* Many beginning actors tend to *pause*—an indication that "nothing" is happening—for their own convenience (because they are not breathing correctly, because they are not

Photo by Kenn Stilson.

**Figure 13.3**   Director Robert W. Dillon, Jr., gives comments to his actors at a dress rehearsal of Southeast Missouri State University's production of *Picasso at the Lapin Agile*. Scenic design by Dennis C. Seyer, costume design by Rhonda C. Weller-Stilson, lighting and sound design by Philip Nacy.

thinking fast enough, because they are not sure of what they are doing), without regard to dramatic effect. During silences, however, dramatic action is still being driven forward. Objectives are still being pursued. Nevertheless, silences should be used sparingly and *only when they are more effective than speech*.

Some playwrights are so conscious of the need to use silences effectively that they take great pains to indicate the proper place for them in their scripts. Actors performing in the plays of Harold Pinter, for example, will find silences to be as much a part of the dialogue as the words themselves.

Timing varies from play to play, from scene to scene, from character to character, and from audience to audience. Thought-provoking plays usually require a slower tempo than does farce, and expository scenes at the beginning almost always require a slower tempo than do climactic scenes at the end. One character moves and speaks more slowly than another, and one audience is quicker at grasping meanings than another. During the final rehearsals, the director will guide the cast in establishing effective tempos for the play, for different scenes, and for different characters. The actors alone have the responsibility to feel out the audience and make necessary adjustments from performance to performance.

Vocal projection is another variable element. An ongoing requirement of the theatre is that the audience hears and understands the lines. This requirement may be satisfied by a variety of voice levels, ranging from a shout to a whisper. Projection does not mean talking loudly but describes the actor's effort to share every moment of the play with the audience. The play, the scene, the character, and the size and acoustical qualities of the auditorium will determine the degree of loudness that is most suitable. Again, variety is necessary. Nothing is more tiresome than listening to an unvaried voice over a period of time. Unmotivated, abrupt changes, on the other hand, are likely to startle the audience and attract undue attention.

Visual projection is equally important. The audience must see the action as clearly as they can hear the lines. Three requirements of movement, business, and gesture are:

1. They must be suitable to the character, the scene, the play, and the general style of the production.
2. They must be clearly seen.
3. Their significance to the total meaning must be readily comprehensible.

At final rehearsals, actors turn much of their attention to auditory and visual projection. The director carefully checks their effectiveness, but the final test can be made only by performing before an audience. To ensure that the cast will pass the test on opening night, producers and directors have preview performances or invite an audience to the final run-throughs.

## Working at Rehearsals

For a talented actor, well trained in techniques of her art, rehearsals are a happy time, though they are not always filled with fun. Preparing a play for production is at best hard work, often fraught with frustration. But during rehearsals you have the greatest opportunity for creative accomplishment. You should begin rehearsals resolved to use all your resources for the good of the production. What is best for the production should be the single criterion for decisions, and nothing makes for a happier atmosphere than sharing this resolve with all members of the cast.

Rehearsals will proceed best if you establish a relationship with the director and with the other actors based on mutual respect. The director determines the working methods, the rehearsal schedule, and the distribution of rehearsal time among the different acts and scenes. You respect both the method and the schedule and cooperate with the director in his way of working. Needless to say, you attend rehearsals regularly and punctually. You are ready to work at the scheduled time, which means you arrive fifteen to thirty minutes early, warm up, and prepare for your first scene. You have an obligation to keep yourself healthy, rested, and in good spirits, so sickness, fatigue, or personal problems do not interfere. To the other actors, you are generous and demanding: insisting that they give their best, generous in giving your best to them.

At the first opportunity, you will also want to get to know the stage manager, to understand her importance to the production and to respect her authority. Although her specific duties vary from theatre to theatre and company to company, the stage manager is the person who, according to Lawrence Stern, "accepts responsibility that the rehearsals and performances run smoothly onstage and backstage."[6] Establishing the proper relationship with this individual is absolutely critical to a productive rehearsal and performance period.

Throughout each rehearsal, you are alert and committed to the work at hand. You give your entire attention to what is going on, both when you are in a scene and when you are waiting for an entrance. You mark directions in your script or in a notebook. Once blocking or business has been given by or worked out in conjunction with the director at rehearsal, you are responsible for retaining it. You bring a supply of pencils (with erasers) to rehearsal with you and record all movements in the margin of your script at the time you are blocked, using standard abbreviations. Drawing diagrams in the margin is a practical way of recording complicated blocking. You must do more, though, than keep track of your blocking. You write down your units, objectives, subtext, comments, and interpretations until your copy of the script becomes a complete score for playing your role. That score becomes an invaluable source of reference during later rehearsals and performances. You take careful notes on your director's oral critiques and refer to them before the next time you rehearse the particular scene. You study, absorb, experiment, probe, watch, listen, and create.

Rehearsals constitute a fluid process during which the production gradually emerges. For you, the actor, the process offers a chance to explore every facet of the character you are portraying. Layer by layer the process of reincarnation occurs, and you relate your character to the performances of the rest of the company and the production as a whole. You recognize that early rehearsals must progress in bits and pieces; therefore, you are wary of going too fast. Each moment of the play must be explored and the problems solved through trial and error. Early decisions can be only tentative; preliminary ideas about a character may actually be reversed as rehearsals progress. The production must develop organically. Without change at each rehearsal, satisfactory progress toward the final shape of the production bogs down.

Rehearsal expectations vary from company to company, but the work habits of all good actors reflect an attitude toward the theatre that is conducive to creativity and free from serious "acting traps" that shackle their efforts. What are these traps? Joseph Slowik has pinpointed four on which Grotowski regularly concentrated while Slowik was observing his company. They are *impatience, half-heartedness, poor work ethics,* and *substitution.*[7]

Impatience leads to a lack of technique, because it causes you to look for shortcuts that disrupt and emasculate your work. Stanislavski called this trap taking the "line of least resistance" in creating a character. The impatient actor relies on tricks, on work that has been successful in a previous characterization, or on actions that have been neither sufficiently grounded in the play's given circumstances nor properly articulated with the other actors' performances.

Half-heartedness means giving less than maximum effort during rehearsals. Good actors simply do not work with anything less than their entire being. They know that truth and believability are difficult to achieve under any circumstances and that without maximum effort they simply will not appear.

Poor work ethics inevitably lead to a rehearsal atmosphere in which creativity cannot take place, in which actors will be afraid to take a chance. Sure signs of poor work ethics are resentment, backbiting, buck passing, and unconstructive criticism, all mortal enemies of the trust necessary for success in the theatre.

Substitution is the most pervasive trap of all, but also the most difficult to define. "Anything less than [a] preciously recognizable human response is a substitute," said Slowik. "It is something behind which the actor hides when he is empty. When audiences seem to be satisfied with less than the 'real thing' actors continue to hide behind substitution, building their careers on one of the most destructive enemies of creativity."[8]

# Playing the Part

We have seen that your first major concern during rehearsals is discovering the total meaning of the play by studying the script, examining other sources, and discussing the interpretation with the director and the other actors. When working with the kind of play that constitutes the great body of Western drama, both

Photo by Kenn Stilson.

**Figure 13.4**   A scene from Southeast Missouri State University's production of *Guys and Dolls*. Directed by Kenn Stilson, choreography by Kari Schroeder, musical direction by Chris Goeke, scenic design by Chris Pickart, costume design by Rhonda C. Weller-Stilson, lighting design by Philip Nacy. Once the show opens, actors must be able to repeat an inspired portrayal at every subsequent performance. Note the joy on the faces of the ensemble.

classic and contemporary—the kind of play in which the dramatist expresses his or her meaning by creating characters involved in some sort of conflict—you must next give immediate attention to understanding the character you are playing and to believing the character's speech and actions. In later rehearsals, you become increasingly concerned with projecting the character to the audience, and you continue to focus on these concerns during the entire run of the play. You must bring the character newly to life at every performance, confident that you are not only performing "natural" actions but also creating a theatrically effective form.

As the play is repeated in performance, the core—the super-objective, motivating forces, simple objectives, and overall physical form of the production—stays the same. Keeping it the same is one of your responsibilities. You are required to perform the play as rehearsed, and the Actors' Equity Association fines and ultimately suspends professionals who fail to respect their obligation. As we explained, however, this requirement does not mean that creativity (and exploration) ceases and that the robot-like actor repeats from memory what has been "frozen" in rehearsal. Rather, you commit yourself at each performance to accomplishing the character's objectives and to establishing relations with objects and other actors as if it were for the first time. Performance demands continual and fresh adjustment to the stage life going on around you. To keep a performance the same, it must always be subtly different; mechanical repetition does not retain vitality.

*Concentration* is the key to success, but you must recall the earlier lesson in Chapter 6 in which we concluded that concentration must take place on two levels. Let us review this important, if sometimes confusing, duality.

On one level, you direct your attention to satisfying the desires of the character. You use your speech and actions to get what the character wants and attempts, and to influence the behavior of the other characters as you try to satisfy your objective. By concentrating on this objective, you are able to believe your actions. They, in turn, produce feelings similar to the feelings the character would have if the situations were real. Your imagination also allows you to use the feelings that arise from your relationship to the other actors.

On another level, you concentrate on expressing the character in theatrical terms. The audience must hear the lines and see the actions. A tempo must be maintained that will be suitable to the play, stimulating to the audience, and dramatically effective. You do your part to create enough variety in the performance to ensure a continual renewal of the audience's interest. To maintain this level of concentration, you must develop what Lynn Fontanne called an "outside eye and ear" to guide you in playing your role. You have the dual function of being both character and interpreter.[9]

In some contemporary works, the creation of character in imaginary circumstances is a minimal part of your responsibility. You express your or the playwright's meaning to the audience in your own person. In these instances the audience becomes a part of the given circumstances of the play, and your task is to find every way possible to communicate with them directly, clearly, and forcefully.

Perform your function with ease and authority. The audience experiences no pleasure watching a performer who is tense and strained and no comfort watching one who does not seem confident in his ability to perform with some degree of credit to himself. Concentration, again, is the keynote to relaxation. When you can turn your full attention to doing a job you know you are prepared to do, you forget your fears and your self-consciousness.

Although many of the suggestions we have made about performing a role are universal, conditions will certainly vary with the experience of the company, the sophistication of the audience, and whether the play is presented for a limited run, for a long run, or in repertory. These distinctions are too complex for inclusion in this text, but you should be prepared to seek advice from your instructor, your director, your stage manager, or a colleague who has experienced the specific conditions under which you will be performing. Keeping a role fresh during a long run is a particularly difficult problem and one that will tax your ability to generate anew exciting objectives and actions every time you step onstage. Naturally, each audience must believe you are performing the role for the first time and, for them, you are. Any reasonably accomplished actor can get excited about opening night; it is the fifth, or seventy-fifth, or three hundred seventy-fifth performance of the same role that taxes your technique.

One of the final tasks the actor must learn is to handle **criticism,** both positive and negative. Although it would be foolish to say you should pay no attention to criticism from the press or your friends, it is important for you to establish the habit of acting for your fellow actors and your director rather than for the critics. Negative criticism is depressing and inevitably affects a show adversely. Praise or flattery usually adds fuel to the fires of self-esteem, a conflagration from which your enemies all too often emerge. Acting is a frightening art, the only one in which the moment of its final creation is also the moment of its acceptance or rejection by the public. Actors often suffer because the audience, on whom they are dependent for their success, does not seem to view their art with the same respect they have for other artists. Uta Hagen explained the phenomenon this way:

> More than in the other performing arts the lack of respect for acting seems to spring from the fact that every layman considers himself a valid critic. While no lay audience discusses the bowing arm or stroke of the violinist or the palette or brush technique of the painter, or the tension which may create a poor entrechat, they will all be willing to give formulas to the actor. . . . And the actor listens to them, compounding the felonious notion that no craft or skill or art is needed in acting.[10]

This book has been dedicated to the purpose of helping you believe in your craft, your skill, and your art. *Believe* is the operative word, the linchpin, of its message. Without a believable foundation for character—believable actions; believable objectives; believable vocal, physical, and emotional technique; and above all, a belief in the script and one's fellow artists—you are doomed to failure. With them, you have a chance to create magic, to move an audience to a deeper understanding of the mystery and the majesty—as well as the failures and the foibles—of humankind.

# Terms and People to Know

**business, stage**   Small actions, such as smoking, eating, slapping, falling, crying, using a fan, and tying a necktie.

**cast list**   The public posting of actors and their respective roles.

**"clear stage"**   A direction to leave the stage, given by the stage manager for everyone not immediately involved in the action.

**composition**   The physical arrangement of set, props, and actors.

**criticism**   Analysis of and commentary on your work.

**curtain call**   The appearance of actors on stage after the performance to acknowledge the applause of the audience. The term applies whether or not a curtain has been used.

**"dress stage"**   A small onstage adjustment to improve the *composition* of the stage picture.

**freeze**   A point in the rehearsal process where you are asked to solidify your major movements.

**"I am"**   An actor's state of being that is "Right here. Right now. Today." At every rehearsal, you must, as your character, relive the moments of action as if they were happening for the first time.

**"places"**   A direction given by the stage manager for everyone to be in the proper position for the beginning of an act.

**projection**   Using external technique to display thoughts and ideas to the audience. Projection deals with dimension, energy, and clarity in order to communicate the meaning to an audience of a certain size occupying a certain space.

**rehearsal, specific types of**

1. **reading**   The initial table work, where the actors read and discuss the world of the play, the super-objective, motivating forces, simple objectives, obstacles, etc.

2. **blocking**   The director's arrangement of the actors' movements on stage with respect to one another and the stage space.

3. **working**   Rehearsal in which either the director or the actors may stop to work on details.

4. **run-through**   An uninterrupted rehearsal of a scene, an act, or the entire play.

5. **technical (cue-to-cue)**   A rehearsal where actors are asked to play only the moment leading up to and during a section of the play where technical elements are incorporated into the production.

6. **technical run-through**   An uninterrupted rehearsal of the play with all technical elements, excluding costumes and makeup.

7. **dress**   Show conditions. An uninterrupted technical run-through with full costumes and makeup.

**reincarnation** An actor's means of transforming his own distinctive qualities into those of the character. The process occurs throughout the rehearsal period and is complete when he has the ability to think, feel, and behave as his character.

**risk taking** A term synonymous with decision making, whether subtle or large. Risk taking is not to be confused with risqué choices.

**stealing** To take the audience's attention when it should be elsewhere.

**straight play** Any play—comedy or drama—that is not musical or classical.

**"take five"** The announcement of periodic five-minute breaks.

# Suggested Plays for Scene Study

The plays listed in this appendix are primarily intended for traditional undergraduate student-actors between the ages of 17 and 24. They are grouped according to the number and gender of players required.

## One Man/One Woman

*12-1-A,
by Wakako Yamauchi

After Ashley,
by Gina Gionfriddo

Angels in America:
Millennium Approaches,
by Tony Kushner

Arcadia,
by Tom Stoppard

Asian Shade,
by Larry Ketron

Beauty,
by Jane Martin

*Before It Hits Home,
by Cheryl West

*Beyond Your Command,
by Ralph Pape

Big Time,
by Keith Reddin

Biloxi Blues,
by Neil Simon

Bliss,
by Benjamin Bettenbender

Boy's Life,
by Howard Korder

Boys Next Door, The,
by Tom Griffin

*Blue Blood,
by Georgia Douglas Johnson

Blue Room, The,
by David Hare

Brilliant Traces,
by Cindy Lou Johnson

Children of a Lesser God,
by Mark Medoff

Chopin Playoffs, The,
by Israel Horovitz

Closer,
by Patrick Marber

*Cloud Tectonics,
by José Rivera

*Denotes strong multicultural roles

*Coming World, The,*
by Christopher Shinn

*Cowboy Mouth,*
by Sam Shepard

*Coyote Ugly,*
by Lynn Siefert

*Crucible, The,*
by Arthur Miller

\**Darker Face of the Earth,
The,*
by Rita Dove

*Dazzle, The,*
by Richard Greenberg

\**Death of the Last Black Man
in the Whole Entire World,
The,*
by Suzan-Lori Parks

*Desire Under the Elms,*
by Eugene O'Neill

*Diary of Anne Frank, The,*
by Frances Goodrich and
Albert Hackett

*Dimly Perceived Threats to
the System,*
by Jon Klein

*Dining Room, The,*
by A. R. Gurney

*Dinner with Friends,*
by Donald Margulies

*Diviners, The,*
by Jim Leonard

*Elephant Man, The,*
by Bernard Pomerance

*Equus,*
by Peter Shaffer

*Evolution,*
by Jonathan Marc Sherman

*Extremities,*
by William Mastrosimone

\**Fences,*
by August Wilson

*Fisher King,*
by Don Nigro

*Fool for Love,*
by Sam Shepard

*Frankie and Johnny
in the Clair De Lune,*
by Terrence McNally

*Glass Menagerie, The,*
by Tennessee Williams

*Grapes of Wrath, The,*
by John Steinbeck

*Heidi Chronicles, The,*
by Wendy Wasserstein

*Henceforward,*
by Alan Ayckbourn

*Here,*
by Michael Frayn

*Hidden Parts,*
by Lynn Alvarez

*How I Learned to
Drive,*
by Paula Vogel

*Hurlyburly,*
by David Rabe

*Interrogation, The,*
by Murphy Guyer (In
*More Ten-Minute
Plays from Actors Theatre
of Louisville*)

*Italian American
Reconciliation,*
by John Patrick Shanley

*Jack and Jill,*
by Jane Martin

*Juvenilia,*
by Wendy MacLeod

*Kentucky Cycle, The* ("The
Homecoming"),
by Robert Schenkkan

*Key Exchange,*
by Kevin Wade

*Lady and the Clarinet, The,*
by Michael Cristofer

*Last Night of Ballyhoo, The,*
by Alfred Uhry

*Last Train to Nibroc,*
by Arlene Hutton

*Les Liaisons Dangereuses,*
by Christopher Hampton

*Lie of the Mind, A,*
by Sam Shepard

*Life and Limb,*
by Keith Reddin

*Loose Ends,*
by Michael Weller

*Lovers and Other Strangers,*
by Reneé Taylor and Joseph
Bologna

\**Marriage, The,*
by Donald Greaves

*Miss Julie,*
by August Strindberg

*Open Admissions,*
by Shirley Lauro

*Out of Gas on Lovers Leap,*
by Mark St. Germain

*Owl and the Pussycat, The,*
by Bill Manhoff

*Prelude to a Kiss,*
by Craig Lucas

*Private Eyes,*
by Steven Dietz

*Raised in Captivity,*
by Nicky Silver

**Rancho Hollywood,*
by Carlos Morton

*Redwood Curtain,*
by Lanford Wilson

*Reeves Tale, The,*
by Don Nigro

*Romeo & Juliet II,*
by Sandra Hosking

*Royal Gambit,*
by Hermann Gressieker

*Ruby Sunrise, The,*
by Rinne Groff

*Same Time, Next Year,*
by Bernard Slade

*Sexual Perversity in Chicago,*
by David Mamet

*Shadow Box, The,*
by Michael Cristofer

*Shivaree,*
by William Mastrosimone

*Shopping and F\*\*\*ing,*
by Mark Ravenhill

*Simpatico,*
by Sam Shepard

**Spanish Eyes,*
by Eduardo Ivan Lopez

*Split Second,*
by Dennis McIntyre

*Stop Kiss,*
by Diana Son

*Strange Snow,*
by Stephen Metcalfe

*Streetcar Named Desire, A,*
by Tennessee Williams

**Talented Tenth, The,*
by Richard Wesley

*Three Days of Rain,*
by Richard Greenberg

*Three Sisters, The,*
by Anton Chekhov

*Trestle at Pope Lick Creek, The,*
by Naomi Wallace

*Twelve Dreams,*
by James Lapine

*27 Wagons Full of Cotton,*
by Tennessee Williams

*Two-Character Play, The,*
by Tennessee Williams

*Two for the Seesaw,*
by William Gibson

*Valhalla,*
by Paul Rudnick

*View From the Bridge, A,*
by Arthur Miller

*Voyeur and the Widow, The,*
by Le Wilhelm

*Waiting for Lefty,*
by Clifford Odets

**Wine in the Wilderness,*
by Alice Childress

*Woolgatherer, The,*
by William Mastrosimone

**Two Women**

*Apostle John, The,*
by Jeff Goode

*Bedtime,*
by Mary Gallagher

*Be Aggressive,*
by Annie Weisman

**Blue-Eyed Black Boy,*
by Georgia Douglas Johnson

*Brighton Beach Memoirs,*
by Neil Simon

*Bright Room Called Day, A,*
by Tony Kushner

*Candy & Shelley Go to the Desert,*
by Paula Cizmar

*Catholic School Girls,*
by Casey Kurtti

*Children's Hour, The,*
by Lillian Hellman

**Colored Museum, The,*
by George Wolfe

*Coupla White Chicks Sitting Around Talking, A,*
by John Ford Noonan

*Crimes of the Heart,*
by Beth Henley

*Criminal Hearts,*
by Jane Martin

*Early Girl, The,*
by Caroline Kava

*Eleemosynary,*
by Lee Blessing

*Family Scenes,*
by Ivette M. Ramirez

*Feed the Hole,*
by Michael Stock

*Final Placement,*
by Mary Gallagher and Ara
Watson (In *Win/Lose/Draw*)

*Flyin' West,*
by Pearl Cleage

*For Colored Girls Who Have
Considered Suicide/When the
Rainbow Was Enuf,*
by Ntozake Shange

*Importance of Being Earnest,
The,*
by Oscar Wilde

*Last Night of Ballyhoo, The,*
by Alfred Uhry

*Laundry and Bourbon,*
by James McLure

*Letters to a Student
Revolutionary,*
by Elizabeth Wong

*Lie of the Mind, A,*
by Sam Shepard

*Living Out,*
by Lisa Loomer

*Low Level Panic,*
by Clare McIntyre

*Mama Drama,*
by Leslie Ayvazian and
others

*Miracle Worker, The,*
by William Gibson

*Miss Firecracker Contest,
The,*
by Beth Henley

*Miss Lulu Bett,*
by Zona Gale

*Mrs. Klein,*
by Nicholas Wright

*My Sister in This House,*
by Wendy Kesselman

*Once Removed,*
by Eduardo Machado

*Our Country's Good,*
by Timberlake Wertenbaker

*Playing for Time,*
by Arthur Miller

*Poof!,*
by Lyn Nottage

*Proof,*
by David Auburn

*Sally and Marsha,*
by Sybille Pearson

*Sans-Culottes in the
Promised Land,*
by Kirsten Greenidge

*Savage in Limbo,*
by John Patrick Shanley

*Shayna Maidel, A,*
by Barbara Lebow

*Spike Heels,*
by Teresa Rebeck

*Steel Magnolias,*
by Robert Harlin

*Streetcar Named Desire, A,*
by Tennessee Williams

*Story, The,*
by Tracey Scott Wilson

*Talented Tenth, The,*
by Richard Wesley

*Top Girls,*
by Caryl Churchill

*Watermelon Boats,*
by Wendy MacLaughlin
(In *25 Ten-Minute Plays
from Actors Theatre of
Louisville*)

*Weldon Rising,*
by Phyllis Nagy

*What Mama Don't Know,*
by Jane Martin

*Whose Life Is It Anyway,*
by Brian Clark (Female
Version)

*Wine in the Wilderness,*
by Alice Childress

*Women of Manhattan,*
by John Patrick Shanley

## Two Men

*Apprentice, The,*
by Jack Gilhooley

*Beggars in the House of
Plenty,*
by John Patrick Shanley

*Below the Belt,*
by Richard Dresser

*Birdy,*
by Naomi Wallace

*Blood Knot, The,*
by Athol Fugard

*Boy's Life,*
by Howard Korder

*Chopin Playoffs, The,*
by Israel Horovitz

*Day the Bronx Died, The,*
by Michael Henry Brown

*Dance and the Railroad,
The,*
by David Henry Hwang

*Dirty Story,*
by John Patrick Shanley

*Equus,*
by Peter Schaffer

*Elephant Man, The,*
by Bernard Pomerance

*Evolution,*
by Jonathan Marc Sherman

*Fences,*
by August Wilson

*Fisher King,*
by Don Nigro

*Fortinbras,*
by Lee Blessing

*Grapes of Wrath, The,*
by John Steinbeck

*Hidden in This Picture,*
by Aaron Sorkin (In *Best
American Short Plays of the
1990s*)

*How I Got That Story,*
by Amlin Gray

*Hughie,*
by Eugene O'Neill

*Hurlyburly,*
by David Rabe

*Joe Turner's Come
and Gone,*
by August Wilson

*Juvenilia,*
by Wendy MacLeod

*K2,*
by Patrick Meyers

*Lie of the Mind, A,*
by Sam Shepard

*Life in the Theatre, A,*
by David Mamet

*Living at Home,*
by Anthony Giardina

*Lone Star,*
by James McLure

*Man Enough,*
by Patty Gideon Sloan

*Man Measures Man,*
by David Robson

*Marriage, The,*
by Donald Greaves

*Medal of Honor Rag,*
by Tom Cole

*Not About Heroes,*
by Stephen MacDonald

*Of Mice and Men,*
by John Steinbeck

*One Flew Over the
Cuckoo's Nest,*
by Dale Wasserman

*Orphans,*
by Lyle Kessler

*Paul Robeson,*
by Phillip Hayes Dean

*Pvt. Wars,*
by James McLure

*Shopping and F\*\*\*ing,*
by Mark Ravenhill

*Sizwe Banzi Is Dead,*
by Athol Fugard, John Kani,
and Winston Ntshona

*Soldier's Play, A,*
by Charles Fuller

*Some Things You Need to
Know Before the World Ends
(A Final Evening with the
Illuminati),*
by Levi Lee and Larry Larson

*Suburbia,*
by Eric Bogosian

*Survival of the Species,
The,*
by Robert Shaffron

*Three Days of Rain,*
by Richard Greenberg

*Tracers,*
by John DiFusco and
others

*True West,*
by Sam Shepard

*Yankee Dawg You Die,*
by Philip Kan Gotanda

*Zoo Story,*
by Edward Albee

## Three Women

*Agnes of God,*
by John Pielmeier

*And Miss Reardon Drinks a Little,*
by Paul Zindel

*Be Aggressive,*
by Annie Weisman

*\*Blue Blood,*
by Georgia Douglas Johnson

*Camping,*
by Jon Jory

*Candy & Shelley Go to the Desert,*
by Paula Cizmar

*Catholic School Girls,*
by Casey Kurtti

*Cherry Orchard, The,*
by Anton Chekhov

*Crimes of the Heart,*
by Beth Henley

*Desdemona: A Play About a Handkerchief,*
by Paula Vogel

*Eating Out,*
by Marcia Dixcy (In *25 Ten-Minute Plays from Actors Theatre of Louisville*)

*Effect of Gamma Rays on Man-in-the-Moon Marigolds, The,*
by Paul Zindel

*Eleemosynary,*
by Lee Blessing

*Family Scenes,*
by Ivette M. Ramirez

*Five Women Wearing the Same Dress,*
by Alan Ball

*Heads,*
by Jon Jory

*Independence,*
by Lee Blessing

*Killing of Sister George, The,*
by Frank Marcus

*Laundry and Bourbon,*
by James McLure

*Maids, The,*
by Jean Genet

*Miss Firecracker Contest, The,*
by Beth Henley

*On the Verge,*
by Eric Overmyer

*Shallow End, The,*
by Wendy MacLeod

*Three Sisters, The,*
by Anton Chekhov

*Uncommon Women and Others,*
by Wendy Wasserstein

*Vanities,*
by Jack Heifner

*Waiting for the Parade,*
by John Murrell

*Women of Manhattan,*
by John Patrick Shanley

## Three Men

*Absurd Person Singular,*
by Alan Ayckbourn

*American Buffalo,*
by David Mamet

*Art,*
by Yasmina Reza

*Below the Belt,*
by Richard Dresser

*Biloxi Blues,*
by Neil Simon

*Boy's Life,*
by Howard Korder

*Compleat Works of Wllm Shkspr (abridged), The,*
by The Reduced Shakespeare Co.

*Hurlyburly,*
by David Rabe

*I Hate Hamlet,*
by Paul Rudnick

*\*Indian Wants the Bronx, The,*
by Israel Horovitz

*La Turista,*
by Sam Shepard

*Lone Star,*
by James McLure

*Lost in Yonkers,*
by Neil Simon

*\* "Master Harold" . . . and the Boys,*
by Athol Fugard

*Mister Roberts,*
by Thomas Heggen and
Joshua Logan

*Of Mice and Men,*
by John Steinbeck

*Orphans,*
by Lyle Kessler

*Pick Up Ax,*
by Anthony Clarvoe

*Pvt. Wars,*
by James McLure

*\*T Bone N Weasel,*
by Jon Klein

*True West,*
by Sam Shepard

*Words, Words, Words,*
by David Ives

**Two Men/One Woman**

*\*12-1-A,*
by Wakako Yamauchi

*\*And Palm-Wine
Will Flow,*
by Bole Butake

*Apartment 3A,*
by Jeff Daniels

*Art of Dining, The,*
by Tina Howe

*Baltimore Waltz, The,*
by Paula Vogel

*Beyond Therapy,*
by Christopher Durang

*Boy's Life,*
by Howard Korder

*Burn This,*
by Lanford Wilson

*Chopin Playoffs, The,*
by Israel Horovitz

*Copenhagen,*
by Michael Frayn

*\*Corner, The,*
by Ed Bullins

*Cover,*
by Jeffrey Sweet (In *25 Ten-
Minute Plays from Actors
Theatre of Louisville*)

*Cowboy Mouth,*
by Sam Shepard

*\*Fences,*
by August Wilson

*\*F.O.B.,*
by David Henry Hwang

*Fool for Love,*
by Sam Shepard

*Friends,*
by Kobo Abe

*Hedda Gabler,*
by Henrik Ibsen

*\*House of Ramon Iglesia,
The,*
by José Rivera

*Hurlyburly,*
by David Rabe

*Italian American
Reconciliation,*
by John Patrick Shanley

*Key Exchange,*
by Kevin Wade

*Lost in Yonkers,*
by Neil Simon

*Luv,*
by Murray Schisgal

*Molly Sweeney,*
by Brian Friel

*Murder at the Howard
Johnson's,*
by Ron Clark and Sam
Bobrick

*Porno,*
by Mario Fratti

*Prelude to a Kiss,*
by Craig Lucas

*Proposal, The,*
by Anton Chekhov

*Sight Unseen,*
by Donald Margulies

*Six Degrees of Separation,*
by John Guare

*\*Slow Dance on the Killing
Ground,*
by William Hanley

*Speed-the-Plow,*
by David Mamet

*Spoils of War,*
by Michael Weller

*Strange Snow,*
by Steve Metcalfe

*Waste Disposal Unit,
The,*
by Bridget Brophy

*Words, Words, Words,*
by David Ives

## One Man/Two Women

*12-1-A,
by Wakako Yamauchi

Abundance,
by Beth Henley

Baby Dance,
The,
by Jane Anderson

Baby with the Bathwater,
by Christopher Durang

Bosoms and Neglect,
by John Guare

Candy & Shelley Go to the
Desert,
by Paula Cizmar

Coyote Ugly,
by Lynn Siefert

Dinner with Friends,
by Donald Margulies

Duck Pond, The,
by Ara Watson (In 25 Ten-
Minute Plays from Actors
Theatre of Louisville)

Extremities,
by William Mastrosimone

Fox, The,
by Allan Miller

*Home,
by Samm-Art Williams

Last Day of Camp,
by Jeffrey Sweet

Lesson, The,
by Eugène Ionesco

Lie of the Mind, A,
by Sam Shepard

Miss Julie,
by August Strindberg

Odd Couple, The,
by Neil Simon

*Our Lady of the Tortilla,
by Luis Santeiro

Painting Churches,
by Tina Howe

Pizza Man,
by Darlene Craviotto

Rancho Hollywood,
by Carlos Morton

Miss Firecracker Contest, The,
by Beth Henley

Miss Lulu Bett,
by Zona Gale

No Exit,
by Jean-Paul Sartre

Proof,
by David Auburn

*Raisin in the Sun, A,
by Lorraine Hansberry

Redwood Curtain,
by Lanford Wilson

Savage in Limbo,
by John Patrick Shanley

*Shayna Maidel, A,
by Barbara Lebow

Street Scene,
by Elmer Rice

Vinegar Tom,
by Caryl Churchill

Words, Words, Words,
by David Ives

# Acting Power Verbs

**A**
abandon
absolve
acquire
acquit
activate
actuate
address
administer
advance
advise
affect
affront
aggravate
agitate
alarm
allure
ally
amalgamate
amaze
analyze
anger
annihilate
annoy

arbitrate
argue
arrange
ascertain
assassinate
assemble
assert
assess
assist
associate
atomize
attract
audit
author
authorize
awe

**B**
back
baffle
bait
balk
bamboozle
band

beat
bedazzle
beguile
bequeath
besmirch
bet
bilk
bite
bother
brave
breach
break
bribe
brief
budget
build
butcher
buy

**C**
cajole
calculate
campaign
capacitate

chafe
challenge
chance
charm
chart
cheat
check
churn
claim
close
coax
coerce
collect
combine
commission
compel
compile
complete
compose
compound
con
conceive
conclude
concuss

conduct
confine
confront
confuse
conquer
conserve
consolidate
constrain
construct
consult
consume
contend
contract
contradict
contribute
control
controvert
coordinate
copulate
correct
correspond
corroborate
corrupt
counsel

counter
couple
cozen
crush

**D**
dash
dazzle
deal
debase
debate
debauch
decapitate
deceive
decoy
defend
defile
deflower
defraud
defy
delude
demand
demean
demolish
denigrate
depart
deprave
deputize
desert
destroy
detect
determine
develop
diagnose
diagram
direct
disable
discipline
disconcert
discover

dishonor
disobey
dispense
disprove
dispute
disquiet
disseminate
dissolve
distribute
disturb
document
double
drag
draw
drive
dupe

**E**
earn
economize
edit
educate
electrocute
eliminate
embarrass
empower
enable
enchant
enforce
engage
engineer
enhance
enlarge
enlighten
enthuse
entice
entitle
entrap
eradicate
escape

establish
evaluate
exacerbate
exalt
examine
exasperate
exceed
excite
exclude
excuse
execute
exhort
exonerate
expand
expedite
exterminate
extol

**F**
face
facilitate
fascinate
figure
fluster
foil
fool
force
forecast
forget
formulate
fornicate
found
funnel
fuse

**G**
gall
gamble
game
garrote

glorify
goad
grant
guide
gull
gyp

**H**
halt
hate
head
heal
heighten
hire
honor
hoodwink
humble
humiliate

**I**
identify
illuminate
illustrate
impel
implement
impress
improve
incite
incorporate
increase
induce
influence
inform
infract
infringe
initiate
innovate
install
institute
instruct

intensify
interpret
interview
introduce
invalidate
inveigle
invent
investigate
invite
irk
irritate

**J**
jam
jar
jeer
jerk
jinx
jockey
join
jolt
jostle
judge
juggle
jump
justify

**K**
keep
kick
kid
kill
kiss
knife
knit

**L**
lance
laud
launch

lead
lean
learn
leave
lecture
lessen
level
liberate
license
limit
link
list
live
log
love
lure

**M**

magnetize
maintain
make
manage
mandate
mangle
marry
massacre
master
mate
maximize
memorize
minimize
mitigate
mock
modernize
modify
mortify
motivate
murder

**N**

navigate

negate
negotiate
nettle
nix

**O**

obliterate
observe
obtain
operate
oppose
optimize
order
organize
originate
overcome
overhaul
overpower
oversee
overthrow
overturn
overwhelm

**P**

perceive
perform
permit
persuade
perturb
pervert
plagiarize
plan
play
pound
prepare
prescribe
present
prevail
process
procure
produce

promote
propel
propose
prostitute
protect
provide
provoke
pull

**Q**

qualify
quell
quench
question

**R**

rape
ravish
reach
realize
receive
recommend
reconcile
record
recruit
reduce
refine
render
repel
replace
represent
require
research
resist
respect
restore
retire
revere
review
revise

revitalize
rile
rout

**S**

sack
safeguard
sanctify
sanction
schedule
secure
seduce
select
sell
serve
shake
shame
shoot
simplify
slash
slaughter
slay
slip
smash
smuggle
solve
spark
speak
speculate
spoil
staff
stake
start
startle
steal
stimulate
stir
stop
streamline
study

succeed
summarize
supervise
supply
swindle
synthesize
systemize

**T**

tame
tamper
tempt
terminate
test
thrash
thwart
train
transact
transgress
translate
transmit
trespass
trick
trigger
triumph
trouble
troubleshoot
trounce

**U**

undermine
undo
unearth
unite
upgrade
upset

**V**

vacate
validate

| venerate | vindicate | wed | worship | **Y** |
| venture | violate | weld | worst | yawp |
| verify | | wheedle | wow | yearn |
| vest | **W** | win | wreck | yell |
| veto | wager | withdraw | | yield |
| vex | warrant | worsen | | |

# Theatre Resources

## Combined Audition Sites

California Educational
Theatre Association (CETA)
http://www.cetaweb.org

East Central Theatre
Conference (ECTC)
(732) 381–2264

Illinois Theatre Association
(ITA)
http://www.iltheassoc.org

Indiana Theatre Association
(ITA)
http://www.intheatre.org

Institute of Outdoor Drama
Auditions
http://www.unc.edu/depts/
outdoor

League of Resident Theatres
(LORT) Lottery Auditions:
Contact your nearest AEA
office.

Midwest Theatre Auditions
(MTA)
http://www.webster.edu/
depts/finearts/theatre/mwta

New England Theatre
Conference (NETC)
http://www.netconline.org

New Jersey Theatre Alliance
(NJTA)
http://www.njtheatrealliance
.org

Northwest Drama Conference
(NWDC)
http://www.cwu.edu/~nwdc

Rocky Mountain Theatre
Association (RMTA)
http://www.rmta.net

Southeastern Theatre
Conference (SETC)
http://www.setc.org

Southwest Theatre & Film
Association (SWTFA)
http://www.southwest-
theater.com

StrawHat Auditions:
Non-Equity Auditions
http://www.strawhat-
auditions.com

Theatre Alliance of Michigan
(TAM)
http://www
.theatreallianceofmichigan.org

Theatre Auditions in
Wisconsin
http://www.dcs.wisc.edu/lsa/
theatre/auditions.htm

Theatre Bay Area General
Auditions
http://www.theatrebayarea
.org

Unified Professional Theatre
Auditions (UPTA)
http://www.upta.org

University/Resident Theatre
Association National Unified
Auditions (U/RTA)
http://www.urta.com

## News & Publications

Backstage & Backstage West
http://www.backstage.com

Broadway.com
http://www.theatre.com

Broadway Play Publishing
http://www
.broadwayplaypubl.com

*Chicago Tribune*
http://www.chicagotribune
.com

*Curtain Up*
http://www.curtainup.com

Dramatic Publishing
http://www
.dramaticpublishing.com

Dramatists Play Service, Inc.
http://www.dramatists.com

*Hollywood Reporter*
http://www
.hollywoodreporter.com

*Los Angeles Times*
http://www.latimes.com

Music Theatre International
http://www.mtishows.com

*New York Times*
http://www.nytimes.com

Playbill Online
http://playbill.com

Rodgers & Hammerstein
Organization, The
http://www.rnh.com

Samuel French, Inc.
http://www.samuelfrench
.com

Theatre Communications
Group
http://www.tcg.org

TheatreJobs.com
http://www.theatrejobs.com

*Variety*
http://www.variety.com

*Village Voice*
http://www.villagevoice.com

*Washington Post*
http://www
.washingtonpost.com

## Unions & Organizations

American Association of
Community Theatre (AACT)
http://www.aact.org

Actors' Equity Association
(AEA)
http://www.actorsequity.org

American Federation of
Television and Radio Artists
(AFTRA)
http://www.aftra.org

American Guild of Musical
Artists (AGMA)
http://www.musicalartists
.org

American Society of
Composers, Authors and
Publishers (ASCAP)
http://www.ascap.com

Association for Theatre in
Higher Education (ATHE)
http://www.athe.org

British Equity
http://www.equity.org.uk

The Costume Society of
America (CSA)
http://www
.costumesocietyamerica.com

Directors Guild of America
(DGA)
http://www.dga.org

Dramatists Guild of America
(DGA)
http://www.dramaguild.com

International Alliance of
Theatrical Stage Employees
(IATSE)
http://www.iatse.com

Kennedy Center American
College Theatre Festival
(KCACTF)
http://www.kennedy-
center.org/education/actf

National Endowment for the
Arts (NEA)
http://arts.endow.gov

Non-Traditional Casting
Project (NTCP)
http://www.ntcp.org

Society of American Fight
Directors (SAFD)
http://www.safd.org

Screen Actors Guild (SAG)
http://www.sag.org

Society of Stage Directors and Choreographers (SSDC)
http://www.ssdc.org

United Scenic Artists (USA)
http://www.usa829.org

United States Institute of Theatre Technology (USITT)
http://www.usitt.com

Writers Guild of America (WGA)
http://www.wga.org

## Professional Theatre Companies

Actors Theatre of Louisville (Louisville, KY)
http://www.actorstheatre.org

Alabama Shakespeare Festival (Montgomery, AL)
http://www.asf.net

Alley Theatre (Houston, TX)
http://www.alleytheatre.org

Alliance Theatre Company (Atlanta, GA)
http://www.alliancetheatre.org

American Conservatory Theater (San Francisco, CA)
http://www.act-sfbay.org

American Repertory Theatre (Cambridge, MA)
http://www.amrep.org

Arena Stage (Washington, DC)
http://www.arenastage.org

Arizona Theatre Company (Tucson, AZ)
http://www.aztheatreco.org

Arkansas Repertory Theatre, The (Little Rock, AR)
http://www.therep.org

Asolo Center for the Performing Arts (Sarasota, FL)
http://www.asolo.org

Barter Theatre (Abingdon, VA)
http://www.bartertheatre.com

Berkeley Repertory Theatre (Berkeley, CA)
http://www.berkeleyrep.org

Berkshire Theatre Festival (Stockbridge, MA)
http://www.berkshiretheatre.org

California Theatre Center (Sunnyvale, CA)
http://www.ctcinc.org

Casa Mañana Theatre (Ft. Worth, TX)
http://www.casamanana.org

Center Stage (Baltimore, MD)
http://www.centerstage.org

Cincinnati Playhouse (Cincinnati, OH)
http://www.cincyplay.com

Cleveland Playhouse, The (Cleveland, OH)

http://www.clevelandplayhouse.com

Coconut Grove Playhouse (Coconut Grove, FL)
http://www.cgplayhouse.com

Contemporary Theatre, A (Seattle, WA)
http://www.acttheatre.org

Dallas Theater Center (Dallas, TX)
http://www.dallastheatercenter.org

Denver Center Theatre Company (Denver, CO)
http://www.denvercenter.org

Florida Stage (Manalapan, FL)
http://www.floridastage.org

George Street Playhouse (New Brunswick, NJ)
http://www.georgestplayhouse.org

Goodman Theatre (Chicago, IL)
http://www.goodmantheatre.org

Goodspeed Opera House (East Haddam, CT)
http://www.goodspeed.org

Great Lakes Theater Festival (Cleveland, OH)
http://www.greatlakestheater.org

Guthrie Theater, The (Minneapolis, MN)
http://www.guthrietheater.org

Hartford Stage Company (Hartford, CT)
http://www.hartfordstage.org

Huntington Theatre Company (Boston, MA)
http://www.huntingtontheatre.org

Indiana Repertory Theatre (Indianapolis, IN)
http://www.indianarep.com

Kansas City Repertory Theatre (Kansas City, MO)
http://www.missourireptheatre.org

La Jolla Playhouse (La Jolla, CA)
http://www.lajollaplayhouse.com

La MaMa e.t.c. (New York, NY)
http://www.lamama.org

Long Wharf Theatre (New Haven, CT)
http://www.longwharf.org

Lorraine Hansberry Theatre (San Francisco, CA)
http://www.lorrainehansberrytheatre.com

Los Angeles Repertory Company (Los Angeles, CA)
http://www.larep.org

Manhattan Theatre Club (New York, NY)
http://www.manhattantheatreclub.com

Mark Taper Forum (Los Angeles, CA)
http://www.taperahmanson.com

McCarter Theatre (Princeton, NJ)
http://www.mccarter.org

Milwaukee Repertory Theatre (Milwaukee, WI)
http://www.milwaukeerep.com

New Dramatists (New York, NY)
http://newdramatists.org

New Harmony Theatre, The (Evansville, IN)
http://www.usi.edu/nht

Old Globe Theatre (San Diego, CA)
http://www.oldglobe.org

Olney Theatre Center (Olney, MD)
http://www.olneytheatre.org

Oregon Shakespeare Festival (Ashland, OR)
http://www.osfashland.org

Orlando-UCF Shakespeare Festival (Orlando, FL)
http://www.shakespearefest.org

PCPA Theaterfest (Santa Maria, CA)
http://www.pcpa.org

Philadelphia Theatre Company (Philadelphia, PA)
http://www.phillytheatreco.com

Pioneer Theatre Company (Salt Lake City, UT)
http://www.pioneertheatre.org

Pittsburgh Public Theater (Pittsburgh, PA)
http://www.ppt.org

Playwrights Horizons (New York, NY)
http://www.playwrightshorizons.org

Portland Center Stage (Portland, OR)
http://www.pcs.org

Public Theater/New York Shakespeare Festival (New York, NY)
http://www.publictheater.org

Repertory Theatre of St. Louis, The (St. Louis, MO)
http://www.repstl.org

Roundabout Theatre Company (New York, NY)
http://www.roundabouttheatre.org

St. Louis Black Repertory Company (St. Louis, MO)
http://www.stlouisblackrep.com

San Jose Repertory (San Jose, CA)
http://www.sjrep.com

Seattle Repertory Theatre (Seattle, WA)
http://www.seattlerep.org

Second City, The (Chicago, IL)
http://www.secondcity.com

Shakespeare Theatre, The (Washington, D.C.)
http://www.shakespearetheatre.org

South Coast Repertory (Costa Mesa, CA)
http://www.scr.org

Southern Repertory Theatre (New Orleans, LA)
http://southernrep.com

Stages St. Louis (St. Louis, MO)
http://www.stagesstlouis.com

Stage West (Ft. Worth, TX)
http://www.stagewest.org

Steppenwolf Theatre Company (Chicago, IL)
http://www.steppenwolf.org

Syracuse Stage (Syracuse, NY)
http://www.syracusestage.org

Tennessee Repertory Theatre (Nashville, TN)
http://www.tnrep.org

Theatre Three (Dallas, TX)
http://www.theatre3dallas.com

Trinity Repertory Company (Providence, RI)
http://www.trinityrep.com

Utah Shakespearean Festival (Cedar City, UT)
http://www.bard.org

Walnut Street Theatre (Philadelphia, PA)
http://www.wstonline.org

Williamstown Theatre Festival (Williamstown, MA)
http://www.wtfestival.org

Yale Repertory Theatre (New Haven, CT)
http://www.yalerep.org

# Endnotes

## Chapter 1

1. Constantin Stanislavski, *An Actor Prepares,* trans. Elizabeth Reynolds Hapgood (New York: Theatre Arts Books, 1973), 122.
2. Robert Cohen, *Acting Professionally: Raw Facts About Careers in Acting,* 5th ed. (Mountain View, CA: Mayfield Publishing Company, 1998), 3.
3. Sonia Moore, *Training an Actor: The Stanislavski System in Class* (New York: Penguin Books, 1979), 26–27.

## Chapter 2

1. Constantin Stanislavski, *My Life in Art,* trans. J. J. Robbins (New York: Theatre Arts Books, 1948), 567.
2. Irina and Igor Levin, *The Stanislavsky Secret* (Colorado Springs, CO: Meriwether Publishing, Ltd., 2002), 7.

3. Jerzy Grotowski, *Towards a Poor Theatre* (New York: Simon & Schuster, 1968), 185.
4. Robert Benedetti, *The Actor at Work,* 8th ed. (Boston: Allyn and Bacon, 2001), 11.

## Chapter 3

1. Sanford Meisner and Dennis Longwell, "Acting Class, Day One, with a Master Teacher," *The New York Times,* 31 May 1987.
2. Arthur Miller, *All My Sons* (New York: Dramatists Play Service, Inc., 1947), 19.
3. Michael Redgrave, "The Stanislavsky Myth," *New Theatre* 3 (June 1946): 16–18, in *Actors on Acting,* ed. Toby Cole and Helen Krich Chinoy (New York: Crown Publishers, 1970), 403.
4. Mel Gordon, *The Stanislavsky Technique: Russia; A Workbook for Actors* (New York: Applause Theatre Book Publishers, 1987), 71.

## Chapter 4

1. Vasili O. Toporkov, "Physical Actions," in *Actors on Acting,* 523–24.
2. Moore, *Training an Actor,* 139.
3. Robert Lewis, *Method— Or Madness?* (New York: Samuel French, 1958), 29.
4. Kenneth Tynan, *Curtains* (New York: Atheneum, 1961), 77.
5. Uta Hagen, *A Challenge for the Actor* (New York: Macmillan Publishing, 1991), 124–25.
6. Stanislavski, *An Actor Prepares,* 213.
7. Moore, *Training an Actor,* 190–91.
8. Constance Congdon, *Tales of the Lost Formicans and Other Plays* (New York: Theatre Communications Group, 1994), 52.

## Chapter 5

1. Richard Boleslavsky, *Acting: The First Six Lessons* (New York: Theatre Arts Books, 1933), 97–99.
2. David Magarshack, "Introductory Essay on Stanislavsky's 'System,'" in *Stanislavsky on the Art of the Stage,* Konstantin Stanislavsky (London: Faber and Faber Ltd., 1980), 41–43.
3. Ibid.
4. Hagen, *A Challenge for the Actor,* 82.
5. Ibid., 170.
6. Lewis Funke and John E. Booth, *Actors Talk about Acting: Fourteen Interviews with Stars of the Theatre,* vol. 1 (New York: Avon Books, 1961), 57–58.
7. Stanislavski, *An Actor Prepares,* 167.
8. David Gardner, *Tom Hanks* (London: Blake Publishing, Ltd., 1999), 97.
9. Barbara Kramer, *Tom Hanks* (Berkeley Heights, NJ: Enslow Publishers, Inc., 2001), 47, 71.
10. Marlon Brando, with Robert Lindsey, *Brando: Songs My Mother Taught Me* (New York: Random House, 1994), 411–17.
11. Steve Martin, *Picasso at the Lapin Agile* (New York: Samuel French, Inc., 1996), 33–37.
12. Magarshack, "Introductory Essay," 37–39.

## Chapter 6

1. Constantin Stanislavski, "Direction and Acting," in *Acting: A Handbook of the Stanislavski Method,* ed. Toby Cole (New York: Crown Publishing, 1955), 24–25.
2. Constantin Stanislavski, *Stanislavski's Legacy,* ed. Elizabeth Reynolds Hapgood (New York: Theatre Arts Books, 1958), 174.
3. Stanislavski, *An Actor Prepares,* 78.
4. Ibid., 79.
5. Magarshack, "Introductory Essay," 39–40.
6. Constantin Stanislavski, *An Actor's Handbook,* ed. and trans. Elizabeth Reynolds Hapgood (New York: Theatre Arts Books, 1963), 25.
7. Constantin Stanislavski, *Building a Character,* trans. Elizabeth Reynolds Hapgood (New York: Theatre Arts Books, 1949), 118.
8. Stanislavski, *An Actor Prepares,* 185.
9. Levin and Levin, *The Stanislavsky Secret,* 13–14.

10. Sanford Meisner and Dennis Longwell, *Sanford Meisner on Acting* (New York: Vintage Books, 1987), 16–77.
11. Levin and Levin, *The Stanislavsky Secret,* 23.
12. Ibid.
13. David Auburn, *Proof* (New York: Faber and Faber, 2001), 42–43.

## Chapter 7

1. Moore, *Training an Actor,* 65.
2. Ibid., 228.
3. Stanislavski, *An Actor Prepares,* 163.
4. Magarshack, "Introductory Essay," 38.
5. Moore, *Training an Actor,* 159–160.

## Chapter 8

1. Stanislavski, *Building a Character,* 7.
2. Magarshack, "Introductory Essay," 77.
3. Stanislavski, *An Actor Prepares,* 258.
4. Michael Chekhov, *To the Actor* (New York: Harper & Row, 1953), 69.
5. Mira Felner, *Free to Act: An Integrated Approach to Acting,* 2nd ed. (Boston: Pearson Education, 2004), 193–194.
6. Charles Marowitz, *The Act of Being* (New York: Taplinger, 1978), 29–30.

7. Harold Clurman, "The Principles of Interpretation," in *Producing the Play,* ed. John Gassner (New York: Holt, Rinehart, 1941), 287.

8. Felner, *Free to Act,* 178–186.

## Chapter 9

1. Boleslavsky, *Acting: The First Six Lessons,* 56–57.

2. Stanislavski, *An Actor Prepares,* 256–58.

3. Clurman, "The Principles of Interpretation," 277.

4. John Dover Wilson, "Mr. T. S. Eliot's Theory of Hamlet," in *What Happens in Hamlet* (Cambridge: University Press, 1970), 305.

5. Clurman, "The Principles of Interpretation," 277.

6. Max Reinhardt, "Regie Book of The Miracle," in *Max Reinhardt and His Theatre,* ed. Oliver M. Sayler (New York: Brentano's, 1924), 64–65.

7. Robert Patrick, *Kennedy's Children* (New York: Random House, 1973), 5.

8. Augusto Boal, *Games for Actors and Non-Actors,* trans. Adrian Jackson (London and New York: Routledge, 1992), xxx. Italics in the original.

## Chapter 10

1. Grotowski, *Towards a Poor Theatre,* 147.

2. Sonia Moore, *Stanislavski Revealed* (New York City: Applause Theatre Book Publishers, 1991), 125.

3. Moore, *Training an Actor,* 238–39.

4. Alan Ball, *Five Women Wearing the Same Dress* (New York: Dramatists Play Service, Inc., 1993), 10.

5. Eugene O'Neill, *Desire Under the Elms,* in *The Bedford Introduction to Drama,* 3rd ed., ed. Lee A. Jacobus (Boston: Bedford Books, 1997), 938.

6. Clifford Odets, *Golden Boy,* in *Six Plays of Clifford Odets* (New York: Grove Press, 1979), 252.

7. Anton Chekhov, *The Three Sisters,* adapted by David Mamet (New York: Grove Press, 1990), 81–82.

8. Constance Congdon, "No Mercy," in *Contemporary American Monologues for Men,* ed. Todd London (New York: Theatre Communications Group, 1998), 19–20.

9. Marsha Norman, *Getting Out* (New York: Dramatists Play Service, Inc., 1979), 61.

10. Galanty Miller, "The Dreaded Word," in *The Best Men's Stage Monologues of 2000,* ed. Jocelyn A. Bearn (Hanover, New Hampshire: Smith and Kraus, Inc., 2002), 32.

11. Lynn Siefert, *Coyote Ugly* (New York: Dramatists Play Service, Inc., 1986), 34–35.

12. Sam Shepard, *La Turista* (New York: The Bobbs-Merrill Company, Inc., 1968), 19–20.

13. Reynolds Price, "Early Dark," in *Contemporary American Monologues for Women,* ed. Todd London (New York: Theatre Communications Group, 1998), 93.

14. Lee Blessing, *Two Rooms* (New York: Dramatists Play Service, Inc., 1990), 20–21.

15. Frank Cossa, *The Queen's Knight,* in *Outstanding Stage Monologs and Scenes from the '90s,* ed. Steven H. Gale (Colorado Springs: Meriwether, 2000), 15.

16. David Rabe, *In the Boom Boom Room* (New York: Grove Press, 1986), 58.

## Chapter 11

1. Edward Bond, *Early Morning* (London: Calder and Boyars, 1968), 21–22.

2. Grotowski, *Towards a Poor Theatre,* 171.
3. George Bernard Shaw, *Major Barbara,* in *Complete Plays with Prefaces,* Vol. I (New York: Dodd, Mead, 1962), 347.
4. Arthur Kopit, *Indians* (New York: Hill and Wang, 1969), 9.
5. James Baldwin, *Blues for Mister Charlie* (New York: Dial Press, 1964), 63.
6. Christopher Fry, *The Lady's Not for Burning; A Phoenix Too Frequent; and an Essay "An Experience of Critics"* (New York: Oxford University Press, 1977), 54.
7. Sean O'Casey, *Three Plays* (New York: Macmillan, 1960), 42–43.
8. Kopit, *Indians,* 47.
9. John Barton, *Playing Shakespeare* (London and New York: Methuen, 1984), 55–56.
10. Ibid., 56.
11. Luigi Pirandello, *Right You Are If You Think You Are,* trans. Eric Bentley (New York: Columbia University Press, 1954), 19.
12. Friedrich Duerrenmatt, *Play Strindberg,* trans. James Kirkup (Chicago: The Dramatic Publishing Company, 1952), 57.
13. Ibid., 58.
14. William Shakespeare, *King Lear* (New Haven, CT: Yale University Press, 1947), 71.
15. Shakespeare, *Measure for Measure* (New Haven, CT: Yale University Press, 1954), 46.
16. Shakespeare, *The Merchant of Venice* (New Haven, CT: Yale University Press, 1923), 4.
17. Charles Gordone, *No Place to Be Somebody* (Indianapolis: Bobbs Merrill, 1969), 12.
18. Ossie Davis, *Purlie Victorious* (New York: Samuel French, 1961), 31.
19. Peter Brook, *The Empty Space* (New York: Atheneum, 1968), 77–78.
20. Laurence Perrine, *Sound and Sense* (New York: Harcourt Brace Jovanovich, 1956), 40.
21. Shepard, *Red Cross,* in *Chicago and Other Plays* (New York: Urizen Books, 1981), 115.
22. O'Casey, *Three Plays,* 101.
23. Davis, *Purlie Victorious,* 31.
24. Reynolds Price, *August Snow* (New York: Dramatists Play Service, Inc., 1990), 10–11.
25. Donald Margulies, *Sight Unseen and Other Plays* (New York: Theatre Communications Group, Inc., 1995), 277–78.
26. Maria Irene Fornes, "Abingdon Square," in *American Theatre Book of Monologues for Women,* ed. Stephanie Coen (New York: Theatre Communications Group, 2003), 11–12.
27. Shepard, *Fool for Love* (San Francisco: City Lights Books, 1983), 46–47.
28. Tina Howe, *Painting Churches,* in *Coastal Disturbances: Four Plays* (New York: Theatre Communications Group, 1989), 160–61.
29. Howe, *Coastal Disturbances,* in *Coastal Disturbances: Four Plays,* 228–29.
30. Craig Lucas, *Reckless* (New York: Dramatists Play Service, Inc., 1998), 19–20.
31. Don Nigro, *The Reeves Tale* (New York: Samuel French, Inc., 2004), 23.
32. Paula Vogel, *How I Learned to Drive* (New York: Dramatists Play Service Inc., 1997), 9.
33. Nicky Silver, *Raised in Captivity* (New York: Theatre Communications Group, Inc., 1995), 21–23.

## Chapter 12

1. Michael Shurtleff, *Audition: Everything an Actor Needs to Know to Get the Part* (New York: Walker, 1978), 1.
2. Ibid.
3. Fred Silver, *Auditioning for the Musical Theatre* (New York: Newmarket Press, 1985), 138.

## Chapter 13

1. Levin and Levin, *The Stanislavsky Secret*, 93–94.
2. Clurman, *The Fervent Years* (New York: Knopf, 1945), 41.
3. Hagen, *A Challenge for the Actor*, 292–93.
4. Moore, *Stanislavski Revealed*, 125.
5. Stanislavski, *An Actor's Handbook*, 43.
6. Lawrence Stern, *Stage Management: A Guidebook of Practical Techniques*, 3rd ed. (Boston: Allyn and Bacon, Inc., 1987), 4.
7. Joseph Slowik, "An Actor's Enemies" (paper presented at the Mid-America Theatre Conference, Omaha, Nebraska, 16 March 1984).
8. Slowik, "An Actor's Enemies," 6.
9. Funke and Booth, *Actors Talk about Acting*, 67.
10. Hagen, with Haskel Frankel, *Respect for Acting* (New York: Macmillan, 1973), 3.

# Bibliography

*This bibliography does not include plays, which can be found in many editions.*

Adler, Stella. *The Technique of Acting.* New York: Bantam Books, 1978.

Artaud, Antonin. *The Theater and Its Double.* Translated by Mary Caroline Richards. New York: Grove Press, 1961.

Barton, John. *Playing Shakespeare.* London and New York: Methuen, 1984.

Barton, Robert. *Acting: Onstage and Off.* 2nd ed. Fort Worth: Harcourt Brace Jovanovich, 1993.

Benedetti, Robert L. *The Actor at Work.* 9th ed. Boston and New York: Pearson Education, 2005.

Boal, Augusto. *Games for Actors and Non-Actors.* Translated by Adrian Jackson. London and New York: Routledge, 1992.

———. *Theatre of the Oppressed.* Translated by

Charles A. McBride and Maria-Odilia Leal McBride. New York: Theatre Communications Group, 1979.

Brestoff, Richard. *The Great Acting Teachers and Their Methods.* Lyme, NH: Smith and Kraus, 1995.

Boleslavsky, Richard. *Acting: The First Six Lessons.* New York: Theatre Arts Books, 1933.

Brando, Marlon, with Robert Lindsey. *Brando: Songs My Mother Taught Me.* New York: Random House, 1994.

Brook, Peter. *The Empty Space.* New York: Atheneum, 1968.

Chekhov, Michael. *To the Actor.* New York: Harper & Row, 1953.

Clurman, Harold. *The Fervent Years.* New York: Knopf, 1945.

———. "The Principles of Interpretation," in *Producing the Play,* ed.

John Gassner. New York: Holt, Rinehart, 1941.

Cohen, Robert. *Acting One.* 4th ed. Boston: McGraw-Hill, 2002.

———. *Acting Professionally: Raw Facts About Careers in Acting.* 5th ed. Mountain View, CA: Mayfield Publishing, 1998.

Cole, David. *Acting as Reading: The Place of the Reading Process in the Actor's Work.* Ann Arbor: University of Michigan Press, 1992.

Cole, Toby, ed. *Acting: A Handbook of the Stanislavski Method.* Rev. ed. New York: Crown Publishing, 1955.

——— and Helen Krich Chinoy, eds. *Actors on Acting.* Rev. ed. New York: Crown Publishers, 1970.

Duerr, Edwin. *The Length and Depth of Acting.* New York: Holt, Rinehart and Winston, 1962.

Felner, Mira. *Free to Act: An Integrated Approach to Acting.* 2nd ed. Boston: Pearson Education, 2004.

Funke, Lewis, and John E. Booth. *Actors Talk about Acting: Fourteen Interviews with Stars of the Theatre.* Vol. 1. New York: Avon Books, 1961.

Gardner, David. *Tom Hanks.* London: Blake Publishing, Ltd., 1999.

Gassner, John, ed. *Producing the Play.* New York: Holt, Rinehart, 1941.

Gielgud, John, and John Miller. *Acting Shakespeare.* New York: Macmillan Publishing, 1992.

Gordon, Mel. *The Stanislavsky Technique: Russia; A Workbook for Actors.* New York: Applause Theatre Book Publishers, 1987.

Grotowski, Jerzy. *Towards a Poor Theatre.* New York: Simon & Schuster, 1968.

Hagen, Uta. *A Challenge for the Actor.* New York: Macmillan Publishing, 1991.

——— with Haskel Frankel. *Respect for Acting.* New York: Macmillan Publishing, 1973.

Harrop, John, and Sabin R. Epstein. *Acting with Style.* 3rd ed. Needham Heights, MA: Allyn & Bacon, 2000.

Henry, Mari Lyn, and Lynne Rogers. *How to Be a Working Actor.* 3rd ed. New York: M. Evans and Company, 1994.

Hethmon, Robert H., ed. *Strasberg at the Actors Studio.* New York: Viking, 1965.

Hooks, Ed. *The Audition Book.* New York: Back Stage Books, 1996.

Hull, S. Loraine. *Strasberg's Method As Taught by Lorrie Hull: A Practical Guide for Actors, Teachers and Directors.* Woodbridge, CT: Ox Bow Publishing, Inc., 1985.

Hunt, Gordon. *How to Audition.* New York: Harper-Collins Publishers, 1995.

Kaiser, Scott. *Mastering Shakespeare.* New York: Allworth Press, 2003.

Kramer, Barbara. *Tom Hanks.* Berkeley Heights, NJ: Enslow Publishers, Inc., 2001.

Lessac, Arthur. *Body Wisdom: The Use and Training of the Human Body.* New York: Drama Book Specialists, 1981.

———. *The Use and Training of the Human Voice.* 3rd ed. New York: Drama Book Specialists, 1997.

Levin, Irina and Igor. *The Stanislavsky Secret.* Colorado Spring, CO: Meriwether Publishing, 2002.

———. *Working on the Play and the Role: The Stanislavsky Method for Analyzing the Characters in a Drama.* Chicago: Ivan R. Dee, 1992.

Lewis, Robert. *Advice to the Players.* New York: Harper & Row, 1980.

———. *Method—Or Madness?* New York: Samuel French, 1958.

Linklater, Kristin. *Freeing the Natural Voice.* New York: Drama Book Specialists, 1976.

Luckhurst, Mary and Chloe Veltman, eds. *On Acting: Interviews with Actors.* New York: Faber and Faber, 2001.

McTigue, Mary. *Acting Like a Pro: Who's Who, What's What, and the Way Things Really Work in the Theatre.* White Hall, VA: Betterway Publications, 1992.

Magarshack, David. "Introductory Essay on Stanislavsky's 'System,'" in *Stanislavsky on the Art of the Stage*, Konstantin Stanislavsky. London: Faber and Faber Ltd., 1980.

Marowitz, Charles. *The Act of Being*. New York: Taplinger, 1978.

———. *Stanislavsky and the Method*. New York: Citadel Press, 1964.

Meisner, Sanford, and Dennis Longwell, "Acting Class, Day One, with a Master Teacher," *The New York Times*, 31 May 1987.

———. *Sanford Meisner on Acting*. New York: Vintage Books, 1987.

Moore, Sonia. *Stanislavski Revealed*. New York: Applause Theatre Book Publishers, 1991.

———. *Stanislavski System, The*. New York: Penguin, 1984.

———. *Training an Actor*. New York: Penguin, 1979.

Moss, Larry. *The Intent to Live*. New York: Bantam Books, 2005.

Novak, Elaine Adams. *Performing in Musicals*. New York: Schirmer Books, 1988.

Olivier, Laurence. *On Acting*. New York: Simon and Schuster, 1986.

Olivieri, Joseph. *Shakespeare Without Fear*. Fort Worth, TX: Harcourt, 2001.

Parke, Lawrence. *Since Stanislavski and Vakhtangov: The Method as a System for Today's Actor*. Hollywood, CA: Acting World Books, 1994.

Poggi, Jack. *The Monologue Workshop*. New York: Applause Theatre Book Publishers, 1990.

Reinhardt, Max. "Regie Book of The Miracle," in *Max Reinhardt and His Theatre*, ed. Oliver M. Sayler. New York: Brentano's, 1924.

Rodenburg, Patsy. *The Right to Speak*. New York: Routledge, 1992.

Schechner, Richard. *Environmental Theatre*. New York: Hawthorn Books, 1973.

Shurtleff, Michael. *Audition: Everything an Actor Needs to Know to Get the Part*. New York: Walker, 1978.

Silverberg, Larry. *The Sanford Meisner Approach, An Actor's Workbook*. Lyme, NH: Smith and Kraus, 1994.

———. *The Sanford Meisner Approach, Workbook Two: Emotional Freedom*. Lyme, NH: Smith and Kraus, 1997.

Silver, Fred. *Auditioning for the Musical Theatre: One of the Country's Leading Musical Audition Coaches Prepares You to Get the Parts You Want*. New York: Newmarket Press, 1985.

Skinner, Edith. *Speak with Distinction*. New York: Applause Theatre Book Publishers, 1990.

Slowik, Joseph. "An Actor's Enemies." Paper presented at the Mid-America Theatre Conference, Omaha, Nebraska, 16 March 1984.

Sonenberg, Janet. *The Actor Speaks*. New York: Crown, 1996.

Spolin, Viola. *Improvisation for the Theatre*. Evanston, IL: Northwestern University Press, 1963.

Stanislavski, Constantin. *An Actor Prepares*. Translated by Elizabeth Reynolds Hapgood. New York: Theatre Arts Books, 1989.

———. *An Actor's Handbook*. Edited and translated by Elizabeth Reynolds Hapgood. New York: Theatre Arts Books, 1963.

———. *Building a Character*. Translated by Elizabeth Reynolds Hapgood. New York: Theatre Arts Books, 1949.

———. *Creating a Role*. Translated by Elizabeth Reynolds Hapgood. New York: Theatre Arts Books, 1961.

————. *My Life in Art.* Translated by J. J. Robbins. New York: Theatre Arts Books, 1948.

————. *Stanislavski's Legacy.* Edited by Elizabeth Reynolds Hapgood. New York: Theatre Arts Books, 1958.

Stanislavsky, Konstantin. *Stanislavsky on the Art of the Stage.* Translated by David Magarshack. London: Faber and Faber Ltd., 1980.

Stern, Lawrence. *Stage Management: A Guidebook of Practical Techniques.* 3rd ed. Boston: Allyn and Bacon, Inc., 1987.

Strasberg, Lee. *A Dream of Passion: The Development of the Method.* Edited by Evangeline Morphos. Boston: Little, Brown, 1987.

Thomas, James. *Script Analysis for Actors, Directors and Designers.* Boston: Focal Press, 1992.

Tynan, Kenneth. *Curtains.* New York: Atheneum, 1961.

Wilson, John Dover. "Mr. T. S. Eliot's Theory of Hamlet," in *What Happens in Hamlet.* Cambridge: University Press, 1970.

Woods, Leigh. *On Playing Shakespeare: Advice and Commentary from Actors and Actresses of the Past.* New York: Greenwood Press, 1991.

Yakim, Moni. *Creating a Character: A Physical Approach to Acting.* New York: Backstage Books, 1990.

# Index